GREATEST BRITISH RAILWAY JOURNEYS

Introduction by Michael Portillo

HEADLINE

First published in 2020 by
HEADLINE PUBLISHING GROUP

First published in paperback in 2021 by
HEADLINE PUBLISHING GROUP

1

Please refer to page 302 for picture credits.

Cataloguing in Publication Data is available from the British Library

ISBN 978 1 4722 7928 6

Designed and typeset by EM&EN
Printed and bound in Great Britain by Clays Ltd, Elcograf S.p.A.

MIX
Paper from
responsible sources
FSC® C104740

HEADLINE PUBLISHING GROUP
An Hachette UK Company
Carmelite House
50 Victoria Embankment
London EC4Y 0DZ

www.headline.co.uk
www.hachette.co.uk

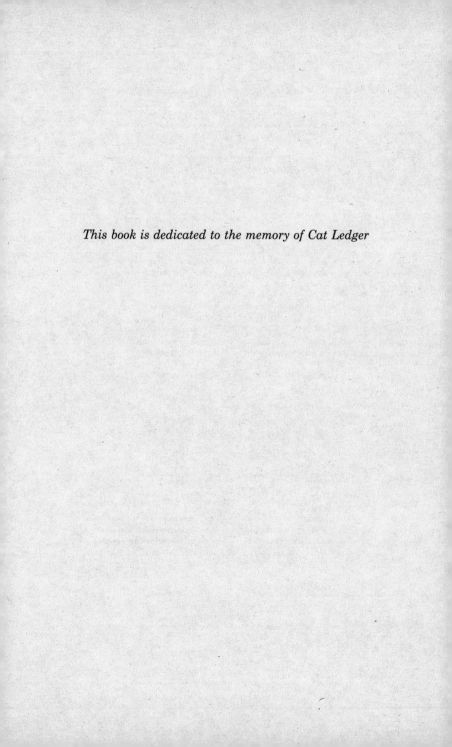

This book is dedicated to the memory of Cat Ledger

Contents

As the railway age got underway, the whole of Ireland was part of the British Empire and the engineering innovators were drawing from the same well. As such, the story of great railway lines and the men who made them in Ireland reflects those in the United Kingdom, with similar outcomes in terms of commerce and communication.

Introduction by Michael Portillo

If you search online for 'Portillo moment', lots of results come up. My humiliating defeat in my parliamentary seat in Britain's 1997 general election has passed into the history books and become a saying in its own right, albeit in a minor way. But another door opened for me, as the saying goes.

Quite soon, I began to receive invitations to make television documentaries. One commission was for a BBC Two series, *Great Railway Journeys*. The show had a different presenter each week, who was encouraged to introduce an autobiographical element to their episode. I made a journey around Spain, where my father, Luis, had been caught up in the Spanish Civil War, and later exiled. The programme included interviews with his brothers, who had fought on the other side of the divide, which helped to make it pretty emotional for me.

Fully ten years later, when a television production company had it in mind to make a series about rail journeys using an antique *Bradshaw's Handbook* to steer the course, the company's chief executive, Lorraine Heggessey, reputedly suggested that I should be the presenter. She had been with the BBC when I had set off across Spain, and remembered my programme. I was initially engaged for a short series; but at the time of writing, we are in our twelfth year of filming railway adventures, with twenty-seven series under our belts.

Our first jaunts were in the United Kingdom, and each year since then we have filmed a series 'at home'. That surprises people, who ask, 'Surely you've been everywhere by now?' I would not quite claim that, but in any case, I have never been embarrassed to return to a place in order to uncover some different part of our history. It has also helped that we have used Bradshaw's books from different eras, enabling us to focus on three time periods: the 1860s; the years immediately before the First World War; and the late 1930s, as war loomed once again.

The programmes have therefore changed their look – and not only because the presenter has grown older! For the mid-Victorian era, the archival imagery available to us consisted largely of illustrations, with the occasional photograph. When we reached 1913, photographs were plentiful and there was even some grainy moving footage. By the time of the 1936 guidebook, moving images abound.

George Bradshaw was born in Salford in 1801 and became a cartographer. He mapped canals and then railways, and spotted a gap in the market. While each rail company made it known when its own trains would run, the range of available services was not collated in a single book. *Bradshaw's Railway Time Tables* were first published in 1839, and from 1841 a new edition was published monthly until 1961.

The timetable's complexity came to be parodied in music hall song, and it soon made appearances in British literature. Setting out to solve a new case, Sherlock Holmes would ask Dr Watson to fetch the Bradshaw's from its place in the bookcase at 221B Baker Street. When Jonathan Harker first encounters Dracula in Transylvania, he is lying on a sofa 'reading, of all things in the world, an English *Bradshaw's Guide*'; for how, without a Bradshaw's, would the vampire plan the transport of fifty boxes of earth from Whitby, where he would land in England, to King's Cross station in London? 'Bradshaw's' became a generic noun for a timetable, much as, in my youth, 'Biro' meant any ballpoint pen, and 'Hoover' any vacuum cleaner.

Because we have passed through a revolution in information technology that has transformed our lives, we can perhaps understand how, in another era, the arrival of the railways changed everything. Before the railways, the world was as described by Jane Austen. Ordinary people walked most of their journeys. Those who were better off had horses, and for special journeys there were horse-drawn coaches. But these ran on rutted roads and were slow and uncomfortable. The upper classes embarked on grand tours, made possible by ship. Such excursions might take months, and storms, rocks and even pirates had to be braved along the way.

Robert Stephenson's *Rocket* had a top speed of thirty miles per hour, quite unlike anything that had travelled on land before. The Liverpool & Manchester Railway had been engineered by his father, George. Inaugurated on 15 September 1830, it was the first service to be operated entirely by steam locomotives (that is, with no need for winches or horses). It was dual-track and signalled, and on the first day, eight locomotives were fielded. It is extraordinary to me that the railway that was opened that first day was already so complete and versatile.

Indeed, in the nearly 200 years since then, the technology of railways has remained recognisable. Steam locomotion has been replaced by electric traction, but metal wheels still run on metal track, generally using a standard gauge first deployed by the Stephensons. In recent years, there has been a high-speed revival of railways in much of Europe, China and Japan, and they are clearly the direct descendants of that first Liverpool to Manchester line. I cannot think of any other Victorian invention that has 'lasted' so well.

Some of the first British railway journeys that we filmed were intended to be nostalgic for me. My mother's father was John W. Blyth, a manufacturer of linen in Kirkcaldy, and a collector of art, in particular Scottish paintings. My mother, Cora, would take me and my brothers to visit her parents. We made the journey thriftily, by night. Marketing hype is not new, and that slow train, on which we tried to snatch sleep while sitting bolt upright, was dubbed 'the Starlight Special'.

What *was* special was the arrival. We lived in a semi-detached house in London and my parents had no car. At Kirkcaldy, John Blyth's chauffeur, resplendent in a double-buttoned tunic, leather driving gloves and cap, met us in the monogrammed maroon Daimler. It purred the short distance to Wilby House, which struck me as magnificent, not least because pictures hung everywhere. A gong was rung for meals. But when allowed to 'get down from the table', I didn't need to go far beyond the garden to see the steam trains plying between Edinburgh and Dundee.

Shortly before reaching Kirkcaldy, the Starlight Special crossed the Forth Bridge. To my young eyes, it was the most magnificent piece of engineering imaginable, and the passage of decades has not lessened my sense of awe.

I am almost as impressed by the Ribblehead Viaduct, but the nostalgia is of a different sort. When I became a transport minister in 1988, British Rail had applied to close the Settle to Carlisle railway in order to save money and avoid expensive repairs to the viaduct. I was keen to refuse permission, because I valued the railway's heritage so much. However, it was tricky, since the government was urging British Rail to reduce its losses.

The Friends of the Settle–Carlisle Line proved to be a formidable force. They alerted rail lovers that the line might soon be gone, and passenger numbers climbed steeply during what might have been its last summer. Meanwhile, an engineer called Tony Freschini found a way to cut two-thirds from the bill for viaduct repairs. With fare income up and restoration costs sharply down, I was able to sign the refusal of closure.

When I travelled on the line filming for *Great British Railway Journeys*, I felt great personal joy because the line had survived. Crowds of people were out in the valleys to film the steam locomotive panting up the gradients through that magnificent scenery. The stations are beautifully kept by local volunteers, and villages along the way flourish thanks to the tourists attracted by the railway.

The third route that evokes memories for me is that short stretch on the Isle of Wight from Ryde to Shanklin, although when I travelled on it during summer holidays, it went on through the Boniface Down Tunnel to Ventnor; and, as it did so, the compartment filled with smoke from the locomotive. That smell, whenever I encounter it today, carries me directly back to childhood. Now, the service is operated by superannuated London Underground stock. It's not the same, but I love the fact that the line remains highly quirky.

During my early journeys of the series, I said the word 'Victorian' as often as I said 'Bradshaw'. Suitably, Queen Victoria featured frequently in our storytelling. She had a fear of speed, which, at first, made her reluctant to use railways. However, her husband, Prince Albert, was drawn to modern things, and he persuaded her aboard. She had to admit that the comfort of her private rail car far surpassed any horse-drawn coach, and she became a frequent user of trains between Windsor station (the scene of a failed assassination attempt upon her) and London, and to and from the South of France. She died at Osborne House on the Isle of Wight, and her coffin was returned by train, first to Waterloo, and then from Paddington on to Windsor.

Railways have been an important part of the modern human adventure. They accelerated the Industrial Revolution, as coal and timber were hauled to cities, factories and ports. They enabled the working class to travel, not least on holiday specials, which carried excited families from grimy cities to sandy resorts. Railways made women more independent, because the previous practice of chaperoning became impractical on frequent and lengthy train journeys. They increased contact between countries, but also played a macabre role in mechanised war.

Over the years, I have enjoyed my journeys very much, and I have met a large number of enthusiastic people with a story to tell me about the past. The history that I have learned has been my biggest stimulus. It has been exciting, at each stop, to discover what happened in that place. Perhaps an entrepreneur established a mill, or King George V arrived on the Royal train, or future prime minister James Ramsay MacDonald grew up in poverty, or unemployed men gathered to march from Jarrow to London.

At school, I learned about the Domesday Book. It is a great manuscript register of England and Wales ordered by William the Conqueror. It simply records exactly what there is in each place. At times, as the number of rail journeys has grown, I have felt as though we were making a new register, logging in each place what was and what is, along with an explanation of why railways might have been important in the transitions from one era to another. If that's what we have been doing, then our work is not yet done. How could it ever be, when there is always more to discover?

Chapter One

FOLLOWING THE
RAILWAY PIONEERS

Today's railway network came from a stable of far-sighted engineers with a vision of how untried, untested technology could change the face and pace of society. These men, with their three-dimensional insight, made blueprints into reality. Two hundred years ago, as an agricultural age gave way to industrialisation, no one was untouched. Although the heyday of railways is arguably gone, we still have the opportunity to ride on the same routes that these railway innovators knew so well.

Kilmarnock to Troon

Series 6, Episode 1

Distance: 10 miles

Michael Portillo: '[This] railway went on to become the earliest in Scotland to use a steam locomotive, and the towns of Troon and Kilmarnock benefitted significantly from its development.'

Early in its 200-year history, this pleasingly green rail route between Kilmarnock and Troon earned itself a raft of distinctions. Scotland's first tracks were laid here, and it's where horse-drawn passenger services – and later, steam locomotives – were initially paraded before a curious public. The country's earliest viaduct was a noteworthy feature of the line too. Perhaps more impressive still, though, is the fact that this historically virtuous stretch of rails wasn't simply abandoned when the rapid developments in technology threatened to leave it behind. As the Industrial Revolution cranked up, new rails were laid in place of the clunky originals and horses were replaced by fast-moving steam engines hauling both coal and people. Today, trains still thunder across parts of the track bed engineered when George III was on the throne.

With coal and minerals being dug at Kilmarnock, and the harbour from which they would be shipped at Troon, some ten miles distant, this trailblazer railway was built to fulfil an industrial equation. Landowner William Cavendish-Bentinck was the son of a British prime minister and was himself an MP.

Yet it's for his far-sighted approach regarding the introduction of the railway that he's best remembered.

At the time, the most obvious solution would have been a canal: waterways were inching their way across maps to carry freight while the Industrial Revolution made its slow start in Britain. But Cavendish-Bentinck's interest had been arrested by short stretches of waggonways being built at collieries, where horses towed carts whose wheels were borne on rails. Could this idea be expanded upon for his own industrial works?

At such a scale, it was virtually untried technology, but one that was much cheaper than building a canal. The alternative, roads, were a poor third choice. Some routes had been improved thanks to the turnpike trusts, a seventeenth- and eighteenth-century toll-driven initiative that reflected an increase in cross-country travel. Other roads, though, were slow and sometimes treacherous.

In the language of the day, the system he sought was known as a plateway, tramway or dramway – concepts that had been associated with wooden railways used for short stretches some fifty years previously. Railways with locomotives were, as yet, something largely unknown, with potential still unseen.

To his consternation, Cavendish-Bentinck discovered that not all his neighbours were poised to embrace the cutting-edge technology of iron rails in the way he was – and the new-fangled system would have to cut across their land. In response, he turned to former colleagues to supply the certainty he needed, and the Kilmarnock & Troon Railway was built after being incorporated by an Act of Parliament, passed in May 1808. For years afterwards, Parliament retained its role in sanctioning proposed lines. In anticipation of his project's enduring success, Cavendish-Bentinck won the right to make improvements to the harbour at Troon at the same time as getting the go-ahead for the railway.

While estimates for the railway may have been cheaper than a corresponding canal, at £38,000 (about £300,000 in today's currency) it was still a substantial sum. Investment came mostly from the Cavendish-Bentinck family. In 1809, Cavendish-Bentinck became the Duke of Portland, following the death of his father, which may well have boosted his finances.

One man, William Jessop, already had some experience of bigger railway projects, having built a link between Croydon and Wandsworth in southern England, where wagons were pulled by horses. Although his health had started to fade, Jessop was brought in to help surmount the obstacles that lay ahead, not least the River Irvine.

The track was made from wrought-iron rails, each one measuring 1 metre by 10 centimetres (3 feet by 4 inches) and weighing 18kg (40 pounds). They were L-shaped, with the upstanding ridge used to guide the wheels travelling on it. Each rail was nailed on to a stone sleeper block, with the nail going into a hole plugged with oak to create a solid fixing.

In an ambitious undertaking, double tracks were constructed from the outset, each 1.2 metres (4 feet) in width, with a generous gap between them, to permit free-flowing traffic. Although the gradient from Kilmarnock to the sea at Troon descended gently, its completion was still something of an engineering feat, while the four spans of the stone-built Laigh Milton Viaduct were another stand-out achievement.

The project was noteworthy enough for the *Scots Magazine* to report on it in 1812: 'The ground, on which these blocks are laid, is beat solid, and the stones are also beat down, after being laid, so as to give them all the solidity possible . . . The space of four feet between the rails is filled with road metal for the horse, to near the top of the ledges of the rails, and the outside to the sole of the rails.'

The line was opened on 6 July 1812 and, having cost nearly £60,000, was considerably over budget. (These were fiscally treacherous times and overspends like this could have cost the railway its future. Records reveal that, by 1813, the Glenbuck Iron Company in Ayrshire, where ore was extracted and processed, had been paid nearly £13,500 for about 72,000 rails. Nonetheless, that company went bankrupt the same year after the failure of its bank.)

To help recoup some of the investment, the Duke did not restrict traffic to his own industrial works, but permitted other operators to use it for a fee. Of course, they needed wagons that fitted the rails and a horse, to provide pulling power. A horse could tow a five-ton load from Kilmarnock to Troon in two hours.

Even before the official opening, one William Wright from Kilmarnock was already operating a passenger service three times a week, with each customer paying a toll by tonnage, which must have been disconcerting for the larger traveller. With the final leg to Kilmarnock still under construction, the entrepreneurial Wright began his trips from Gargieston, two miles short of the town centre. The journey took up to two hours and the only suspension was provided by a layer of straw. It didn't take long for the iron rails to be clogged with dirt, making it a bumpy and even dangerous ride.

The *Glasgow Herald* reported on 'a melancholy accident' that happened four miles from Troon in 1811, when a horse's harness gave way. 'The waggon tumbled down a precipice of seven or eight feet perpendicular. One man unfortunately was killed and some so severely hurt that their lives are despaired of . . .'

Still, it wasn't enough to deter travellers. Advertisements of the era reveal that one service, in a stagecoach-type wagon called *Caledonia*, offered an 'inside' day return for 2s 6d in 1814, while a single ticket was 1s 6d. Those passengers who opted to perch on the outside of the *Caledonia* paid 1s 6d return, or a shilling for a single fare. To add to its list of accolades, it may well be that the Kilmarnock & Troon service also had the first booking office.

Within a few years, the Duke spotted the potential of steam locomotives and bought one, believing it would enhance transport on his system. He almost chose a new rack-and-pinion design drawn up by inventor John Blenkinsop, one of the luminaries of the time, who was ultimately overshadowed by George Stephenson. By 1817, though, the Duke was convinced by a Stephenson design; however, it sat uncomfortably on the Scottish track. Its capacity to haul loads was limited, and its substantial weight kept breaking the iron rails. By now, technology was leaping forward. From being a visionary on the front edge of a wave, the Duke had been overtaken by rail design and a standard track width that didn't jigsaw with his own.

Undaunted, he set to, determined to keep pace. In 1837, wholesale changes were made to the line, including the construction of a new wooden bridge to replace the Laigh Milton Viaduct, in order to reduce the sharpness of the curves on the line. Despite the costs, the Kilmarnock to Troon line was an attractive enough proposition to be leased by the bigger and further-reaching Glasgow, Paisley, Kilmarnock & Ayr Railway by the mid-1840s. The Duke's project was a success: it set a standard for Scotland, and dividends were paid on company shares almost until the dawn of the twentieth century.

View from the train

For today's travellers, a different experience awaits. The line is longer, of course, and the wooden viaduct has been replaced by a third bridge that now carries trains across the River Irvine.

Having fallen into disrepair, the original Laigh Milton viaduct was improved in a 1996 scheme and is now suitable for use by walkers, with plaques highlighting its historical significance. Look down by the water's edge and it's still possible to see evidence of the nail-driven stone sleepers that held the rails in place for decades.

Troon has a different station, built in 1892 by Scottish architect James Miller, who also designed stations at Fort Matilda and West Kilbride, as well as commercial buildings in Glasgow. This station replaced one dating from 1839, which stood on a more easterly site. The modern railway services that scythe through Burns country are indebted to the platelayers from 1812, who provided a section of the track for them. Troon is now famous for its golf course and, during competitions, an extra 100,000 people a day pour through the station doors.

Stockton to Darlington

Series 8, Episode 3

Distance: 26 miles

Michael Portillo: 'In the thirty years after . . . railway lines opened between Stockton and Darlington, Britain was transformed. Bradshaw's readers would already take for granted rail journeys behind powerful and reliable locomotives. In a generation, the train had become an essential part of daily life.'

No one can be conclusively credited for inventing locomotives, but one man made such a significant contribution that he soon became known as 'the Father of Railways'. George Stephenson was hailed as an eminent engineer after the success of the Stockton & Darlington Railway in 1825, the first steam-hauled railway in the world, which carried 600 passengers on its inaugural run.

Two years before that, Stephenson, together with his son Robert, had started a locomotive factory in Newcastle. At the time, they were still experimenting with a new generation of engines that would replace the cumbersome static models of the past.

Although the technology was untried, they persuaded a newly formed railway company to abandon its plans for a horse-drawn plateway and back locomotion instead. However, Stephenson wasn't simply a gifted mechanical engineer and an intuitive civil engineer: he was also a diligent organiser who saw potential where others saw problems, and was always aware of what railways could offer. There were no blueprints to follow, thus it was his all-round ability and prophetic vision that catapulted him to the forefront of the rail revolution. Ultimately, George and Robert set robust guidelines for railway systems that everyone else in Britain and around the world then followed.

George Stephenson was born in 1781, the son of illiterate parents who lived nine miles outside Newcastle. George was working as a colliery engineman before he learned to read and write at night school. He continued in the pits after his marriage in 1802, making shoes and mending clocks to earn extra cash. Soon widowed, pit bosses got an early glimpse of his genius when he fixed a misfiring pump engine at a mine in Killingworth, saving his employer money. He went on to design an engine that could pull coal up an incline, albeit at just a few miles per hour.

For him, it was a steep learning curve. Heavy engines caused cast-iron tracks to buckle, so he helped redesign the rails using wrought iron. He found adding more wheels to the locomotive better distributed its weight. The price of failure was huge, but there were good reasons to invest in steam engines, keenly felt at the time. Horses needed food, which was in short supply even though the end of the Napoleonic Wars in 1815 had promised better trading conditions after years of shortages. But it was a poor harvest that year, blighted by a volcanic eruption in distant Indonesia. Corn Laws were imposed that kept cereal prices high, protecting landowners, who were producers, but punishing the poor. Suddenly the economies of keeping a horse were turned on their head and the advantages of having a machine that carried more freight faster than ever before was an irresistible proposition. It's why Stephenson's employers gave him a free hand.

Success at the Hetton Colliery, where an eight-mile stretch of railway was installed as the first system that didn't use horsepower, gave him unshakeable faith that bigger and better things were possible. The Stockton & Darlington Railway, which won assent from Parliament in 1821, was waiting in the wings. It was to be twenty-six miles long and would link a rich seam of coal from mines in south-west Durham to a riverside, at a time when coastal traffic played a fundamental role in carrying freight around the country.

If the elder Stephenson was the Father of Railways, then its great uncle was Edward Pease, the son of a woollen manufacturer and a prominent Quaker, who was the leading figure of the Stockton & Darlington Railway company. His initial aim was to put mines in County Durham on an equal footing with those then achieving dominance on Tyneside, becoming contenders in the race to get coal to London. He was sold on the idea of railways after talking to Stephenson, so much so that he bought into the Stephenson family firm. But to get the necessary financial backing from banks, Pease not only had to prove the commercial good sense of the scheme, but also to explain, without much evidence to prove it, that Britain was on the cusp of a transport revolution. His powers of persuasion were such that fellow Quakers, and many of his family members, provided the cash needed for the project. Without his involvement, there's an argument to say the railway might never have got off the ground.

Although locomotives had made a grand entry on to the industrial stage, there was a general acceptance during the early days of the railway that horses towing carts would play a part in operations. Therefore, Stephenson picked a gauge that corresponded with the width of a wagon. At one end, the gradients were thought to be too steep for either locomotives or horses, so winding engines were used. The cargo was turned over to horses in the middle part of the line, while locomotives flexed their might at a point where the track was flat. The route included the stone-built Skerne Bridge, the oldest railway bridge still in use today.

The first steam engine to run on the line on its opening day was *Locomotion* No.1, built by the Stephensons and taken by horse and cart from the factory. In addition to pulling ten wagons of coal and one of flour, there was a carriage for passengers, something of a departure in prevailing thought, which tended to focus on cargo alone.

At one junction, six of the coal wagons were uncoupled, with the contents distributed to the poor, and two new wagons were hitched up; one containing local dignitaries and the other a town band. Throughout, the route had been lined with enthusiastic sightseers, but by the time the train reached Stockton, the crowds were estimated to be 40,000-strong. Church bells were rung, the band played and a seven-gun salute was repeated three times.

Unfortunately, the pandemonium of the welcome repeated itself in the following weeks on the line. There were problems caused because it was a single track with only four passing loops in every mile. Without signals or communications between users, either mechanised or horse-drawn, fights broke out about who had priority. With both Stephensons engaged in other projects, it was down to a local manager, Timothy Hackworth, to orchestrate some manner of harmony, while also improving the rudimentary braking and reversing capacities of the locomotives, training drivers and redesigning the wheels so they didn't mangle the track. At this stage, no station was planned.

Despite a rapidly elevating status, George Stephenson never lost his strong regional accent. Early in his career, he had designed a mining lamp in about the same time frame as designer Humphrey Davy, who accused Stephenson of stealing his idea. After several run-ins with London-based scientists, Stephenson felt sure his Geordie brogue was inducing some people to believe his grasp of engineering was in some way second-rate. (The row about the safety lamp rumbled on for years, resulting in the design by Stephenson being used almost solely in the north east.) Accordingly, he ensured his son Robert had a broad education before he started working, although Robert was still a teenager when he, George and Pease officially opened the family firm that took his name. While he had a big hand in the design of *Locomotion*, Robert wasn't there to see it in action, as he had left the works in 1824 for a spell working as a mining engineer in Bolivia.

The Stockton & Darlington Railway was a local railway tailor-made to fit the needs of the immediate area. However, it was extended to Middlesbrough by 1830. It eventually spawned other lines, including the South Durham & Lancashire Union Railway, which opened in 1861 and crossed the Pennines to Furness. In 1863, both became part of the North Eastern Railway. The Stephensons' company grew until its site covered six acres, and they employed some 1,200 people at its peak.

Yet as a cornerstone of the railway story, it played its part in transforming the whole nation. Soon thousands of people were employed building railways and then running them. Countless more were manufacturing rails, locomotives and carriages, as well as producing bricks to line tunnels and quarrying stone for bridges.

As a result of the railways, people could travel vast distances domestically, try new food and sell produce at different markets. It was a platform for foreign travel too. And it's for all these reasons that George Stephenson is feted.

Liverpool to Manchester

Series 1, Episode 1

Distance: 33 miles

Michael Portillo: 'Before the railway, it took some thirty-six hours to cover the thirty miles by canal. This line cut journey times to just two hours: a revolution for intercity travel.'

New, improved steam engines were making an impact early in the nineteenth century, with Britain poised on the brink of a transport revolution that would have a significant effect on the population and its prosperity. Rails were already tried and trusted, but which of the steam engine designs vying for eminence would triumph? Merchants and factory owners keen to exploit a new age of manufacturing won parliamentary approval for tracks to link the cotton factories of Manchester with the busy port of Liverpool in 1826, although in the process some MPs scoffed at the idea that any locomotives running on them would exceed twenty-five miles per hour. Initially, the group had been set on using stationary engines with winding wires, which would haul wagons along newly laid tracks. Steam engines were already indispensable in agriculture and industry, but the majority stayed rooted to the spot.

However, after the shareholders employed George Stephenson – already a distinguished engineer – he persuaded them that locomotive power was the way forward for the pioneering Liverpool & Manchester Railway. His forward-thinking was pivotal – and, of course, as a locomotive builder, he had a vested interest – but there was plenty of hard graft needed before his vision could be celebrated.

A team of navvies armed with picks, shovels and wheelbarrows set to work, and there were challenging obstacles for them to overcome. For the thirty-three-mile route to be completed, it would require a tunnel to be excavated under a city, for the first time ever. Stephenson was on hand with plans for the 291-yard (266-metre) shaft. Not for the first time, he was developing proposals that other railway engineers would later follow.

The railway also included a viaduct, comprising nine arches made from yellow sandstone and red brick, across the Sankey Valley. High enough to clear the masted ships using the Sankey canal below, it was the earliest major railway viaduct in England. There was also a two-mile-long rock cutting at Olive Mount to complete. For the businessmen involved, while the ambition of the track-laying was not a point of contention, the rolling stock to be used on it most certainly was. To determine the best out of an array of options, they decided to hold a competition on a level, straight section of track that had been completed at Rainhill, between Liverpool and Manchester.

The Rainhill Trials were held in October 1829. Entering was no small undertaking. Anyone who wanted to take part had to first transport their engines to the north-west in pieces, inevitably using a combination of canals, carts and ships, then reassemble them on site. Strict rules were put in place to ensure a fair result among ten hopefuls, governing fuel, water and weight. The aim was to see how each competing engine fared over ten short trips that equalled the thirty-three-mile journey. Five contenders were immediately eliminated as they could not kick-start their engines in time to take part.

Cycloped was ready to be put through its paces – quite literally, as it was powered by a horse on a drive belt. While that sounds far-fetched today, it would have seemed a probable winner at the outset, coming off the back of a horse-drawn age. The term horsepower remains central to engineering, even today. But it was the first to retire, soon followed by the inaptly named *Perseverance*, a late-arriving Scottish entry, which quickly spluttered to a halt.

The stage was set for *Novelty*, from London, which soon roared up to a speed of twenty-eight miles per hour, to ringing cheers from the 15,000-strong crowd – until a furnace explosion brought it to an untimely halt. *Sans Pareil*, from Darlington, where the first English railway had begun four years previously, was also suffering technical hitches. This left the canary-yellow and white *Rocket*, designed by Robert Stephenson, a clear path to victory and the £500 first prize. Its maximum speed of thirty-six miles per hour was four times faster than the mail riders of the day, and it could carry loads far heavier than any horse-drawn cart could transport. Compared with static competitors, *Rocket* instantly proved more versatile. Winding engines and horse-drawn freight were almost immediately consigned to history, and the age of the locomotive dawned.

A year after the Rainhill Trials, the Liverpool & Manchester Railway was ready for its official opening. Guest of honour at the ceremony, on 15 September 1830, was the Duke of Wellington, the Tory prime minister, who was unpopular in northern towns for his opposition to progress in general, and votes for working men in particular. With regard to the railways, he said: 'I see no reason to suppose that these machines will ever force themselves into general use.'

The Prime Minister rode in one of a fleet of specially made carriages that set out from Liverpool with fanfare, pulled by the locomotive *Northumbrian*, which was being driven by George Stephenson himself. Further down the same train was William Huskisson, former President of the Board of Trade and Colonial Secretary, and an enthusiastic advocate for railways.

Two parallel tracks had been constructed, with one reserved for the prime ministerial train alone. An hour into the journey, the train had reached Parkside, where it stopped to take on water. Some passengers chose to stretch their legs by walking along the neighbouring track, oblivious to any dangers that railways could pose. Huskisson sought out the Duke of Wellington, hoping to repair a political rift from two years earlier that had resulted in Huskisson leaving the government. Without warning, Stephenson's *Rocket* came hurtling along, sending panicked passengers scattering. (It was long before any form of communication along the rails had developed.) Most stepped clear of the lines, but Huskisson clung to the door of the Duke's carriage. Unfortunately, it wasn't latched, and it swung slowly outwards into the path of the oncoming engine. Already in poor health, Huskisson was terribly injured, suffering a crushed leg. Stephenson took charge and ensured the injured man was sent to nearby Eccles for medical care as quickly as possible. Despite the proud engineer's best efforts, chaos ensued, not least because an angry crowd soon blocked the by-now delayed train carrying the Duke. With Stephenson's careful choreography now out of kilter, there were locomotives obstructing the line that the prime ministerial party wanted to use for a quick getaway. As for Huskisson, he died later that night, becoming the first railway fatality.

An account that appeared in *Mechanics Magazine* described what happened after the ceremony as travellers returned to Liverpool. The train, already powered by two engines, picked up another three, although hopes for an incremental increase in speed were dashed.

> We went still slower than before, stopping continually to
> take water – query, to take breath – and creeping along at
> a snail's pace, till we reached Sutton inclined plane; to get

up which the greater part of the company were under the necessity of alighting and making use of their own legs. On reaching the top of the plane, we once more took our seats, and at 10 o'clock we found ourselves again at the company's station in Crown Street, having accomplished the distance of 33 miles in 4 hours and 40 minutes.

Despite the tragedy and its confusing aftermath, the first scheduled passenger service, carrying 140 people, set off as per the timetable the next day. In Crown Street and Manchester's Liverpool Road, the cities each had a new intercity terminus. Neither would endure for very long. The Crown Street premises were shut in 1836 with the opening of Lime Street station, while the Manchester site operated for just fourteen years before becoming a goods yard when the weight of passengers meant a new station was needed, leading to the construction of Manchester Victoria.

The rapid turnover in stations reflects how the railway industry frequently now risked becoming the victim of its own success. Following the Rainhill Trials, the railway company invested heavily in *Rocket* and its sister locomotives, which already bore improvements by the time they arrived. But technology was now moving so rapidly that their design was outdated within three years. Despite its fame and an instantly recognisable silhouette, *Rocket* quickly became obsolete. And there was still considerable opposition to the railway to overcome, especially from canal owners and shareholders. Nearby Worsley once considered itself the birthplace of a transport revolution, thanks to the Bridgewater Canal, which linked coal mines there with Manchester city centre. Now it was being thrust unwillingly into the shade by the close proximity of the railway. The canal ran both above and below ground, not only providing transport from the coal face, but also helping to drain the mine. It had an aqueduct with three sandstone arches to carry it over the River Irwell. Opening in 1761, it's thought of by some as the trigger for the Industrial Revolution. But canal users of the 1830s must have watched with some trepidation as the Liverpool & Manchester Railway crossed it at Patricroft, at considerable speed. (Worsley didn't get its own station until 1864, with travellers using the Liverpool & Manchester line and changing at Eccles.)

Canal users were right to be worried. Within twenty years, there were 6,200 miles of rail in Britain, providing inexpensive and flexible travel for passengers and freight at an ever-increasing pace.

Greystones to Dublin

Series 8, Episode 12

Distance: 19 miles

Michael Portillo: 'Here is a daring feat of engineering built
by the Father of Irish Railways.'

It is the line that first introduced the Irish to passenger trains,
combining the ingenuity of two great engineers: William
Dargan, dubbed 'the Father of Irish Railways', and England's
Isambard Kingdom Brunel. For would-be entrepreneurs, its
construction was also a salutary lesson on the perils of the railway business: greedy landowners, vested interests, challenging
geology and, particularly, burgeoning costs. The fact that it was
built in spite of these obstacles was as much a testament to
innovative engineering skills as it was to the can-do attitude
underpinning the Victorian economy.

The opening of Britain's first public steam railway, the
Stockton & Darlington, in 1825 soon convinced a group of Irish
businessmen that this new technology was a runner. In February 1831, the directors of the Dublin & Kingstown Railway
Company obtained parliamentary approval for a six-mile track
between Westland Row, in the heart of Dublin city, and Kingstown (today known as Dún Laoghaire). The leading promoter
was stockbroker James Pim. His home overlooked Kingstown
harbour, and he could see the potential for wealthy commuters
like himself to replace interminable coach journeys along an
overcrowded, pot-holed, mud-strewn road. But Pim was also a

Quaker and philanthropist. He believed a slice of his wealth should, in any case, be used in the cause of progress.

Studies by the Dublin & Kingstown Railway made clear the popularity of the existing road. It carried 70,000 journeys a month, of which 48,000 were by horse and carriage, 6,000 by horse-riders, and the rest by carts and gigs. Averaged out at 2,300 journeys per day, this would produce, even by conservative estimates, an annual income of £30,000 on railway operating costs of £10,000. And that sum didn't even take into account the ongoing expansion of Kingstown harbour, which was being improved to accommodate the increased freight and passenger traffic from new iron-clad steamships. This would, in turn, lead to more potential users for the railway as the harbour became busier.

Pim had made detailed studies of new railway lines in England; he had contacts with merchants and bankers in Liverpool, Bristol, Cardiff and London; and he was meticulous in his planning. This helped ensure government backing from both the Board of Works, which had agreed a £75,000 stake in the Dublin & Kingstown Railway, and the War Department, which saw it could disembark troops quickly into Ireland in the event of yet another armed rebellion or, worse, a French invasion ahead of an attack on England. All in all, Pim's project was what today's investment analysts would call a no-brainer. The Board of Trade insisted on Charles Vignoles as chief engineer, while William Dargan, who would go on to build 60 per cent of Ireland's rail network, was appointed contractor.

Dargan had made his name in canal and road construction and the skills needed to build a coastal railway – sea embankments, bridges, cuttings – were similar. More importantly, he knew how to get the best from his labourers, the gangs of tough 'navvies' who roamed the country seeking work. Dargan had a reputation for treating his workers well, ensuring they were paid on time and helping out if they were short of food. During the famine years, he became known among them as 'the man with his hand in his pocket', sometimes telling malnourished workers to go home and build up their strength without fear their pay would be docked.

But before work could start, compensation deals had to be struck with landowners. This proved far more expensive than expected. The somewhat batty peer Baron Cloncurry insisted he could no longer enjoy privacy for his cherished swims in the sea, while the other principal objector, the Reverend Lees, played hardball in order to screw the company out of every penny he could. At one point, Dargan even considered tunnelling under the land in question, but this idea was rejected as being too difficult, dangerous and expensive. The dispute was eventually settled by paying the churchman an outrageous £7,500, while Cloncurry took £3,000 on the proviso that a bridge over the line was built 'in the best Italianate style' so that he and his dogs could still stroll to his favourite bathing area. He also demanded, and got, a granite bathing hut, the design of which was based on a Greek 'pleasure dome for men'.

With the all-clear from the lawyers, Dargan recruited 1,000 labourers from across Ireland and England to pickaxe and shovel their way along the railway's route. These men were seen almost as a race apart by polite society – one Dublin clergyman, the Reverend St George Sargent, described them as 'the most neglected and spiritually destitute people I ever met' – and to start with, they were poorly paid. In June 1833, after a group of so-called agitators persuaded the navvies to down tools, their simmering discontent evolved into a riot, which received an over-zealous police response. The situation calmed down only when Dargan persuaded his directors to pay a better piecework rate based on the number of wheelbarrows of earth shifted.

Construction then continued on schedule, although a series of landslides and the collapse of a culvert bridge in Dublin following flooding in late 1834 threatened to delay the grand opening. But again, Dargan's force of will triumphed and on 17 December 1834, the 9 a.m. Dublin to Kingstown locomotive *Hibernia* pulled away just 30 minutes late. The track was lined by a crowd of some 4,000 cheering onlookers, while the *Dublin Evening Post* noted that 'the carriages were filled by a very fashionable concourse of persons and the greatest eagerness was manifested to witness the first operation of the work'. The one minor problem, according to *The Times* of 22 December, was that springs between carriages were not 'sufficiently elastic' to prevent sudden jolts when the train stopped. As a result, 'three or four gentlemen had on one occasion today their heads knocked together', although 'the majority had hard Irish heads and did not mind a few knocks'. Overall, the Dublin & Kingstown Railway, now arguably the world's first commuter railway, was hailed a magnificent achievement. Investors collected dividends of 10 per cent on profits for many years, and the company's board enjoyed a gratifying revenge on the avaricious Reverend Lees (now a railway enthusiast) by denying him a station convenient to his home.

The success of the line was now the springboard for an even greater engineering challenge – an extension along the rocky outcrop of Bray Head towards Greystones and Wicklow. By 1844, Dargan had built track as far as Dalkey, using part of a former quarry tramway, and among guests at the opening ceremony was none other than Isambard Kingdom Brunel. He used the occasion to make a business proposition to the Dublin & Kingstown Railway board; would they consider a joint venture to extend the line much further – right down the south-east coast to Wexford? The carrot was Brunel's plan to build a railway line across South Wales to Fishguard, connecting with a ferry link to Rosslare, near Wexford. A rail link from there on to Dublin would create a continual flow of passengers and freight traffic. The board were convinced, and two years later, the Waterford, Wexford, Wicklow & Dublin Railway Company was formed. But it would be nine years before Brunel and Dargan managed to complete the twenty-four-mile link to Wicklow.

The reason for that lies partly in the geology of the Wicklow Mountains as they tumble down to their foothills along the Irish Sea coast. The quartzites of Bray Head, in particular, comprise hard-to-drill Precambrian rocks, and their vertical strata meant they were vulnerable to collapse during tunnelling. An additional problem lay in coastal erosion and the resulting landslips. But the project was also badly affected by the economic shock of the Great Famine (1845–49). Investors fought shy of pumping ever more cash into the new line, and work was constantly delayed. Brunel also had other commitments in England. By 1848, construction was at a standstill.

It seems odd that Brunel and Dargan didn't opt for a more straightforward, if longer, route that would have taken the track inland. One theory has it that Lord Meath did not want the vista from his Kilruddery residence spoiled, and so offered the Bray Head land for free. Whatever the truth, the engineering partnership remained focused on the coastal route, blasting three tunnels, bridging a 300-foot ravine (and then replacing the original bridge after it was destroyed by a storm swell), moving the line 10 feet to avoid a landslide and even bolting cantilevered roofs over sections of track to protect trains from falling stones. Not until 1850 did the 500-strong workforce manage to overcome Bray Head. Five years later, the line opened as far as Wicklow, eventually reaching Wexford in 1872. Dargan and Brunel had fulfilled their goal of bringing a railway to the far south, although not for nothing did it earn it the nickname Brunel's Folly. By the early twentieth century, it was clear that four new tunnels would have to be bored, each pushing the route further away from the waves that were undermining the original foundations. Passengers travelling between Greystones and Dublin today can still see the abandoned tunnel entrances, architectural ghosts of the Victorian age.

Newcastle to Berwick

Series 3, Episode 16

Distance: 63 miles

Michael Portillo: 'To unite the English and the Scottish required a monumental piece of Victorian engineering by Robert Stephenson.'

In the mid-1840s, engineers struggled to keep pace with the frenzy of railway construction as passengers yearned for simple journeys and railway company owners demanded meaningful profit. There was no central strategy that governed the way the railways developed, and as the network crawled across the British map, there was pressure to fill in the gaps. One such example was in the north-east corner of England, where the process of industrialisation was fizzing. Scottish engineers linked Berwick with Edinburgh in 1846. A year later, tracks were laid between Tweedmouth and London – but passengers making the journey between Edinburgh and London had to take to a horse and carriage followed by a ferry to get from one line to the next, as the two were separated by the River Tweed.

The missing piece of the jigsaw would be the Royal Border Bridge, a mighty structure built by Robert Stephenson that not only created a continuous link between the two capital cities, but helped to sweep away centuries of hostility between the two nations. By now, Victorians were so invested in progress that Berwick Castle's Great Hall – where King Edward I, 'the hammer of the Scots', took reluctant oaths of allegiance from Scottish nobility in 1296 – was demolished.

Born in 1803, Stephenson junior lived in lockstep with the railway age for his entire life. He was still a teenager when he began helping his father George orchestrate the Stockton & Darlington line. After that, he was an engineer and advisor, both with his father and in his own right, on numerous railway projects in Britain, as well as helping to export the technology across the globe. He undertook the London & Birmingham Railway, which was authorised in 1833. At 112 miles long, this was a hugely challenging project, especially as the necessary skills were still in their infancy. Today he is best remembered for the many bridges he built for railways, which still dominate various points of the British skyline.

The speed at which projects were demanded by railway-hungry customers, and the stress of getting designs safely *in situ* from paper plans, was immense. The earliest iron bridge in Britain to carry trains pulled by locomotives was his High Level Bridge in Newcastle, also on the Newcastle & Berwick Railway line, which was completed in 1849 and was the first bridge to carry rail and road traffic, with a toll levied there until 1937.

The Royal Border Bridge was being built at the same time, but this was entirely a stone structure. Stephenson and his colleague Thomas Harrison flipped between the two, distilling the best construction practices for both. Stephenson was particularly diligent at Tweedmouth when it came to the foundations, with piles driven down to bedrock through 12 metres (40 feet) of dense gravel, with a steam-driven pile driver (invented in 1843 by Scots-born James Nasmyth) being put through its paces. Deep coffers, enclosures that are pumped out while work takes place, were sunk to aid construction by a workforce some 2,700 strong. The bridge was built with 227,000 cubic metres (eight million cubic feet) of stone, while the inner faces of the arches needed two and a half million bricks, which were set in cement and then faced with stone. The result was spectacular. Built on a curve, the viaduct has fifteen arches over land, which were completed before the remaining thirteen over water were built. Each span measures 18.6 metres (60 feet), which has the bridge at 658 metres (2,160 feet) in length. At its greatest height above the riverbed, the rails are 37 metres (120 feet) in the air. With foresight, iron bars were embedded into the masonry to break up any ice floes drifting down the river. (In 1881, large ice blocks crashed into pillars that supported the Solway Firth Viaduct, opening up two major gaps.)

The figures above prove 'the Tweed viaduct' was a giant undertaking, but there was an impatience about the project that meant a temporary wooden bridge was built to get the railway moving, which was opened to trains in September 1848. By now, railway investor and politician George Hudson had bought up the line so it became the York, Newcastle & Berwick Railway. It's said Hudson distributed £3,000 worth of bribes to secure the Yorkshire to Newcastle leg of the network, gleefully anticipating a quick profit by planning to operate the first railway line between London and Edinburgh. Alas, he was trumped north of the border by the North British Railway Company, so his ambitious plans were thwarted.

The sense of grandeur introduced by the Royal Border Bridge seemed to be infectious, as there were unusually fine stations on each side of the river. In Berwick, the station grew up from the ruins of Berwick Castle, once a magnificent medieval stronghold, now with a railway platform spanning an area that was once the preserve of kings. Tweedmouth station stood in splendid isolation on the other bank, built with tall chimney stacks, decorated gables and a five-arch portico. Its cost, at more than £8,500, was about four times the average for the era. The Royal Border Bridge was opened by Queen Victoria and

Prince Albert on 29 August 1850, on the same day as Newcastle station. The Queen had given her permission for the use of 'Royal' in the bridge's name. Yet the word 'Border' is misleading, as the bridge is entirely in England, with the start of Scottish territory still some two-and-a-half miles north of Berwick.

Despite the success of the six-span iron High Line Bridge, stone viaducts remained popular, crossing some of the country's most spectacular ravines. In 1858, the Hownes Gill Viaduct opened just eighteen months after construction started, providing a link in the Stockton & Darlington line to replace the winching system that had been designed by Robert Stephenson in 1834. Its dozen arches, measuring 213 metres (700 feet) in length, were built with 2.5 million firebricks. For designer Thomas Bouch, it was a triumph: one of many achievements he enjoyed in bridge-building, tramway-laying, railway-laying and ferry-loading. However, the mighty Hownes Gill Viaduct was not the only common ground to link Bouch and Stephenson.

Both knew the ignominy of being responsible for a bridge that collapsed with tragic consequences. For Stephenson, it was the bridge that crossed the Dee, built for the Chester to Holyhead line. The accident happened on 24 May 1847, just as work on Stephenson's Newcastle and Berwick bridges was commencing. Of the twenty-five people on the train, including the driver, fireman and coach, there were five fatalities when the last of three bridge spans gave way as the locomotive was crossing.

While Stephenson was convinced that the train had derailed, investigations pointed to a fracture in a cast-iron girder being the cause of the accident. This is now recognised as metal fatigue, something that was barely understood at the time. The disaster was one of the first investigated by the newly instituted Railway Inspectorate. At the time, a local inquest questioned whether Stephenson was negligent. More compellingly, a jury decided: 'There are upwards of one hundred bridges similar in principle and form to the late one over the river Dee . . . all are unsafe.' Still, Stephenson's reputation proved robust enough to withstand the criticism, and he remained in charge on the bridges at Newcastle and Berwick.

For Bouch, the outcome was far graver. He had been the engineer in charge of the Tay Bridge, opened on 1 June 1878, then the longest railway bridge in the world, across Scotland's longest river. It was a feat for which he had been knighted. But eighteen months later, the 5.20 p.m. train from Burntisland to Dundee, consisting of four third-class carriages, one second-class and one first-class, was being lashed by a fearful storm as it began to cross the bridge. Observers saw the train lights at first horizontal, and then vertical as the locomotive drove into a chasm. The central girders of the bridge had given way, leading to the worst rail catastrophe of the era. Bouch was woken by a telegram and went to the scene, where he saw the lattice girders of the bridge looking like a broken skeleton, and the river filled with boats, searching for survivors. Finding bodies turned into a week-long operation. There were an estimated seventy-five deaths, but not all the passengers' bodies were recovered. The stopped silver watch of one victim showed the time as 7.16 p.m.

After the inquiry that followed, which specifically referenced substandard construction and poor maintenance, Bouch was squarely blamed for the disaster. Immediately, he was relieved of responsibility for the Forth Bridge, which he had been commissioned to design, and he died a broken man in 1880. One obituary said of Bouch: 'In his death, the profession has to lament one who, though perhaps carrying his works nearer to the margin of safety than many others would have done, displayed boldness, originality and resource in a high degree, and bore a distinguished part in the later development of the railway system.'

By comparison, Robert Stephenson's reputation escaped almost unscathed. But there's little doubt that the pressure of his work took a toll. Outwardly he was confident, serving as an MP from 1847, and playing an integral part in the organisation of the Great Exhibition in 1851. At the time, he was credited with building one third of Britain's railways: some 2,000 miles of track.

However, when he was building the Britannia Bridge across the Menai Strait, something of the inner torment of an engineer was revealed. When the Admiralty refused to have the Strait closed for the construction work, Stephenson was compelled to float wrought-iron tubes into place and then have them jacked up to bridge height, an untested procedure. The official painter for the project observed Stephenson as the operation was successfully carried out, noting: 'As his nerve tension increased with the suspense . . . involuntary tears were seen to be trickling down his face.'

Could the stress that each engineering challenge presented have contributed to Stephenson's early death, and that of his friend, Isambard Kingdom Brunel? Both died in the autumn of 1859, after suffering years of failing health, Brunel at fifty-three and Stephenson at fifty-six. Joseph Locke, another leading engineer of the age, whose achievements are often eclipsed by those of Stephenson and Brunel, died the following year, aged fifty-five.

View from the train

From a vantage point on the Royal Border Bridge, the landscape is spectacular for miles distant. In the foreground, there is the seventeenth-century Berwick Bridge and the Royal Tweed Bridge, which opened in 1928. Now part of the East Coast Main Line, the configuration of modern railway paraphernalia doesn't look the same here as it does elsewhere. That's because the Royal Fine Art Commission was consulted on plans that aimed to reduce the visual impact when the line was electrified in 1989. The first significant maintenance on the bridge, when the land-based arches needed repair, was carried out four years later. In 2010, the bridge was illuminated to mark its 160th anniversary.

Oxford to Pershore

Series 3, Episode 11

Distance: 53 miles

Michael Portillo: 'While the railways affected everywhere, many places were left unspoiled. This is still a land of green pastures.'

It's been called the last pitched battle between two private armies on British soil. Armed with pickaxes and shovels, rival gangs of navvies clashed after work stalled on what's now known as the Cotswold Line. In command of one group was a contractor who called in magistrates and constables to defend himself and his men. Heading the other was one of Britain's most distinguished engineers, Isambard Kingdom Brunel.

With his stovepipe hat and fat cigar, standing against a backdrop of colossal engineering projects of the era, Brunel endures as an emblematic figure of the Victorian age. Although his boundless ambition sometimes trumped his technical expertise, Brunel has nonetheless been dubbed 'the man who built Britain'. Indeed, he's still so revered he was named the second most famous Briton of all time in 2002, behind wartime leader Winston Churchill.

But in July 1851, he was a man battling financial pressures and the frustrations of a works schedule that was overdue. He'd been put in charge of building the Oxford, Worcester & Wolverhampton Railway after it was incorporated on 4 August 1845, a project that enjoyed significant input from the Great

Western Railway. Given the breadth of his workload, tracts of the project were contracted out, common practice at the time, but something that put distance between the engineer and his scheme. One such contractor was Robert Marchant, who went unpaid after he was deemed to be dragging his heels at Mickleton, a Gloucestershire village lying close to both Warwickshire and Worcestershire.

With each end of the line virtually complete, it was this middle section and its tunnel that was causing investors a headache, and Brunel was told by Great Western Railway to take personal control of the matter.

A report in the *Illustrated London News* in July 1851 outlines what happened. In short, a group of replacement navvies was marched to the tunnel by an agent representing Brunel, but Marchant refused to give way, despite a scuffle. Indeed, he claimed that he was owed money and that tools on the site were his property. Marchant then called in magistrates and policemen, armed with cutlasses.

The magistrates read 'the Riot Act', a piece of law dating from 1714 by which local authorities could compel any group numbering more than a dozen to disperse. For a while peace reigned, but Brunel, while appearing to play along with the magistrates' requests to withdraw, had in fact sent out a call for re-enforcements to navvies working on other lines under his personal umbrella. Men from nearby Warwick, who'd been building the line from Oxford to Birmingham, began marching to Mickleton Tunnel, their boots tramping through sleepy villages during the night until the army of men poised to move against Marchant numbered about 2,000. With the advantage of this manpower, Brunel was eventually victorious, as Marchant could see he was sorely outnumbered, having only about 150 workers. He withdrew, and both sides agreed to arbitration.

But let there be no mistake. Brunel was exerting his charisma to manipulate the men in his employ and seemed happy to break the law in order to achieve his aim. Later, shareholders were told the tunnel had been reclaimed 'without absolute violence', but there's no doubt there were clashes among the men, who had been relieved of the tedium of track-building and brought together in a uniting cause trumpeted by Brunel. Conversely, one must assume, there were orders issued by Brunel to temper any fighting. While these were rough-hewn men who were expert at wielding hefty tools, there were no deaths – although one man had his little finger bitten off during the ruckus. The tunnel was finally completed in the spring of 1852. The Oxford, Worcester & Wolverhampton line launched with a Latin motto that roughly translated to 'persevere through difficulties to true things'. Later known as the 'Old Worse and Worse', it was amalgamated with two other lines to form West Midland Railway in 1860, before becoming part of Great Western Railway three years later, just one of numerous companies soaked up by the conglomerate.

Brunel had long been associated with Great Western Railway, which itself had been started in 1835 to link London and Bristol. But before working with the company, he worked on two projects that were, by any standards of the day, abject failures. Born in 1806, he was the son of a Frenchman, who fled the French Revolution, and the English woman he married. As a result, Isambard was schooled in both France and England, although arguably he learned most at the knee of his father, Marc, a talented artist and mathematician.

Marc designed and made numerous successful projects, such as a sawmill in Battersea and a machine to manufacture soldiers' boots. But, at the time, industrial infrastructure was expensive and didn't necessarily persuade critics. Despite being a Fellow of the Royal Society, Marc was put in debtors' prison in 1821 after some costly projects failed to materialise. Only after he made plans to move to Russia did the British government clear his debts and secure his freedom. Three years later, Marc was given the task of tunnelling under the River Thames between Wapping and Rotherhithe to relieve chronic traffic congestion. Eighteen-year-old Isambard was on hand to help.

Among his designs, Marc had a tunnelling shield that compartmentalised tunnellers at different heights on a 'pastry cutter', which was thrust forward on jacks. Even so, the evolving tunnel suffered flooding several times, with the toxic waters of the Thames claiming several lives. After one incident in which Isambard was nearly killed, the project, by now almost bankrupt, was put on ice.

Already acknowledged as a workaholic, the young Isambard's frustration with the confines of ill health and financial constraints were apparent. In 1829, he wrote in his diary: 'What a life, the life of a dreamer. I'm always building castles in the air. What time I waste.'

As he recuperated in Bristol following the Thames Tunnel incident, Isambard spotted a competition for a bridge design to span the River Avon and decided to enter. In just seven weeks, he produced blueprints for four suspension bridge designs, which would span the Avon Gorge, taking traffic an awe-inspiring 75 metres (245 feet) above the water. By far the most eye-catching design was one that featured lofty towers in an Egyptian style flanking the bridge's ends. It was the longest span ever suggested and competition judge, Thomas Telford, who had designed the Menai Suspension Bridge linking Anglesey to North Wales, declared it an impossibility. Indeed, Telford scrapped all the competition entries, proposing his own design instead. People were so outraged the competition was staged again, and this time Isambard was victorious.

He began work on the bridge in 1831, still aged just twenty-five. But that rapidly came to an end after the Queen Square riots later that same year. Disgruntled working men rioted when Sir Charles Weatherall visited the city. He was a judge and politician who opposed expanding the number of people who could vote. At the time, just 6,000 had a say at elections when the city's population was 104,000. In the ensuing clashes, Isambard was made a special constable to help keep law and order. Although the rioting was over in three days, investors were sufficiently horrified by what occurred there to withdraw funding from the bridge.

Now Isambard had two major but incomplete engineering projects behind him. Having sucked the available budgets dry, the Thames tunnel and the footings for the Clifton Suspension Bridge seemed like enduring monuments to his failure. He had irons in the fire, he noted, but none of them were hot.

But 1831 was a pivotal year for Isambard for another reason. He took his first ride on the Liverpool & Manchester Railway, which had recently started its scheduled service, and noticed immediately how, in modern parlance, it was a boneshaker.

'The time is not far off when we shall be able to take our coffee and write while going noiselessly and smoothly at 45 miles per hour,' he observed.

View from the train

Today's traveller, upon leaving Oxford and its graceful spires on the Cotswold Line, witnesses the city give way to rolling hills that typify an area further characterised by the honey-coloured stone used for its buildings. You'd be forgiven for not knowing it was a Jurassic limestone formed at a time when the area was covered in a warm sea. But as rail exploration of the area continues to unfold, it soon becomes clear that a stone that's amber in the north of the Cotswolds and golden at the heart of the region is bleached almost white in Bath. The luminosity of Cotswold stone is so prized it's previously been spirited from the area for projects including Windsor Castle, Eton College, Blenheim Palace and the Houses of Parliament. For many, warm-stoned Cotswolds villages and pubs are quintessentially English.

However, a railway navvy from Isambard's time would have been looking for something entirely different. As the tracks made steady progress, he would have been eyeing barley in the fields bordering the line, aware that this was a key ingredient for beer. Traditional breweries were established in the area, at a time when it was felt beer was a health drink – or healthier than water, anyway. Moreover, it was patriotic to drink domestically brewed beer rather than imported wine. Old-style breweries – being tall – would have been visible for several miles distant. The luckiest navvies were brought beer from breweries by horse and cart, and it would have been dark in colour from the highly roasted malt.

Exeter to Newton Abbot

Series 4, Episode 20

Distance: 20 miles

Michael Portillo: 'I've arrived alongside the coastal beauty
of what Bradshaw's would call South Devonshire. This was
the scene of some of Isambard Kingdom Brunel's greatest
railway engineering successes and worst failures – and
both his triumphs and disasters prove his genius.'

In 1833, when Isambard Kingdom Brunel became chief engineer of the Great Western Railway, he could see, in his mind's
eye, passengers with a single ticket taking a west-bound train,
then climbing aboard a company ship and heading to America.

Before that happened, he had to survey a route that would
take a London train into Bristol, construct the first ocean-
going, steam-powered ship, and build the station where the
inclusive ticket could be bought. As it happened, his ship –
the *Great Western* – was making regular crossings before the
first locomotive completed the land part of the trip. Although
the railway line project was riddled with hitches, go-it-alone
Brunel set about them with dogged determination. However, his
confident – sometimes intolerant – exterior masked inner concerns. On Boxing Day in 1835, as he was talking up the Great
Western main line at every opportunity, he wrote in his diary:
'Everything at this moment is uncertain . . . it can't last. Bad
weather must surely come. Let me see the storm in time and
gather in my sails.'

Initially, Isambard had been asked by Great Western Railway to work in concert with George Stephenson. But he declined the proposal, saying that, by working in that way, the company 'would not obtain that individual responsibility which alone can secure to them the best advice, and they might become seriously embarrassed by differing opinions . . .'

And while both men were fine engineers, there were some substantial differences in approach. The most starkly obvious was Isambard's avid preference for a broad gauge. George Stephenson had stuck with his standard gauge, measuring 143.5 centimetres (4 feet 8½ inches), for all the railways in which he had a hand. This seemed to Brunel to be a hangover from the age of colliery locomotives, with the penalty being that journeys were unnecessarily slow and uncomfortable. He argued that a broad gauge, measuring 213.4 centimetres (7 feet) offered travellers better accommodation, and meant that more freight could be carried on each journey. As a consequence, there was an issue that began to loom large as railway building accelerated. In an era when literally dozens of different companies were involved in railway construction without a national strategy in place, the network could not be properly linked up.

Undaunted, Brunel went ahead with the route between London and Bristol, with wide tracks laid through the Thames Valley and the Marlborough Downs, and also began work on the longest tunnel to be built so far. Critics said that at one-and-three-quarter miles (2.8 km) long, and through notoriously unstable geology, the Box Tunnel, between Bath and Chippenham, was an impossibility. Brunel sank shafts, and labourers worked between them in six sections. Each week, one ton of explosives was expended in making progress from one end to the next, as well as one ton of candles, so the men could see what they were doing. As they worked, pumping mechanisms had to be increased as water continually leeched from the hillside.

By 1841 the tunnel was open, completing the intercity line, albeit at a cost of a hundred men's lives. It was wide enough to accommodate two broad-gauge tracks throughout, and the line was so flat that it was nicknamed 'Brunel's billiard table'. His genius was such that observers believed he had lined up the shaft so that the rising sun could be seen in the tunnel on his birthday, 9 April. When later commentators realised the sun appeared fractionally off-centre on that date, that theory was thought quirky, until one researcher realised a perfect alignment actually happened three days earlier – on the birthday of Brunel's younger sister.

Travellers using the line at today's high speeds don't get the chance to admire the classical design of the tunnel's west portal as their train plunges into the tunnel. The one at the eastern end is less grand.

Likewise, they won't necessarily be aware of Brunel's bridge at Maidenhead, which has two wide brick arches and was initially derided by those who felt it could not bear the weight of trains. Opened to rail traffic in 1839, Great Western Railway insisted wooden scaffolding used during construction was left in place to support the bridge. Brunel had no option but to concur, but lowered the scaffolding slightly so it played no role before the planks were eventually swept away in a storm.

But there was trouble for free-spending risk-taker Brunel further down the line. By 1844, Bristol and Exeter were linked by a (broad-gauge) track masterminded by Brunel. The next leg, heading west to Plymouth, needed to be engineered. The obvious route for the track bed went close to the sea at Dawlish, then into the steep escarpments of Dartmoor. Even for someone of Brunel's calibre, it was going to be a challenge to get locomotives to smoothly and safely tackle these curves and gradients. To counter this, Brunel chose the virtually untested system of atmospheric railways, powered by vacuum rather than steam, and on the face of it a more agile option.

It was, he noted, swift, silent and smokeless, and, at first glance, presented itself as a step change in the Industrial Revolution, cleaning up the transport industry at a stroke, with pollution restricted to the engine houses. He was among many inspired by the Dalkey extension, a two mile tramway outside Dublin that extended an existing railway line, which used a single pump station to provide propulsion. One man who wasn't impressed was Robert Stephenson, who cautioned his friend against it.

For the South Devon Railway line, the atmospheric railways relied on a cast-iron traction pipe with a slot in it for a piston attached to a leading carriage. Engine houses with distinctive square chimneys were pitched at regular points along the line to suck air out of the pipe, creating a vacuum, and it was this that pulled the carriage. To keep the pipe airtight, it was furnished with leather flaps to cover the slot.

The South Devon atmospheric railway opened in 1847, although locomotives were borrowed from Great Western Railway at first to consolidate the service. It turned out the system was underpowered, and coal consumption at the engine houses was far higher than anyone anticipated. But the underlying difficulties were climate-related. In the autumn, the leather flaps got drenched; in the winter, they froze; and in hot weather, they dried out and became brittle. As the seasons progressed, the innovative system proved itself unviable, and, the following year, Brunel himself advised it should be abandoned. The cost to shareholders was, once again, considerable.

Despite the tough terrain, the rail link to Plymouth was completed by 1849. Along the route stood Newton Abbot, a small market town whose fortunes were transformed with the arrival of the railways. Workshops were built there for locomotive and carriage repairs, and it became known as 'little Swindon' after the town where the mighty Great Western Railway was based.

Brunel weathered the impact of some reputational damage. He was also preoccupied with other projects, particularly his ships. The *Great Western* had been the longest ship in the world when it was launched in 1837. Brunel then turned his attentions to building iron ships, with the *Great Britain* becoming the first iron-hulled, propeller-driven ship to cross the Atlantic in 1845. But it was the *Great Eastern*, designed to cruise non-stop from Britain to Australia, that started sucking up Brunel's energy. The project was plagued with difficulties and predictably ran over budget by some margin. During its maiden voyage on 6 September 1859, it was rocked by an explosion before it left British waters. The disaster was of little consequence to Brunel, who had suffered a stroke the previous day and died ten days later, aged fifty-three. Inevitably, his detractors pointed to a clutch of failures that marred his career, the atmospheric railway being one of them. The gauge dispute was resolved in Stephenson's favour with an Act of Parliament in 1846 that standardised measurements. Some thirty years after Brunel's death, the last of Great Western Railway's broad-gauge track was ripped up and replaced with standard gauge, making every line on the network compatible. His insistence on its superiority had come to nothing.

Although the *Great Eastern* seemed a monstrous folly, it was used to lay cables across the Atlantic. And the successful achievements of the man fondly known as 'the little giant' in Victorian society were dazzling. The stand-out Royal Albert Bridge crossing the Tamar was his design. The tunnel under the Thames that he worked on with his father Marc is still in use today, as part of the London Overground service. And the

Clifton Suspension Bridge, a project he called 'my first child', was finally completed after his death, by way of tribute.

Daniel Gooch, engineer and close colleague, described Brunel as 'bold but right', saying: 'The commercial world thought him extravagant; but although he was so, great things are not done by those who sit down and count the cost of every thought and act.'

View from the train

After the train pulls out of Exeter, it's soon alongside the Exe estuary, with its mudflats rich in bird life, especially in the winter. Indeed, for the majority of the journey, the sea seems just touching distance away. The line goes into Teignmouth and along the Teign estuary before coming to Dawlish, where the proximity of the sea can prove alarming. Pictures of modern engines emerging through sea spray during autumn and winter storms are fodder for train spotters. Severe weather in 2014 led to waves breaching the sea wall and the subsequent collapse of the railway line into the sea, leaving Cornwall severed from the railway network. An estimated 20,000 tonnes of earth and stones slipped into the sea. While there have been many efforts to improve the resilience of the line, it's still prone to floods. Watch out for the atmospheric railway's pumping houses, still dotted along the route.

London to Greenwich

Series 2, Episode 16

Distance: 4 miles

Michael Portillo: 'The railways created the need for standardised time in Britain, and in other countries too. That
gave rise to time zones. Since 1884, time around the globe
has been set by reference to Greenwich.'

Telling the time is a skill taught to young children without
much ado these days. Yet it hasn't always been that easy – and,
in fact, it was only thanks to the advent of railways that the
country learned how to tell the correct time.

At the outset, the declaration of time was a regional issue
dictated by the sun, which led to Bristol being fourteen minutes
behind London time and Plymouth twenty minutes. So the right
time in one location was quite wrong in the next. Wherever they
were in the country, train guards generally carried a fob watch
bearing London time, for better clarity.

When it came to early railway timetabling, it caused considerable confusion for unwary travellers, as well as for train
operators, who needed much more precision, not least to avoid
accidents on the network. Greenwich was already been responsible for determining accurate time for mariners, as *Bradshaw's
Guide* explains:

The Royal Observatory occupies the most elevated spot in
Greenwich Park. For the guidance of shipping, the round

globe at its summit drops precisely at 1 p.m. to give the exact Greenwich time.

Prior to a voyage, navigators in ships in the teeming London docks would set their chronometers to what became known as Greenwich Mean Time. It seemed only natural for train companies to fall in line by taking a cue from Greenwich. Emerging technology helped it to do so, as the railway wasn't the only major change of the era. In 1837, innovators William Fothergill Cooke and Charles Wheatstone demonstrated the first electric telegraph communication between Camden and Euston stations. Today, the mile between them seems little further than shouting distance, but communication in real time between two places was hitherto unknown.

A close relationship between these two game-changing inventions began, with Greenwich – as the nation's trusted time-keeper – able to send out the exact time to stations across the country via the telegraph. Bradshaw's railways guides quickly adopted 'railway time' in publications, anticipating this was likely to be the universal choice. Much later, a conference was held in Washington, USA, to confirm that international time zones extended from the meridian line that runs through Greenwich.

For author Charles Dickens, railway time was yet another sign of the ubiquitous nature of the railway in Britain:

There were railway hotels, coffee-houses, lodging-houses, boarding-houses; railway plans, maps, views, wrappers, bottles, sandwich-boxes and timetables . . . there was even railway time observed in clocks, as if the sun itself had given in.

As it happened, the capital's first railway line had already arrived in Greenwich before the invention of the electric telegraph, initially leaving from Tooley Street, which would soon become known as London Bridge station. Authorised by Parliament in 1833, there was a delay as the company scrabbled to find the necessary cash from a public that was still unsure about railways, especially given their extraordinarily high cost. It was the first railway built for passengers rather than freight.

The capital's first station was Spa Road in Bermondsey, with trains running from there to Deptford from February 1836. Its appearance in railway history was fleeting, though, as Spa Road was closed within two years.

Trains ran on an impressive brick-built viaduct some 6.75 metres (22 feet) above street level, which sidestepped the issues caused by Thames floodwater and rose above the difficulties caused by crossing existing roads. In total, there were 878 arches, built with 60 million bricks, mortared in at a rate of about 10,000 a day. The project was so hungry for bricks it caused a city-wide shortage. A considerable number of those bricks were used to build walls along the viaduct, which stood 137 centimetres (4 feet 6 inches) high, to stop trains tumbling off the tracks. In hindsight this was, of course, a somewhat quaint and misplaced concern. Yet, for the same reasons of safety, the operator used specially low-slung carriages, rising just four inches above the tracks, and the line was lit with gas lamps to light the train's way in the dark – even though gas and sparks from a locomotive firebox were a potentially hazardous combination.

Among the other lessons learned by engineers at the time were that the granite sleepers set into concrete were noisy and quick to damage rolling stock, and that the bricks used in the arches had a tendency to shift because of the softness of the black, peaty ground: they needed strategically placed iron ties to secure them. Early in construction, two viaduct arches collapsed completely because of the ground's instability.

At first, there seemed little guarantee the railway would be a success. Greenwich was amply served by boats from London and most people were content with the rapid services. However, on the Whit Monday following the official opening, the line carried 13,000 passengers, indicating any previous prejudices had been swiftly overcome. Between 1836 and 1840, the line ferried more than 1.25 million passengers a year between London Bridge and Greenwich. This reflected a growing tourism, with people drawn to Greenwich as a break from squalid London. Attractions included the park – opened to the public in the 1850s – the Royal Observatory and other less familiar sights. Originally, Tudor royalty had come here to escape the city, staying at the Palace of Placentia, 'the pleasant place'. Henry VIII, Edward VI, Queen Mary and Queen Elizabeth I were all born there.

Before the palace was abandoned, the Queen's House was built nearby in a Palladian style at the start of the seventeenth century. Later, the palace became came the Royal Hospital for Seamen at Greenwich, built to house naval veterans. At one point, 2,700 former seamen were living there. These were hard-bitten men who'd led a gruelling life on wooden ships, facing enemy fire during a series of maritime spats as Britain laid the foundations of its empire. Without the Royal Hospital, which offered them food, clothes, lodgings and a weekly allowance, they would certainly have been destined for the indignities of the workhouse. *Bradshaw's Guide* reveals that every mariner 'pays sixpence a month towards the support of this noble institution', continuing:

> The pensioners, who are of every rank, from the admiral to the humblest sailor, are qualified for admission by being either maimed or disabled by age . . . widows of seamen are exclusively appointed nurses.

Incongruously, the building, designed by Sir Christopher Wren, includes the spacious Painted Hall, the walls and ceiling of which are a Baroque masterpiece painted over the course of two decades by artist Sir James Thornhill and referencing the intrigues of Britain's social history. It was here Nelson's body lay in state after he was killed at the Battle of Trafalgar in 1805.

When the train service began, blue-uniformed pensioners would have been in evidence on the streets of Greenwich. Indeed, some of the travellers may have been visiting relatives there. The last Greenwich pensioners left the site in 1869, when it became the Royal Naval College. Bradshaw's was a fan of the elegance of Greenwich, saying: 'We cannot but hope that the park and heath may be preserved for ages to come, as an oasis in the desert, when the mighty city has spread its suburbs far beyond it, into the hills and dales of the surrounding country.'

At the time, the housing in Greenwich catered for middle-class residents, with pockets of poverty in and around the viaduct arches. As the train went back up the line towards London, there was much more evidence of want among the residences.

Hot on the heels of the London & Greenwich Railway came the London & Croydon Railway, which paid fees to share the line as far as the Corbetts Lane Junction before using its own lines for the remainder of the journey. By the 1840s, with four different companies using the viaduct to enter London Bridge station, the approach had to be widened. Eventually, the London & Croydon Railway built its own terminus at Bricklayers Arms to sidestep the charges. Lines in the area grew more congested as the century wore on. Greenwich remained the terminus until 1878, when an extension was built to Maze Hill, running beneath the grounds of Queen's House and the Royal Hospital.

A book describing Tooley Street, also published in 1878, illustrates how the docks offered an extraordinary array of work to nearby residents:

. . . we find ourselves in Tooley Street, whose name, we are told, is a strange corruption of the former appellation, St. Olave's Street, and whose shops exhibit a singular mixture of the features which are found separate in other parts of the district—wharfingers, merchants, salesmen, factors, and agents; outfitters, biscuit-bakers, store-shippers, ship-chandlers, slopsellers, block-makers, and rope-makers; engineers, and others, together with the usual varieties of retail tradesmen—all point to the diversified, and no less busy than diversified, traffic of this street.

It was a place, the book observed, where the crane and the pulley never seemed to be idle.

Settle to Carlisle

Series 1, Episode 7

Distance: 73 miles

Michael Portillo: 'This railway is valued both for what it is today and for the ambition of those Victorian engineers.'

Engineers who redrew the British landscape with railway lines, bridges and viaducts were venerated in Victorian society. Yet it's fair to say that no matter how bold their ambition or fine their drawings, no locomotives would have run without the heroic efforts of navvies, who provided the necessary muscle to turn boardroom dreams into reality.

The Settle to Carlisle line is still celebrated for the twenty-four elegant arches of the Ribblehead Viaduct, picturesque against the Yorkshire Dales. When it was given the go-ahead, directors at Midland Railway believed the service would yield up lucrative Scottish markets. Today, it's noted as the last main line in Britain hewn out of the bedrock by pickaxe.

Navvies undertook back-breaking toil, often in high winds and driving rain, forging a path for track layers using only shovels and wheelbarrows, easily shrugging off daily perils. But their reputation wasn't rooted in extraordinary blind courage, physical fortitude and breath-taking stamina. It was hard drinking and riotous behaviour for which they are best remembered. 'Navvy' is the short form of navigator, the name given to men who had dug the canal system a generation earlier. A loose third were Irish, escaping the privations of the famine there by working in England. Others were agricultural labourers attracted by wages some three times greater than those earned in the fields. Weavers were also struggling to make a living as the circumstances of cotton trading changed, and so they often switched jobs to make ends meet. Distinctive in their dress, navvies wore caps and waistcoats as well as jackets to protect against the fiercest winter weather, and were usually pictured smoking clay pipes.

At the height of Railway Mania in the mid-1840s, there were some 250,000 navvies at work around the country, each typically capable of shifting twenty tons of rubble every day. These men were nomadic, seeking one job to follow the next. Not for them the joys of rail travel. They would walk across country to a new site, the journey in navvy lingo called 'in tramp'. The term stuck for men who lived in the open. At first, the men relied on accommodation in towns close to railway construction sites. However, they became notorious for drinking sprees – or 'randies', as the men called them – making themselves unpopular guests. Fights and theft were also symptomatic of a navvy influx, and such were the numbers of workers required, even large rural towns struggled to offer sufficient rooms. Reluctant railway companies soon found themselves needing to build living spaces alongside the evolving tracks.

The result was a series of squalid shanty towns, where sanitary conditions were poor and diseases such as cholera, dysentery or typhus were rife. An overall death rate of three men per mile was not considered excessive. But by 1866, when the Settle to Carlisle Line proposals had been given parliamentary approval, Victorian social reformers had been shocked by the numbers of deaths among working navvies and a wave of concerned paternalism swept across the industry. As a consequence, the navvy accommodation on this project would be far better than anything the men had previously experienced.

Recent investigations into the settlement at the Rise Hill
Tunnel have discovered there were temporary houses built on
the high moors able to accommodate a couple, their children
and upwards of fourteen lodgers in a dormitory arrangement.
Made from wood, they were homely, with pictures on the walls,
decorated china cups and ornaments around the fireplaces.
Toilet facilities were in an outhouse, an arrangement similar to
those in many brick-built homes at the time.

Almost all navvies were men, with the exception of Rachel
Hamilton, a pipe-smoking Irishwoman living in Glasgow in the
1870s. At 6 feet, 4 inches tall, and weighing around seventeen
stone, she found a job as a navvies' foreman in Glasgow. Otherwise, women at the camps were cooks and cleaners. The daily
diet the men had was nothing short of extraordinary, featuring
condensed milk for breakfast, several loaves, a few steaks and
no fewer than ten pints of beer issued throughout the day. It
was an era when beer was deemed healthier to drink than
water – and the intoxication probably helped to dull lingering
aches and pains.

On the surface, there were static team-powered engines
used to winch open wagons laden with building materials
from the bottom of the hill up to the site. It was tempting for
workers to hitch a ride, and two women died at Rise Hill when
the winched wagon they were in derailed after the supporting
rope broke. Another man was decapitated when he lay down
on the tracks, drunk, to sleep. Below ground level, the men
depended solely on their physical prowess to make progress,
despite the damp, cramped conditions and a lack of light. The
deepest ventilation shaft at Rise Hill measures 44 metres
(147 feet), giving some indication of the depths the men went to
in order to forge the tunnel.

The winter of 1870 was especially harsh. One man, plagued
with illness, cut his throat in one of the outhouses, rather than

face another day of labouring in bleak conditions. There were also accidents with the gunpowder used to loosen the cold, hard ground as the company pressed on, hoping speed would lead to savings.

This was just one settlement out of many. Another served the 2,000 men devoted to the construction of the Ribblehead Viaduct, looming more than 30 metres (100 feet) from the valley bottom. Historian Gerald Tyler found that more than 200 people were buried nearby, many the victims of a smallpox outbreak. More than half were aged under thirteen. The widows of workers received £5 compensation, equivalent to about a month's wages. A plaque at St Leonard's Church in Chapel-le-Dale – where the graveyard was extended to accommodate victims – remembers those who, 'through accident', lost their lives in the construction of the railway. The plaque was paid for by fellow workers and the Midland Railway Company.

That workers contributed to this plaque reflects a culture fashioned by railway companies everywhere to divest well-paid navvies of their cash as quickly as possible. Apart from paying for accommodation, workers had to buy food at premium prices from the railway company, which was the sole provider of sustenance to men marooned in the middle of nowhere. To ensure they were not tempted by travelling merchants, workers were sometimes paid in tokens. But bosses turned a blind eye if suppliers watered down the beer, put sawdust in bread or sold rotten meat. Free-spending men were often paid next door to a public house, also run by the railway company, so their money literally walked back through the door and into the cash register. Little was done to prevent such exploitation.

Men who worked alongside such privation surely wanted to let off steam, especially given the dangers of their work. Yet their behaviour slowly began to modify, an effect of Christian missions setting up in tandem with railway camps, and also the growing influence of the temperance movement. Perhaps, too, better circumstances had the civilising effect for which the Victorians were hoping. When the Settle to Carlisle Line was opened to passengers in 1876, all traces of the navvy camps disappeared beneath the bracken.

As the railway building boom slowed, many men found permanent jobs associated with the industry and lived in a growing number of railway towns, providing far better living standards for their families. By 1900, more than 620,000 people – nearly five per cent of the population – worked for the railways. Others found work abroad: their reputation for hard work went before them, and British navvies were welcomed at railway building enterprises in Europe, South Africa, Canada and Australia, commanding greater pay than local men to reflect their legendary work rate.

While the ingenuity of singularly great contributors to the railway age are commemorated with statues, there are just a few plaques to mark the navvies: and these are for those who perished at work. Yet the legacy that all these men bequeathed Britain is a far-reaching network that's still in use every day. Perhaps the tunnels and tracks here have become a monument to those men. After British Rail issued a closure notice on the Settle to Carlisle Line in 1984, the nation decided it was worth saving and mounted a wide-ranging and enthusiastic campaign to save it. In 1989, the government backed the line and today it is thriving, with passenger numbers exceeding 750,000 a year, as well as forty freight trains rumbling along the line each day.

The view from the train

Although the navvies who built the line would have known of twenty-one stations dotted along its length by the time they finished, there are just eleven open today. Dent is the highest station on the National Rail network in England, offering sweeping views across the Yorkshire Dales. By the station there is a snow hut, built to provide shelter for fifteen men who kept the lines clear of snow in the depths of winter. There are four-teen tunnels (the longest, beneath Blea Moor, measuring 2.4km or 2,629 yards) and twenty viaducts in addition to the one at Ribblehead.

Tenterden to Bodiam

Series 10, Episode 15

Distance: 10 miles

Michael Portillo: 'My Bradshaw's timetable for 1907 reveals that the journey time from Tenterden to Bodiam, a distance of about ten miles, was thirty minutes, so about twenty miles per hour. It was a new line built with innovatory rail technology: lighter, nimbler . . . slower.'

As the twentieth century approached, not everyone in Britain had reaped the benefits of the railway age. Typically, it was rural areas that had been left behind, remaining isolated after plans to link them via branch lines to major routes were deemed unnecessary by Parliament or too costly by railway builders. With an ongoing agricultural slump, farms were feeling the pinch due to their remote locations.

All this changed in 1896 with the Light Railways Act, which offered up a short cut to get the necessary permissions and cash backing from the Treasury in exchange for smaller, slower railways. The Act aimed to cut through ponderous bureaucracy by having a three-man commission appointed by the Board of Trade to consider fresh proposals, which now might come from councils as well as entrepreneurs.

Builders of these slimmed-down railways were no longer obliged to seek an Act of Parliament – but nor would they be permitted to run trains at the same pace as elsewhere, at a time when speeds of sixty miles per hour were the norm, and

100 miles per hour was within the grasp of new locomotives running on the main lines. The Act replaced existing – but barely used – legislation dating from 1864 designed to help small railways.

Light railways could better cling to tricky contours, use inexpensive building materials and were less exposed to the costs of rigorous safety measures. Yet, perhaps curiously, there was no official definition of a 'light railway' attached to the Act, and a number of them ran on the same standard gauge as the rest of the network, looking for all the world like regular trains.

However, one man at the forefront of these new-style networks had a vision for an alternative railway network, although his efforts to change the way the railways looked and ran have been largely forgotten. Holman Fred Stephens was the son of two Pre-Raphaelite artists and named for Holman Hunt, another painter and also his godfather. Holman was also a great nephew of the naturalist Charles Darwin. Yet it wasn't to art or exploration that Holman was drawn, but engineering.

He began his working life at the Neasden workshops for London's Metropolitan Railway. The workshops were built in the middle of fields in 1880, soon followed by an estate of houses constructed for workers in what became known as the railway village. Aged twenty-two, he became resident engineer for the Cranbrook & Paddock Wood Railway in Kent, which had a history of economic difficulties from its inception in 1877 to its opening fifteen years later. It was also known as the Hawkhurst Branch Line. After spending two years trying to get the project past the finishing post, Holman had first-hand experience of the problems that faced costly transport schemes in country areas – but also better understood why they were so badly needed.

In 1894, he became a member of the Institution of Civil Engineers, which allowed him to design and build railways. So, when the Light Railways Act was passed, he was qualified to become a promotor, engineer, locomotive superintendent and director of newly drawn-up ventures.

His long-standing nickname, Holly, was replaced with 'the Colonel', after he joined the Territorial Force for decades of service. (His First World War medal card reveals that he achieved the rank of Lieutenant Colonel, although he wasn't entitled to any medals after the conflict because he did not serve overseas.) In fact, building work on his first two 'light railways' began before the Act was passed, and they had been described as tramways, specifically to sidestep the weight of paperwork attached to the building of transport infrastructure. These were the Rye & Camber Tramway, less than two miles in length, with a 91-centimetre (3-feet) gauge, which served three stations after it opened in 1896, and the gloriously named Hundred of Manhood & Selsey Tramway, with a service on the standard gauge railway starting in 1897. Both were built under the Railway Construction and Facilities Act of 1864.

The first railway to fall into the sphere of the Light Railways Act was the Rother Valley Light Railway, which ran for a dozen miles from Robertsbridge to Rolvenden, officially opening in the spring of 1900. The Colonel had an eye for expansion and was hoping to extend as far as Maidstone, although this proved a pipe dream. But it did get as far as Tenterden, and was renamed the Kent & East Sussex Light Railway in 1904 to reflect this change. The railway performed sterling service for Guinness drinkers, transporting hop-pickers to Bodiam, where the crop was grown, and taking the fruit of their labours away.

The Colonel worked on passenger services at Ffestiniog in North Wales, the Isle of Wight and the Isle of Sheppey, in addition to a line that linked north Devon and Cornwall, another that took a stretch around Plymouth, and one linking Shrewsbury to Wales. In addition, there were industrial lines in Derbyshire, Warwickshire, Kent and Shropshire, ferrying stone, ironstone, coal and lead. He wasn't finished, either, having big ideas about the spread of light railways. Many other projects that Stephens was involved with fell at an early hurdle, but what tended to distinguish the railways in his empire was the way they were run on a shoestring. Economy was his watchword: he laid down girders to bridge streams and culverts rather than building bridges, and constructed cattle grids rather than level-crossing gates.

As part of an overriding desire to save cash, the Colonel introduced the concept of railmotors: petrol driven buses that ran on the rails. Earlier, he had flirted with a steam-driven railmotor, but this proved unreliable. However, the combustion engine evolved rapidly during the First World War, and Stephens saw the opportunity. He bought some hybrid vehicles, with bus bodies attached to one-ton lorry chassis, and adapted them for rails by attaching flanged wheels, using them back-to-back in pairs to avoid the apparently intractable issue of reversing. Ford's chassis were chosen because it was easy to get spares.

The Ford Railmotor Set No. 1 arrived at the Kent & East Sussex tracks in 1922, with each adapted vehicle having twenty seats, a bonnet, indicators and headlights. They looked so similar to road transport it was jarring to see the railmotors at stations, and even more so when the drivers had to crank the starting handle at the front to make the engine splutter into life. Film cameramen were there to capture the moment they departed from the platform.

Railmotors were not particularly popular with travellers, who suffered grievously from the absence of shock absorbers as they bounced around on the wooden slatted seats inside. Initially, the position of the fuel tank meant the buses quickly filled with fumes. Excessive vibration made the radiator leak, so there were water supplies on board. If it was a damp or cold morning, there would be problems scaling an incline, because the wheels slipped. But while they suffered from reliability issues, they were considerably cheaper than even the smallest locomotive. Only one driver was needed, so there was an immediate saving in crew costs. A second set was bought, at a cost of £542 and 17 shillings, from a Norfolk company, paid for in monthly instalments over the year. In total, there were eight pairs built from new used on the Colonel's railways, and he clearly had plans to construct still more, at an even better price.

In 1927, Stephens advertised for two 'good second-hand motor omnibuses, not less than 14 seaters, 4ft 6in – five ft wheel track'. There's no evidence his efforts to save money with hand-me-down vehicles came to anything, but the advertisement indicates his determination to drive down costs. This was not to make better profits, but in order that light railways with limited numbers of passengers might survive. He was quick to switch rolling stock from one line to the next – an advantage of standard gauge, as it could get to its intended destination under its own steam. So railmotors appeared in Selsey, at Shrewsbury and at a railway in the Derwent Valley, in which the Colonel played a part.

The Colonel died in 1931 in a hotel in Dover, where he lived. The Kent & East Sussex Railway went into liquidation the following year, but financially limped on until passenger services were ended in 1954, and freight in 1961. Just twenty years later, it was back up and running as a heritage line, justifying the Colonel's immoveable faith in the value of light railways in rural areas. In his book *The Light Railway Era*, John Scott-Morgan explained the appeal of light railways like this:

The railways [the Colonel] managed possessed something that the main line railway could never hope to have. Indeed, [his] railways had a deeply human spirit that lack the humbug and hypocrisy of the railway rule book, deeper

rooted than any railway official could ever hope to understand . . . They went through some of the most beautiful
country that Britain could offer and as the trains passed
along their timeless path, from little stations and sleeper-
built halts, from dawn to dusk, they seemed to take with
them the hopes and the dreams of the country folk they
served so well.

At any rate, the Colonel's personal successes stack up better
than those of the relevant railway legislation. While some nay-
sayers declared small lines would soon be criss-crossing the
country, the overall effectiveness of the Light Railways Act isn't
clear. Certainly, the cost per mile of light railways was far lower,
as they were conforming to less stringent standards. By 1918,
only 900 miles of railway had been constructed, mostly in the
guise of conventional lines constructed on the cheap by railway
companies. Of the £1 million earmarked by the Treasury for
light railways, only £203,000 had been taken up. It turned out
that even the smallest branch lines benefitted financially when
they were part of a bigger family, so that rolling stock could
go further, and it partly reflects why small railway companies
started in Victorian times joined up with others to become
larger.

Few of the light railways, either in Stephens' empire or outside it, survived into the modern era. Increasing competition
from buses, lorries and cars played a significant part in their
downfall.

Chapter Two

IRON ROADS FOR KING COAL AND OTHER COMMERCE

With railways providing cheap and swift haulage, coal – which was the fuel of choice – was taken from mine to city (for factories) or seaside (for ports, and global distribution). In its wake, there was buoyant trade in just about every commodity, including fish, milk, biscuits – even dead bodies. Just as it transformed trade, so the railway changed the experience of passengers, as people began to work to a timetable and started to experience busy lives. As Robert Hughes noted, in his book *The Shock of the New*: 'The view from the train was not the view from the horse. It compressed more motifs into the same time. Conversely, it left less time in which to dwell on any one thing.'

Cardiff to Merthyr Tydfil

Series 3, Episode 14

Distance: 24 miles

Michael Portillo: 'The fortunes of the communities of South Wales have ridden the rollercoaster of Industrial Revolution in the nineteenth century, deindustrialisation in the twentieth century, and are now adjusting themselves for life in the twenty-first century.'

Modest amounts of mining had taken place in South Wales for centuries, yielding fuel for heating cottages and small-scale smelting. But those early users had little idea that the coal lying in extensive fields beneath their feet burned more brightly than coal mined elsewhere in the country, and left little ash. It was only the arrival of the railways that meant 'black gold' could be taken from collieries to the coast and people could cash in on the earth's riches. A tale of two towns reveals just how transformative it would be.

Demand for Welsh coal had already increased prior to the age of the train, when a colony of ironworks was established in South Wales at the end of the eighteenth century. Stationary steam engines, used for hauling or pumping, became an increasingly familiar sight in the area.

Another early steam pioneer, Richard Trevithick, built a high-pressure steam engine to drive a hammer at the Penydarren Ironworks in Merthyr Tydfil in 1802. Soon afterwards, he adapted it by adding wheels, so it could move under its own steam. As a result of a 500 guinea wager, Trevithick set his machine on a ten-mile trial carrying five wagons and seventy men along the iron plates of a tramroad. It completed the trip in just over four hours, at an average speed of 2.4 miles per hour. Despite achieving this significant moment in industrial history, his fortunes took a different direction and Trevithick would die, unheralded and alone, in 1833.

However, he had put down a marker, giving a glimpse of what the future could hold, and Merthyr appeared resilient as an industrial centre. As one century gave way to the next, coal that was surplus to the requirements of the ironworks was being sold in a steady stream in domestic markets and abroad. Opening in 1794, the twenty-five-mile-long Glamorganshire Canal was used to ferry twenty-ton loads of coal from Merthyr Tydfil to Cardiff three times a fortnight. Once it reached Cardiff, the coal could be tipped into barges heading for London or the continent, although the dock facilities were limited.

At the time Trevithick installed his hammer-driving steam pump up in Merthyr, the town's population numbered more than 3,000, while Cardiff's was a modest 1,870, making it the twenty-fifth largest town in Wales. But things were about to change. Two advances, which took place almost in tandem, helped transform Cardiff's fortunes. The Taff Vale Railway had a dynamic effect on South Wales in general, and Cardiff in particular. With the soaring fortunes of coal and railways always closely intertwined, the opening of the Taff Vale Railway in 1841 brought greater prominence to the city than ever before, and it would soon outstrip industrial Merthyr in size and significance.

The other component in Cardiff's success story was the presence of modern docks. One was built by the Second Marquess of Bute, resident of Cardiff Castle, in 1839, giving the city extensive facilities it had previously lacked. The dock was constructed at enormous cost – some £350,000 – and Bute was forced to mortgage some of his extensive estates in Glamorganshire to complete the project. It also created long-running divisions between Bute and the ironworks owners, as well as anyone who had an interest in the now-redundant Glamorganshire Canal. But it meant that the new railway could deliver coal right into the heart of the docks.

The Taff Vale Railway engineer was Isambard Kingdom Brunel, who for once abandoned his favoured broad gauge for standard in order to better fit the route, which mirrored the valley through which the River Taff flowed. Only in the city did he deviate from boundaries forced on him by nature. There, he diverted the course of the river, providing some reclaimed land that would become the site of a station. He built a single-track line, with passing spaces available at stations. By law, the trains were limited to twelve miles per hour, but the journey time was still dramatically cut by comparison with the canal. The Taff Vale Railway acted as an artery, with some hundred miles of lines fanning from it into the ore-rich hills, and those were extended as the years passed. But from the get-go, the line was extremely busy, with two trains a minute passing through Pontypridd, the busiest station on the line. By 1850, the Taff Vale Railway was carrying 600,000 tons of coal every year, and paying a six per cent dividend. But as mining activity increased, the Taff Vale Railway was no longer enough. It was joined by the Rhymney Railway in 1858 and, in 1882, by the Rhondda & Swansea Bay Railway. The mushrooming of routes reflected a discontent by both colliery owners and dock operators with the way the Taff Vale Railway was running things.

One issue was resolved with the appearance of these new lines, but another remained. Some coal owners and railway company directors were still unhappy with dock capacity and the prices they were being charged for freight. They eyed the monopoly fiercely held by the quickly congested Cardiff docks with envy. As a result, rival docks were opened at Penarth in 1865 and Barry in 1889, where the tidal issues that hampered shipping movements at Cardiff were not an issue. One of three engineers brought in to design Barry Docks was Henry Marc Brunel, son of the legendary Isambard Kingdom Brunel. Another was John Wolfe Barry, the designer of London's Tower Bridge and the son of a renowned architect. After the docks and the railways that served them were built, Barry became a holiday resort for the first time, and in twenty years, its population rose from eighty-five people to 27,000.

Cardiff hit back with the development of Roath Basin in 1874, followed by Roath Dock in 1887 and the Queen Alexandra Dock in 1907. At its peak, Cardiff had a quay frontage that measured almost seven miles, with more than 120 miles of railway tracks in one square mile to service waiting ships. In the busy halls of Cardiff's Coal Exchange, built in the late 1880s in grand style to compliment what was, by then, the biggest coal-shifting port in the world, mine owners, ship owners and ship agents busied themselves making deals that took Welsh coal across the globe, with most of the action happening around lunchtime. The first million-pound deal was struck there in 1904. By now, the population of Cardiff had grown 100-fold, and it became the capital city of Wales in 1905.

In the race for tonnage, Barry was the outright winner, becoming the busiest coal port in the world. But although the development of the docks at Barry succeeded in drawing huge volumes of trade away from Cardiff, the Taff Vale Railway continued to flourish, carrying some 14 million tons of coal and coke in 1897, with its 216 locomotives clocking up a mileage of 2,800,000 a year. It was a reflection of the industrial might now wielded in the region.

The Board of Trade annual returns for 1913 show that coal output in South Wales amounted to more than 20 million tons, almost a fifth of Britain's total output, revealing that production in the coal fields there had doubled since 1889. Nobody realised the boom wouldn't last. In Merthyr Tydfil, it was a different story. Workers there showed their discontent with pay and social conditions as early as 1931 with the Merthyr Rising, which ended with the hanging of one so-called agitator. A report in 1841 highlighted that more than 1,500 people were living in homes that measured 2.1 metres by 1.4 metres (7 feet by 4 feet 6 inches), perched on top of iron slag heaps. Each housed a family, with the cramped conditions a breeding ground for disease. Poverty continued to loom large there, more so after the decline of the ironworks. Although the Merthyr furnaces provided railway tracks for Britain and the world, their inland location became a hindrance and, with new production processes gaining favour, investors looked elsewhere.

In 1850, historian Thomas Carlyle found people there 'unguided, hard-worked, fierce and miserable-looking' and described iron foundries as 'a vision of hell'. By the 1860s, Bradshaw's had very certain views about the town:

> Visitors should see the furnaces by night, when the red glare of the flames produces an uncommonly striking effect. Indeed, the town is best seen at that time, for by day it will be found dirty, and irregularly built, without order or management, decent roads or footpaths, no supply of water, and no public building of the least note, except Barracks, and a vast Poor- House, lately finished, in the shape of a cross, on heaps of the rubbish accumulated from the pits and works. Cholera and fever are, of course, at home here . . .'

Ultimately, both Cardiff and Merthyr Tydfil, having experienced the economies of boom and bust, emerged into a future divorced from the harsh realities of coal and iron.

London to Great Yarmouth

Series 3, Episode 1

Distance: 121 miles

Michael Portillo: 'Famous for its herring, the railways and this station enabled Great Yarmouth to take full advantage of the fish stocks of the North Sea. The catch could reach markets all over the country – and, indeed, abroad – and brought the town prosperity.'

With the arrival of the railways in 1844, Great Yarmouth became a boom town, with three noteworthy-strings to its bow. Most eminent was fishing, a line of work that thrived after the tracks linking Yarmouth to London were opened. Fishing had been a pivotal industry since the tenth century, and the fleet based there enjoyed a special seasonal bonus: herring. Herring brought wealth and certainty to the east coast town, with an abundant catch being skimmed from the shimmering shoals that billowed in the North Sea every autumn. Known locally as 'silver darlings', herring had always been salted and barrelled for transport to London or beyond. But thanks to trains, the freighting of preserved fish could go on in far greater quantities than ever before, alongside ample fresh supplies. By 1848, the Eastern Counties Railway were transporting 70 tons of fresh fish from Yarmouth and Lowestoft each week. Moreover, there was now a market for fresh fish in faraway towns and cities, including the Midlands and Manchester.

Jaw-dropping quantities of herring were caught here in the good times. From 1852, a unit of measurement known as a 'cran' was used among North Sea fishermen. A cran was a standard box of fish, containing about 37½ imperial gallons. Usually that worked out to about 1,200 fish but, depending on size, the number could vary to anywhere between 700 and 2,500. In the record-breaking season of 1913, an extraordinary 1,360,000 crans of herring were landed at Great Yarmouth. Poignantly, given the global conflict that was about to erupt, fishing there would never be the same again.

By then, sail-driven luggers had given way to steam-powered drifters, which increased catch capacity. Although only 25 metres (80 feet) in length, each drifter towed nets extending ten miles to capture the fish as they made their annual migration along Britain's North Sea coast to their breeding grounds off France. Local boats from Great Yarmouth – and sometimes from great rivals in Lowestoft – were joined by large numbers of Scottish boats with the same sea-borne riches in their sights. Almost all were tied up on Saturday nights, but local men were quick to set off on Sundays in order to steal a march on their Scottish opposition, who traditionally observed the Sabbath and stayed at home.

When the vessels returned, they were met on the quayside by an army of women, commonly from Scotland, who were there to help gut, pickle and cure and pack the produce. Dressed in a uniform of sorts – scarf, a stiff, waxed apron and rolled-up sleeves – the women dealt with the fish after seemingly endless baskets of them were winched from the boats. Without gloves to protect against cold and odour, the women gutted fish at speed, then speared them for smoking or salted them in barrels. While they were at work, the women sang songs from their native Scotland. At the end of the day, or before it began in earnest, they were often busy knitting garments, both for themselves and to sell.

When the herring season was at its height, the quay was smothered with barrels, stacked high as they awaited collection. Railway lines had been networked as close to the boats as feasibly possible, to ease transport issues. The town was served by three separate termini, so had options when it came to the dispatch of herring. Typically, trains carried coal (for the drifters) and salt (to preserve herring) on their way down to Great Yarmouth, and returned up the line laden with fish. With kippers still standard breakfast fare, fishing seemed a sound career choice as late as the 1950s and early 1960s – but the sea had something to say about it. While fishermen had rejoiced at fat catches, they hadn't acted on fears of over-fishing. By the mid-1960s, the shoals that had kept generations at sea in Great Yarmouth were no more. Reputedly, the last drifter to sail out of Great Yarmouth was the *Wydale* at the close of the decade.

Reflecting the long-term decline, boats had diminished in number by then, but the loss of the industry didn't just affect fishermen. The outlook was equally bleak for basket, net and rope makers, as well as coopers, coal merchants and ice makers. The town's railways felt the loss too. In 1959, the Midland & Great Northern Joint Railway, known as the 'muddle and get nowhere', was closed. The local service between Ipswich and Yarmouth, which ran via Beccles, finished in 1966.

In the town itself, Yarmouth Beach station closed at the same time as the Midland & Great Northern Joint Railway, while Yarmouth South Town, which had a direct service from London Liverpool Street, shut its doors in 1970, after a sustained reduction of trains. But there were some glad railway tidings in 1954 that helped validate the vibrancy of Yarmouth's second-string industry, tourism.

An acceleration in the service of London-bound trains meant the 121-mile distance could be completed in less than three hours, and in the summer the town's remaining station, Yarmouth Vauxhall, was swamped by visitors. On Saturdays in high season, an additional twenty-four services were incorporated into the timetable to cater for them.

Yarmouth had long been a destination for well-heeled trippers, with visitors in the eighteenth century heading there for the perceived benefits of the bracing sea air. (If they bathed at the time, it was probably in the Bath House rather than the North Sea.) The train brought still more visitors, broadening the social profile of the town's clientele considerably. In the early twentieth century, it was the destination of the annual works outings of various companies, including Bass Breweries. At the same time, a new kind of seasonal accommodation was gaining popularity: the holiday camp, offering a bare-bones approach that was nonetheless popular. By the time a service dubbed 'the Holiday Camps Express' ran non-stop from London to the east coast, holiday camps had evolved into something that offered care-free entertainment. They became particularly popular after the end of the Second World War.

People came to see the town as well as the beaches, particularly The Rows, its attractive grid of narrow streets hemmed inside the old town walls. As Charles Dickens explained: 'A Row is a long, narrow lane or alley quite straight, or as nearly as maybe, with houses on each side, both of which you can sometimes touch at once with the fingertips of each hand, by stretching out your arms to their full extent.'

The closeness of the buildings, he said, sometimes made the passages seem like tunnels. Laid end to end, the Rows would have extended seven miles. This dark – and, at times, menacing – backdrop, with its sewage smells, is where the final third of Yarmouth's rail-linked commercial enterprises took place.

As medical curiosity increased, there was a need for dead bodies that anatomists, armed with sharp scalpels, could investigate, usually in front of a class of would-be doctors. At first, the necessary bodies were those of people hanged at scaffolds. But as demand outstripped supply, gangs known as 'resurrectionists' haunted graveyards to dig up fresh corpses that could be sold for the purposes of dissection.

At night, the resurrectionists would creep into graveyards and dig up bodies using a wooden shovel, depositing them in a sack carried on their backs (another name for them was 'sack men'). The only way the bereaved could save their recently deceased loved ones from being dug up to go under the knife was by maintaining a guard over the grave.

Yarmouth was not the only town to suffer from the attentions of sack men, but with St Nicholas's being the largest church in the country, and a quick passage to London by sea, the practice flourished there. In 1832, the Anatomy Act permitted doctors and teachers to work under licence and gave them access to the bodies of the poor who died in workhouses and had no one to pay their burial expenses. Bodies in graveyards might now have been safe, but the bodies of the poor were likely to reach the anatomists' tables instead, despite a widely held horror at the prospect. And with the number of medical students increasing, there was a growing demand for the dead.

In Yarmouth, the issue came to the fore after 1883, when Irish professor Alexander Macalister began a thirty-six-year stint at Cambridge University as chair of anatomy. With the number of medical students increased by a factor of four, he grasped his Bradshaw's and travelled by train down the branch lines from Cambridge to secure bodies from various towns, including Yarmouth, paying a princely £12 for each. Moreover, he made a deal with railway companies to transport the recently dead to Cambridge, or sometimes London. Without the benefit of refrigeration, it was important the dead arrived at their destination as quickly as possible. Thanks to 'the dead carriage', Macalister was able to revive his university department. But his reputation, and the careers of the doctors he taught, were built on the shoulders of the poor and dispossessed. The practice ended as late as 1901, when the case of a pauper's body whisked away from Great Yarmouth came under scrutiny. Public mores had changed over the late Victorian period so much that the practice was no longer considered appropriate.

Newcastle to Lindisfarne

Series 6, Episode 15

Distance: 60 miles

Michael Portillo: 'Newcastle history stretches back almost 2,000 years, during which time it has been controlled by the Romans, Saxons and Danes. Its pride and prize is the river Tyne. In the nineteenth century, its shipbuilding yards were some of the busiest in the world.'

Newcastle's nineteenth-century industrial wealth didn't rely solely on the exploitation of natural resources in the region. There were considerable amounts of human ingenuity that went into the mix, as the history of railways has amply illustrated. Yet beyond trains and tracks, there were further inventions that made the city pre-eminent. One was the way it handled heavy freight, a novel system invented by a man who remains barely celebrated outside Newcastle, where he was born in 1810.

William Armstrong never left the north-east, despite engineering skills that illustrated time and again that he was a class apart from his contemporaries. Instead, the world's elite would visit him to acquaint themselves with his latest thinking. Thanks to Armstrong, the city became a major manufacturer of ships and arms that played a critical role in Britain's victory during the First World War.

As a young man, Armstrong had been dispatched to train as a solicitor by his corn merchant father, also called William.

But it was engineering that excited the younger man, who was also a keen fisherman. During an angling trip to the River Dee in 1835, he was first struck by the possibilities of using water to drive machinery. On his return, he began work on the design and construction of a rotary engine powered by water. Over time, he made adaptations so it ended up as a piston engine, and from that was born the hydraulic crane. The crane was tall with a tank at its top, filled by a steam pump. Slow release of the water provided the necessary pressure. Why was the crane so significant? By now, immense amounts of coal were being trucked to the quayside at Newcastle, but it took time – and no small amount of effort – to load the waiting barges with it. When the cranes were in action, the operation was carried out far more quickly and efficiently, ultimately saving money.

It wasn't Armstrong's only contribution to city life, either. He and his partner in the law firm pioneered and paid for a system that would pipe the waters of the Whittle Burn, a tributary of the Tyne, into the city in 1845. This, of course, improved the health of the population as well as the wealth of company owners there. It also gave him an opportunity to demonstrate the hydraulic crane, using excess water being piped to the quayside. Thereafter demand was such that he gave up working as a solicitor and instead founded an engineering firm at Elswick, a mile and a half from the heart of Newcastle, in 1847.

By 1850, he was employing 300 men, and produced forty-five cranes that year. By 1863, he had 3,800 men on the payroll, building 100 cranes a year as well as a range of other items, which were being sold all over the world. His commercial interests were then directed to shipbuilding and armaments. After reading about the difficulties confronted by British soldiers in the Crimean War, he created a lighter, more accurate gun. At the outbreak of the American Civil War, he sold weapons to both sides. In 1867, he struck a deal with Newcastle's Low Walker shipyard that meant he would provide guns for the ships being built there.

Always an agile businessman, he developed a hydraulic accumulator, a far bigger affair that he used to power a swing bridge over the Tyne. It slid into action for the first time in 1876, and replaced a stone bridge that had been blocking ship access to the Elswick factory. The swing bridge is still in use today. The first major ship to pass through it was the *Europa,* which went to Elswick to collect a 100-ton gun for the Italian navy. Similar technology was used for the lifting mechanism at London's Tower Bridge. By 1884, Elswick was itself a shipyard, and by the end of the century, employed one in four working men in Newcastle.

A film taken prior to Wakes Week, a paid holiday, at the Elswick factory in 1900 reveals hordes of men, most in flat caps and a surprising number in ties, many with jaws clenched around a pipe – although the occasional cigarette smoker is visible – milling about on the factory concourse.

Outside of his business interests, Armstrong donated enough money for a College of Physical Sciences to be built, which would later morph into the city's university. Then there was a donation that helped build the Hancock History Museum, as well as twenty-six acres of land given as a public park. But his transformative effect on Newcastle isn't his only legacy. As well as a townhouse in Jesmond, he had a country house built at Rothbury for himself and his wife Margaret in 1864. Additions to it by noted architect Richard Norman Shaw, as well as the inclusion of Armstrong's fine art collection, made it one of the stand-out residences of the age.

It was here that the King of Siam, the Crown Prince of Afghanistan, the Shah of Persia, two future Japanese prime ministers and various Chinese diplomats came to seal deals with Armstrong. The Prince of Wales was also a guest. A fan of hydraulic power all his life, Armstrong ensured the grounds had lakes that could power equipment inside the house, including lights, a laundry room and the kitchen's rotisserie. Writing in 1881, draughtsman and journalist Thomas Raffles Davison described Cragside in glowing terms:

Imagine a great hill covered from bottom to crest with huge grey boulder stones, and halfway up, cut out of a steppe on the hillside, the site and placing of a building of the most picturesque kind imaginable. Then, having chosen the site and placed the house, call forth your gardeners by the hundreds, and bid them make amongst and around those crags and boulders cunningly winding walks, every one formed of steps of the natural grey stone. Then bring your evergreens and rare heathers by the tens of thousands, plant them over and about the place till there is hardly a spot of bare soil left; then with the rarest and commonest ferns plant every crevice among the boulders. Form two artificial lakes in the valley near the house, so that you can defy suspicion of the manufacture. Make a carriage approach from opposite ends of the valley, so easy and pleasant that it might have been transplanted from Hyde Park . . .

Armstrong himself was so involved in fashioning Cragside that he acknowledged 'it has been my very life'. But he still had sufficient energy – as well as the necessary financial reserves – to overhaul Bamburgh Castle, which he bought in 1894 for £60,000. Sadly, he didn't live to see the medieval castle rebuilt to mimic its former glory. A lifelong advocate of water and solar power, he predicted the end of coal as the country's primary fuel, although its fall from grace has happened earlier than he predicted.

When he died, on 27 December 1900, at the age of ninety – a few weeks before Queen Victoria – *The Times* said in its obituary: 'With his death Newcastle loses her greatest citizen and the country at large one of the worthies of the expiring century.'

Still, industrialisation wasn't the preserve of big cities alone. Even on Lindisfarne, the Holy Island off the Northumbrian coast that became Christianity's centre in the north east, industrial processes sprang up. In 1860, the country's largest lime kiln complex was built there, with giant brick arches that had a monastic feel. Stone was brought here from a quarry at one side of the island, on carts led by horses down a waggonway, and layered in one of six kilns with coal. It might take several days before the kiln was filled and a fire lit. With temperatures of 1,200–1,500°C (2,190–2,730°F), the stone was transformed to quick lime and then used in agriculture and for mortar in buildings. Ships unloaded coal and more limestone at a nearby pair of jetties and took away quick lime. The enterprise was run by a company from Dundee, but employed some thirty-five men locally, including blacksmiths as well as labourers. However, the lime kiln business was not as robust as, for example, shipbuilding. In little more than twenty years, the trade had petered out, with owner William Nicholls ruing a poor investment.

At the time, the East Coast Main Line had a station on the mainland at nearby Beal, which opened in 1847 as the closest station to Holy Island and the first choice for pilgrims, who traditionally approached the island by walking across the causeway. (That station's doors finally closed in 1968, leaving Berwick the nearest option.)

Motherwell to Cumbernauld

Series 6, Episode 3

Distance: 11.75 miles

Michael Portillo: 'I can understand why educated tourists in the nineteenth century would gasp in awe visiting a plant like this. I feel the continuity of history in a facility that manufactured the steel for the *Titanic* and the *Lusitania* and still supplies steel plate for British warships today. I never saw anything on such a scale: the crashes, the bangs, the heat, the steam. The whole thing is deeply impressive.'

At the turn of the nineteenth century, Motherwell was a rural settlement with a population of 600, dwelling in acres of unbroken green with the clean scent of fresh cut hay to fill their lungs. In a country that was distinguished by its stunning vistas, Motherwell was widely acclaimed for its beauty, with campaigner and politician William Cobbett saying it was 'the place of all places in Scotland I should like to live at'.

What a difference a steelworks makes. Energetic entrepreneur David Colville opened one here at a time that the town's citizens still numbered less than 14,000, having expanded during the Industrial Revolution. Just twenty years later, as the twentieth century dawned, the population had swollen to 37,000. While Motherwell's pastoral scenes were sacrificed on the pyre of industrialisation, there was a quid pro quo benefit, with a third of those living there finding enduring employment in iron and steel production.

Railways underpinned the success of the enterprise by transporting raw materials to the steelworks and taking the finished products to its markets. Moreover, the iron and steel produced there went into railway infrastructure, notably in Scotland, as well as the locomotives themselves and the lines they ran on.

Colville had been a tea and coffee merchant before turning his business acumen on to the provision of cast and wrought iron. His first premises was a malleable ironworks sited in nearby Coatbridge, which had rich iron deposits and a handy canal link.

The expansion of the railways meant he could build a new outlet in Motherwell, the Dalzell Ironworks, bringing sons John and Archibald into the family firm. The ironworks opened in 1871, and the Colvilles embraced the latest technology in steel manufacture a decade later. In 1921, a golden jubilee booklet published by the company revealed what had happened at ground level, all those years previously: 'Father and sons threw themselves with characteristic enthusiasm into the work of construction at Dalzell. It is on record that they personally saw every stone of the foundations laid and even shared in the actual physical labour involved in the building of the works.'

The booklet goes on to describe the early years of the factory's operations, when it had twenty puddling furnaces, two ball furnaces and two differently sized mills, with 200 men working there by the spring of 1872. After the Tay Bridge collapsed in December 1879, it was the Colville firm that provided some of the iron bars for the new bridge, helping to secure the company's reputation.

But even greater projects beckoned after the Colvilles turned to the manufacture of steel, the virtues of which were still being discovered. Cast and wrought iron had been used in

industry in general, and on the railways in particular, sometimes with indifferent results. Technology found a fitting and
durable replacement in 1856 when Henry Bessemer came up
with a pear-shaped converter that would render molten pig
iron from the furnace into steel. Quickly evolving alongside
techniques from other industrial innovators, the process was
fast and inexpensive.

Yet Bessemer's system was soon eclipsed by the 'open-hearth
method', also known as the Siemens–Martin Process, which
used large, shallow furnaces and quickly became popular as it
was better suited to English iron ore. The key to its success was
a heated brick chamber that meant super-high temperatures
could be achieved to burn off excess carbon. Colville dispatched
a third son, his namesake David, to work at the Steel Company
of Scotland in Glasgow to find out first-hand how the process
worked, and to study its potential. Having banked this experience, the Colvilles felt sufficiently confident to offer their steel
for use in the construction of the Forth Bridge.

When it opened in 1890, the spectacular Forth Bridge had
the longest cantilever bridge span anywhere in the world and
was the country's first major steel structure.

Before it was built, travellers depended on a ferry service to
cross the broad waterway. Plans for a tunnel, proposed as early
as 1806, had come to nothing. At the height of his career, Sir
Thomas Bouch drew up plans for a bridge, but these were abandoned when his Tay Bridge collapsed. That epic catastrophe left
the way clear for John Fowler and Benjamin Baker to come up
with new, dynamic blueprints, which won parliamentary consent in 1882. Vital statistics for the bridge are extraordinary:
at its highest point, it rises 110 metres (361 feet) above the
water below; 53,000 tonnes of steel were braced together with
6.5 million rivets; and when it's painted, 240,000 litres of paint
are required. The red bridge has now been given world heritage

status for its distinctive style and the part it played in engineering history.

But in the process of its construction, at least fifty-seven lives were lost among the 4,000-strong workforce. Men died from drowning, being crushed, getting struck by a falling object, or falling themselves. One man died of decompression sickness while the piles were driven into the river bed. Engineer Gustave Eiffel believed the death rate was tolerable: 'That would appear to be a large number according to the general rule, but when the special risks are remembered, this number shows as a very small one.'

About one third of the steel in the bridge came from Motherwell, which by now was known by a new moniker of 'Steelopolis'. Where Colville had led, many heavy engineering companies followed, and Motherwell now had a round-the-clock soundtrack of thundering industrial production. In America, the advent of cheap steel made Andrew Carnegie into a billionaire. In Motherwell, it had a similar effect on the Colvilles, but on a smaller scale.

Of course, steel contributed enormously to the development of railways, but it wasn't the only industry hungry for steel at the time. Back to the jubilee booklet: 'In 1879 . . . a further ten acres of ground alongside the existing Iron Works was acquired and five Siemens Open Hearth Furnaces, each of ten tons capacity, were there erected. At the same time, a Steam Hammer, Plate Mill and Shearing Plant were installed: so that the Works could undertake the manufacture of both Ship and Boiler plates.'

In 1900, the shipbuilding industry on the River Clyde employed tens of thousands of men, who put together some of the world's most admired ships. About a fifth of all ships launched across the globe that year came out of Clyde shipyards. Nearby, the Colville's works were busy keeping abreast of demand. Meanwhile, locomotives forged in Scottish steel were hoisted on to ships by enormous cantilever cranes.

By the time the First World War broke out, the number of open-hearth furnaces at Dalzell had increased to thirty, with some 2,800 employees on the payroll. As the demand for steel rose higher than ever before due to the conflict, the company continued to expand, largely by purchasing other concerns. In 1921, with some 18,000 workers now in its employment, it had welfare supervisors, staged concerts and even had a sports-ground. A mansion house near Motherwell was made available for recuperating soldiers during the war before being turned into a summer camp for boys, as well as housing a technical library for aspiring engineers.

The demand created by the Second World War – when women manned the plants while workers were recruited for the armed services – implied a need for more expansion still, and in 1954, the Ravenscraig steelworks at Motherwell began to take shape. Part of the Colville empire, it was completed by 1959, anticipating a busy future. But the new facility barely got a chance to flex its industrial muscles before the economic winds changed direction. There was increasing competition from around the globe, particularly Asia, where labour costs were low. By now British steelworks were using outdated technology and couldn't attract renewed investment.

The monstrous buildings that were once indicative of a hive of steel-making activity have been pulled down at Ravenscraig and there are plans to build housing on the site. Dalzell has been recently reopened after being closed down. Motherwell is not the only victim of the collapse in steel manufacturing in this country, with towns like Consett, Corby, Redcar and Ebbw Vale suffering the same grim decline.

While the plant at Ravenscraig was relatively short-lived, its history was far more illustrious than that of the first

Cumbernauld station. Opened in 1848 by the Caledonian Railway on the Scottish Central line, it was available to customers for just one year before being shut again, one of the early casualties in the railway story in which anticipated demand had failed to materialise. In 1870, Cumbernauld opened for a second time for passenger trains, although the population was still small. Only when plans to impose a new town on the landscape there in the mid-fifties came to fruition did the railway service have economic merit. One of the incoming factories made Irn-Bru, known as Scotland's 'other drink' (the first being whisky). Befitting for a town linked to Motherwell by rail, Irn-Bru was also marketed as: 'Made in Scotland, from girders'.

Epping to Ongar

Series 3, Episode 4

Distance: 8 miles

Michael Portillo: 'From the 1870s onwards, Essex suffered an agricultural depression. Farmers from outside who seized the opportunity to repopulate these bankrupt farms had to relocate lock, stock and barrel, having to transport their dairy herds huge distances.'

For decades, arable farmers in Essex reaped rich rewards thanks to ample sunshine pouring down on an unchallenging landscape. With the east side of the country traditionally drier than the west, its annual harvest of corn was reliably abundant – until it wasn't. A series of bad harvests at the end of the 1870s dented the fiscal resilience of traditional farmers in the area, and they cursed the vagaries of the British weather as the agricultural slump took hold. In fact, the weather was not so much to blame as were the cheap foreign imports that undermined the sanctified position farmers had previously enjoyed. The story of the region's failing grain farmers extended across much of the century.

In the first part of the century, British arable farmers had benefitted from the Corn Laws, which were introduced in 1815 after the Napoleonic Wars and applied to all cereals. These laws meant tariffs were levied on imported grains to protect British farmers, typically the country's biggest landowners at the time.

Certainly, the Corn Laws kept bread prices high, which hit the poorest in the pocket.

When the Corn Laws were scrapped in 1846 by the Conservative prime minister Robert Peel, it was partly in response to Ireland's Great Famine, as the potato blight that caused it had also spread to England, deepening the crisis. In scrapping the laws, the hope was that the price of basic foodstuffs would fall. That didn't particularly go according to plan, and the following three decades were acknowledged as a golden age for British agriculture – but one that didn't last. In the end, it was a change in the law across the Atlantic that would usher in mighty and unforeseen changes in Britain's new free-trade environment.

The Homestead Act was passed in 1862 by the United States government, giving the green light for settlement of the mid-West. Soon, the cereal yields from the prairies seemed as vast as the horizon. Within twenty years, the railway mileage in America had tripled, so farmers found it easier than ever before to get their produce to the coast, no matter how remote their location. And from major ports, steamships benefitting from better technology were achieving record-breaking ocean crossing times, with the cost of freight tumbling by more than half in the decade after 1873 as a result. In short, American corn was cheap and available.

This all led to a catastrophic collapse in cereal prices in Britain, which consequently failed to recover. The prime minister, Benjamin Disraeli, refused to reconsider the free-trade approach that politicians had agonised over, although he agreed to a Royal Commission that would investigate the causes of the rural depression. After three years, it found farmers were being hard pressed by domestic costs, which then rendered them impotent against foreign imports. As a result, the Board of Agriculture, a government department specially concerned with farming, was set up in 1889. It is the ancestor of today's Department for Environment, Food and Rural Affairs.

By 1894, cereal prices had fallen to a 150-year low. At the outbreak of the First World War. Britain imported four-fifths of the wheat the country consumed, and forty per cent of all meat.

In Essex, farmers had failed to identify the dangers or adapt with the changing economic times and many went to the wall. The majority of labourers they had employed were compelled to find new jobs in nearby London. When tenant farmers failed, it was down to landlords to maintain an income by attracting new men to work the soil. Some strategically placed advertisements found farmers from Scotland and others from the West Country, making their way to Essex to begin a new life. Determined not to repeat the pattern that had cost their predecessors so dearly, they didn't just bring their families, but also their dairy herds, bringing a different agricultural profile to the area. And their belief that the county would be 'the land of milk and money' paid off.

Rail links meant the livestock could be transported there on specially rented trains, implying that the migrants had some money in their pockets to cover those initial costs. The trickle of travelling farmers in the 1880s appears to have turned into more of a flood by the early twentieth century. Their hunch about dairy farming was a good one, and the herds soon settled in on the rolling fields, keeping milking parlours busy. Happily, the railway was on hand to take milk from local stations to London, to help nourish its 6.7 million-strong population.

Farmers were served by a railway station at Ongar, opened by the Great Eastern Railway in 1865 as the terminus on a spur from better-connected Loughton. Ongar received fourteen trains a day. Milk traffic doubled between 1894 and 1899, so a special milk dock was built at Ongar to accommodate it. There was also capacity for milk trains at the preceding station, Blake Hall, an attractive red-brick building instituted at the insistence of a local landowner as a condition for allowing the railway to cross his land, but standing in isolation, away from any homes.

Milk was transported in churns for many years, but after 1927, milk tank wagons marked with the logos of nationally known dairies became a familiar sight on the railways. Each one contained 3,000 gallons, enough to supply the 'daily pinta' for some 35,000 people. In 1923, a breath-taking 282 million gallons of milk were ferried across the country by rail. (In Bradshaw's day, a cow produced 11 litres of milk a day, but that was already on the increase during the twenties. Now breeding practices and faster milking means the yield is 30 litres a day.)

Ongar was eventually taken over by the London Underground's Central Line from 1957, at a time when the railways were coming under acute pressure from road transport. Just as milk was increasingly being taken by trucks, so rail passengers turned to cars. It all spelled the closure of Blake Hall in 1981, it having earned for itself the title of the least-used station on the entire Underground service, with just six daily passengers. In the same year, all milk in Britain was finally removed from the tracks, following a slow and steady decline, and the oft-seen milk tank wagons became a railway relic.

To some, Ongar and Blake Hall had been unlikely survivors of the Beeching cuts of the 1960s, which saw the network radically pruned as a result of a report written by Sir Richard Beeching. Blake Hall lost its Sunday service and had its weekday trains reduced, which meant it was hobbled, but not shut. A film made to explain to the public why so many cuts were being made perfectly explained the position both stations found themselves in. Viewers were told that trains had been losing out for a long time to cars, buses and lorries on all fronts.

Freight carried by rail might travel on six trains over the course of its journey, spending considerable time waiting to be shunted on to the right service before reaching its final destination. As for branch lines, the commentator explained: 'We are still suffering enormous financial losses with stopping passenger trains, which [utilise] a lot of expensive equipment to carry a handful of passengers rather slowly and, in the meantime, [hold up] other trains which [could] travel faster if they had the chance.'

The aim was to shut hundreds of stations and depots, a 'necessary part' of building up the more economically robust side of the railway. Thanks to those with a different perspective, Ongar is still part of the railway story.

While no longer part of the network, the Epping to Ongar service has been recreated as a heritage railway, manned by enthusiasts with a diesel locomotive built in 1957, to keep its history alive.

The View from the Train

Although just twenty miles from the concrete of the capital, the journey between Epping and Ongar is verdant, something that hasn't changed markedly in 150 years. According to a 1860s Bradshaw's:

> Essex composes part of that tract of country on the eastern side of England which forms the largest connected space of level ground in the whole island, not one lofty eminence or rocky ridge being found in several contiguous counties.
>
> The surface of Essex is not however totally flat, having many gentle hills and dales . . .

As if to underline just how rural the area is, a story in the London *Evening Standard* in 1976 told how, during that year's long, hot summer, a tube driver operating with his door open was attacked by a rabbit at Blake Hall.

London to York

Series 8, Episode 1

Distance: 210 miles

Michael Portillo: 'Has this been an exercise in national nostalgia? Yes, in part it was: a commemoration of the days when British engineering ruled supreme. But the fact that, over the last ten years, a dedicated group of people has put the *Flying Scotsman* back in steam and back on the tracks demonstrates that British ingenuity and skill also exist in the present.'

An icon of British mechanical expertise, the *Flying Scotsman* is surrounded by admirers wherever it goes. Acknowledged as the most famous train in the world, it's easy to make assumptions about the *Flying Scotsman*'s history, but in fact, it's tale is complex, something the National Railway Museum is keen to underline. When people see today's refurbished locomotive, with its sleek bodywork searing through British countryside, leaving a white plume in its wake, they imagine it's a spectacle that their grandfather witnessed while in short trousers. That's probably not the case. Much of this confusion comes about because the engine – built in 1923, weighing in at 97 tons and at a cost of £7,944 – was named after a railway service that predated it by forty years. If that wasn't enough, there's plenty more to fog its history. In its hundred-year lifetime, this eminent train has been assigned three classes, paraded four colours, been known by six numbers, been attached to nine different tenders and blown steam through at least fifteen different boilers.

The rail link between London and Edinburgh known as the *Flying Scotsman* began in 1862. Given that the train had to stop for lunch at York and offer further comfort breaks along the way, as it was the era of no onboard facilities, journey times of a little more than ten hours were to be expected. Yet twenty-five years later, what began as an undercurrent between railway companies became a rip tide, as competitors went all out to prove their industrial and engineering prowess by fighting to achieve the fastest times between the two capitals. The *Flying Scotsman* service ran on the East Coast Main Line, from King's Cross via York and Newcastle, with the cooperation of the Great Northern, North Eastern & North British Railways. A rival service came out of Euston through Crewe and Carlisle, on the West Coast Main Line operated between London & North Western and Caledonian Railways.

Throughout the 1880s, the services vied for superiority, but the contest came to a head in the summer of 1888 when both sides made commitments to cut the times of their journeys in what became known as 'the Race to the North'.

As locomotives were achieving speeds of more than sixty miles per hour, the companies were able to lop off some two and a half hours from the journey times.

The East Coast consortium was arguably the winner, on one occasion reaching Edinburgh in sprightly seven hours and twenty-seven minutes. Although none of the companies admitted even to the existence of a race, a truce was finally called, perhaps because trains were being pushed to their limits, which came with the associated safety risks. Other trains on the network were held back to give a competing train the edge and passenger comfort was freely compromised. Suddenly aware of the potential hazards they were running, both sides agreed on minimum journey times to take the pressure off train cabin crews.

However, a similar scenario erupted seven years later, this time with Aberdeen as the target, and the start of the grouse-shooting season the trigger. At the time, huge aristocratic house parties migrated north and some fob-watch wearers among them were keen to turn the journey into a race. Once again, carriages were stripped out to reduce weight, and slow-moving travellers were hurriedly bundled aboard as timetables were abandoned. Ultimately, the 525-mile trip was covered in eight and a half hours, with a peak speed of some seventy-seven miles per hour recorded. Speed was important to customers, but there were other considerations too, including facilities. In 1893, the daytime service to Edinburgh running on the Western Main Line introduced the first train with a corridor running from end to end.

As the writer Aldous Huxley famously noted, speed 'provides the one genuinely modern pleasure', and designing faster trains remained an enticing prospect for railway companies. Fast forward twenty-eight years on from the Race to the North (during which time Britain had fought two wars) and the *Flying Scotsman* train was unveiled. Its debut came at a strategically significant time for railways in Britain.

While railways were not integral to the Boer War, they were front and centre in the plans for the First World War, which was, as historian A. J. P. Taylor put it, 'an unexpected climax to the railway age'. During the conflict, the country's numerous railway companies had been taken over by the government's Railways Executive Committee. While these were difficult times, it became apparent that the nation's railways would function better if the number of companies running them was pruned. With the 1921 Railways Acts, 120 smaller railway companies were replaced with what became known as 'the Big Four'; Great Western, London Midland & Scottish, Southern, and London & North Eastern Railways. Chief Mechanical Engineer of London & North Eastern Railways was Nigel Gresley.

As a young man Gresley had taken on an apprenticeship at the Crewe works of the London & North Western Railway, despite his wealthy background, before rapidly rising through the ranks. He was behind all kinds of innovations, but perhaps one of the most fundamental fed in to the *Flying Scotsman*'s speedy service. The length of the journey demanded that two crews were needed to get it done safely, and the train had to halt so the changeover could take place. Gresley inserted a small corridor in the tender, so that a fresh driver and fireman could make their way to the front of the train while it was still thundering along, ready to take over when their shift started. That's in addition to storage for up to eight tons of coal and fifty-five gallons of water – although eventually water could be mechanically scooped up along the route. The *Flying Scotsman* was designed and built at Doncaster, which was known in railway circles as 'the Plant'. (Already central to railway history, it's here the first sleeping cars were built in 1873, the first dining cars in 1879, and corridor coaches three years after that.) By 1928, the *Scotsman* had the prestige of providing the first non-stop service to Edinburgh. Then, in 1934, it became the first steam engine to record speeds of 100 miles per hour.

Although he's best recalled as being the genius behind the *Flying Scotsman*, Gresley designed other ground-breaking engines too, as well as carriages and other railway paraphernalia. He was also the inspiration behind the famous locomotives *Mallard* – still the fastest steam locomotive in the world, having clocked 126 miles per hour in 1938 – and *Green Arrow*. Consider the challenges being made on the domination of the train by the motor car at the time, and Gresley's work seems bolder still.

One celebrated account of riding on the footplate of the *Flying Scotsman* before the Second World War appears in a railway anthology by Ludovic Kennedy, in which he brands the train 'one of the most famous of all travelling hotels'.

> . . . with its Cocktail Bar and Beauty Parlours, its dining saloons, decorated in more or less credible imitation of the salons of 18th century France, its waiters and guards and attendants of all sorts, its ventilation and heating apparatus as efficient as those of the Strand Palace Hotel . . .

> . . . you never for a moment cease to hear, and to feel the effort of the pistons. The shriek of the whistle splits your ears, a hundred other noises drown any attempt at conversation. Though the engine is well sprung, there is a feeling of hard contact on the rails all the time – something like riding on an enormously heavy solid-tyred bicycle . . .

> . . . And continuously the fireman works, and continuously the driver; one hand on the throttle lever, the other ready near the brake handle (a handle no bigger than that of a bicycle and yet controlling power sufficient to pull up a train weighing 500 tons) keeps watch on the line ahead for a possible averse signal.

In 1963, after completing an estimated two million miles, the *Flying Scotsman* retired, just five years before all steam locomotives left the British railway network. Thanks to wealthy railway enthusiasts, the train was saved from the scrap heap and even made trips to America and Australia. Even so, age inevitably caught up with all the working parts. In a ten-year, £4 million restoration, the engine was stripped down so every nut, bolt, rivet and spring could be scrutinised. While the boiler, pipe work and front third of the frame was replaced, the wheels and rods are original. This culminated in a triumphant return to British tracks in 2016, with the *Flying Scotsman* 'running like a sewing machine'.

View from the train

Gliding out of King's Cross, in sight of the vast St Pancras train shed, the *Flying Scotsman* passes through nine tunnels before passing over the forty arches of the Digswell Viaduct at Welwyn, opened in 1850. Stations at Stevenage, Hitchin, Huntingdon and Peterborough all bear a likeness, being the work of one man. Architect Henry Goddard was also responsible for the Great Northern Hotels at Peterborough and Lincoln. Prior to Grantham comes the long descent where *Mallard* achieved its speed record.

Chapter Three

EMPIRE LINES

Queen Victoria came to the throne as the railway revolution was gathering momentum and oversaw the extraordinary technological advances that became the hallmark of her reign. Like many, she was initially terrified of the screeching metal monsters that were thrust upon society, often making their presence known in tranquil fields or through serene vistas, by any standards a blot on the landscape. But Victoria came round to the idea of train travel as safety and comfort improved, albeit with her train moving at a sedate pace. Like the rest of the nation, she understood that, in most instances, the advantages outweighed the drawbacks. With Ireland at that time appearing in Imperial pink on world maps, the story of railway building there was a concern for the government. Ultimately, the railways underscored the wealth of the Empire, although the riches were not equally shared.

Dublin to Drogheda

Series 3, Episode 2

Distance: 31 miles

Michael Portillo: 'Walking the magnificent viaduct at Drogheda reminds me how the railways transformed Ireland in Bradshaw's day.'

The opening of the Dublin & Kingstown Railway in 1834 launched Ireland's rail boom amid frenzied excitement among investors. They knew a gilt-edged opportunity when they saw one, and a main-line railway along the eastern seaboard between the two great cities of Dublin and Belfast was, in terms of business and dividends, about as gilded as they come. But there was trouble ahead.

One problem was that whereas the Dublin & Kingstown Railway had been built in glorious isolation, with no serious competition from other railway companies, the picture was soon very different. Within two years, the Belfast-based Ulster Railway had started work on a line south to Armagh, via Lisburn, Lurgan and Portadown; while the Dublin & Drogheda Railway was heading north from the Irish capital. In an ideal world, these two would have seamlessly linked up, but in nineteenth-century Ireland, with all its political, religious and class rivalries (let alone the vested business interests at play), this was never going to happen.

The Ulster entrepreneurs wanted the first stretch of their line to run inland to Armagh for good reason. It would be a key commuter route, giving Belfast's burgeoning textile and manufacturing factories the ability to recruit workers along the densely-populated River Lagan valley. By early 1837, navvies were already hard at work and the railway was confident it could later press on with an extension down to Dublin. Unfortunately, the Dubliners had different ideas. They had already won permission for a route straight up the coast.

Horrified at the prospect of serious competition, and the pointlessness of two separate lines between the cities, Ulster Railway asked the Dublin & Drogheda Railway to shift its proposed route inland towards Armagh. There was an obvious business motive for this – after all, trains travelling between Armagh and Belfast would pay for use of the line – but Ulster Railway also felt there were sound engineering reasons why the coastal route was inferior. The hills between Dundalk and Newry, they feared, would require too great a track gradient. An Irish Railway Commission was appointed to try and settle the argument, and in 1838 it recommended the inland route.

For months, this delayed work on the Dublin & Drogheda Railway, which by 1840 had progressed just two miles north of Dublin. But in the end, the promoters handed the contract to the redoubtable William Dargan, the engineer who had conquered so many geographical challenges on the Dublin & Kingstown line. Dargan was also the main contractor for the Ulster Railway, although even his reputation could not help resolve the impasse between the companies. Besides, the Irish Railway Commission's report of 1838 had created a new controversy – a full-blown 'gauge war'.

The Commission had decided that the gauge between rails should be 6 feet, 2 inches (just under 1.88 metres). This was considerably wider than the British standard gauge of 4 feet, 8½ inches (just over 1.43 metres), which the Dublin & Kingstown Railway had used. Confident that the issue had been resolved, the Ulster Railway went ahead with the recommended wider gauge, only to discover that its southern rival had opted to build a much narrower gauge, of 5 feet, 2 inches (just under 1.58m). This had been done on the recommendation of its chief engineer, Sir John MacNeill. MacNeill argued that the narrower would save money while still being safe and practical. Each side urged the other to change tack so that all trains would be able to run in both directions. Unsurprisingly, each refused. With the future of the entire network at stake, the Board of Trade, the government regulator on rail standards, was called upon to arbitrate. It appointed its Inspector-General of Railways, Major-General Charles Pasley, to make the ruling.

Pasley was a respected, experienced soldier who had created the science of military engineering from scratch. He was also extremely bright – one story has it that he translated the New Testament from Greek at the age of eight – and he knew that to appease all sides he would have to conduct an inquiry. He took evidence from engineers across Britain and Ireland, eventually concluding that an acceptable gauge for Ireland was somewhere between 5 feet and 5 feet, 6 inches. In what one observer later wryly called 'an exercise in advanced mathematics', Pasley then produced a classic political fudge and split the difference. Ireland's rail gauge would be 5 feet, 3 inches (1.6 metres), a dimension followed to this day, but shared with few other countries.

There followed a predictable uproar in Belfast. The Ulster Railway had already completed a single track as far as Portadown using the wider gauge; now it had to spend an unbudgeted £20,000 laying a third line between those rails to meet the new narrower standard. The Board of Trade agreed that the Ulster Railway should be compensated by other rail companies that would benefit from the conversion (there were plenty lining up

across the North) and made this a legal requirement in various
Irish Railway Acts from 1850 onwards.

Meanwhile, down south, the Dublin & Drogheda Railway
was making good progress, running trains as far as Skerries,
twenty miles north of Dublin, by early 1842. Two years later, the
line was fully operational. As the first train prepared to depart
for Drogheda on 24 May 1844, John MacNeill, now inaugural
professor of engineering at Trinity College, Dublin, was knighted
beneath the arches of the Sherriff Street viaduct. This was a
recognition of his problem-solving engineering nous, although
it had been Dargan's practical application that ensured the line
opened on schedule. Not until 1848 would the Ulster Railway
reach its declared goal of Armagh and, even then, the underlying problem remained: how to link Armagh and Portadown to
Drogheda and, *ipso facto*, Belfast to Dublin.

By this point, though, a new player had entered the game.
Incorporated in 1845, the Dublin & Belfast Junction Railway
was authorised to build the elusive connecting line. Once again,
MacNeill and Dargan were at the heart of it. Work began at
various locations under Dargan's contracting team and they
relished the challenge, first overcoming the soft marshland
south of Portadown before faithfully implementing MacNeill's
extraordinary design for the Craigmore Viaduct across the
Newry Valley (see Dundalk to Portadown, page 155). By the late
1840s, the Dublin & Belfast Junction Railway, which had been
opening its line in stages, stretched from Portadown to a station
in the north of Drogheda. Only one final piece of the engineering
jigsaw remained: to be considered a true, uninterrupted, north–
south main line, the railway still had to cross the valley of the
River Boyne, which was 167m (548 feet) wide, in order to reach
Drogheda's other station, and the link south to Dublin.

Prior to the construction of the Boyne Viaduct, train passengers heading north towards Belfast, or south towards Dublin,

had to alight at Drogheda stations on either side of the river and be ferried a mile through the town by horse and cart across St Mary's road bridge. A viaduct was the obvious solution, but the famine years had caused an economic recession and MacNeill's design – of latticework iron girders (rather than a timber framework) fixed on to fifteen stone piers, or foundation bases – was expensive. The Dublin & Belfast Junction Railway raised a £120,000 loan from the British Exchequer and accepted a tender of £68,000 from Bristol contractor William Evans, who had built the tubular Conwy Railway Bridge in North Wales. This tender was far lower than the top price quoted (£105,786) and did not allow for unforeseen construction problems, of which there were many.

For a start, the plans given to Evans were not originals produced by Dargan, but rather inaccurate copies. That meant additional track-bed work had to be completed before the Boyne was even reached. Meanwhile, a dispute had emerged between the Dublin & Belfast Junction Railway's chief engineer, James Barton, and its consultant, MacNeill, over the latter's load-bearing calculations. That was settled in Barton's favour, but then Evans discovered the geology report for Pier 14 bore little resemblance to reality. Instead of finding bedrock just below the river bed, workmen had to dig down by hand for some 15 metres (50 feet), labouring in the appalling conditions of a 'cofferdam': a square tank comprising four metal plates set around the pier's foundations. It allowed river water to be pumped out, but also leaked incessantly, and Evans's plan to mix stones with soil to try to plug the gaps was refused by harbour commissioners on the spurious grounds that stones might later obstruct navigation. Evans was forced to use bale upon bale of sheep's wool, triggering a local rumour that the viaduct was founded on cotton wool.

Against this background, pressure was mounting to have some form of rail crossing ready in time for Dublin's Great Industrial Exhibition of 1853. Temporary wooden scaffolding around the viaduct was reinforced, and on 15 May 1853, it was tested using a train and two wagons carrying around fifty labourers – an event which attracted an 8,000-strong crowd. The 'volunteer' passengers all completed the trip safely, and the Board of Trade declared the bridge fit for use, provided trains did not exceed five miles per hour, and weighed less than 80 tons. Even so, the crossing must have been a chastening experience for exhibition visitors travelling down to Dublin. By now, work was proceeding only on grudging cash advances from the Board. Rocketing costs forced Evans into bankruptcy, although he stayed with the project to the bitter end.

Still the squabbling continued. The Board was determined to recover some of its costs by charging rail passengers a levy of eight pence – a move anathema to both Dublin & Drogheda Railway and Ulster Railway, who promptly stopped cooperating with the Dublin & Belfast Junction Railway. The row was eventually resolved, and October brought good news when a foundation for Pier 14 was finally found. Yet still the work dragged on, hampered by pay strikes, a collapsing cofferdam and financial constraints. A new completion date of July 1854 came and went, and it was not until 5 April of the following year that the viaduct was officially declared open. By Victorian standards, this was an unusually unceremonious occasion. Railway directors and government officials alike were just glad it was all over.

Slough to Windsor

Series 3, Episode 6

Distance: 2.5 miles

Michael Portillo: 'The advent of the train enabled Queen Victoria, much more quickly than any of her predecessors, to visit her realm, to view her subjects and to vary her residences. This is Windsor, a town of great significance to royals and rails.'

In common with a number of her subjects, Queen Victoria initially regarded trains with trepidation, fearful their enhanced speed would cause bodily injury or even outright insanity. But when she finally plucked up enough courage to take a trip in 1842, persuaded by her husband, Prince Albert, trains brought her considerable joy and immeasurable convenience. As it happened, her reign between 1837 and 1901 reflected the railway's golden age.

Fitting, then, that her first journey, between Slough and Paddington, saw eminent engineer Daniel Gooch at the locomotive's controls and Isambard Kingdom Brunel standing beside him: two giants of the engineering world. Beside them stood a Royal footman, whose scarlet uniform was duly ruined by locomotive smoke. Soon afterwards, the Queen confessed in a letter that she was 'quite charmed' by the railway, having made the half-hour journey 'free from dust and crowds and heat'.

She wasn't the first royal to travel by train. Queen Adelaide, wife of King William IV, took to the railways in 1840, and two year later was given exclusive use of a carriage built by the London & Birmingham Railway. Prince Albert was also already a veteran of the rails. Great Western Railways trains had been stopping at Slough since 1838, although objections from nearby Eton College incorporated into parliamentary consent for the line prevented the halt becoming an actual station for several years. When it was finally constructed after the constraints were rescinded, Slough station, mindful of the potential for royal passengers, was reminiscent of a French chateau. Given the proximity of its main line, which ran through Slough and headed west, it was only a matter of time before Great Western Railways eyed a branch line to the royal town – but plans ran into the same implacable opposition from Eton, the country's most elite and well-connected public school. Headmaster Dr John Keate, remembered for his faux Napoleonic dress and as a noted flogger of pupils, believed the arrival of the railway would provoke a breakdown in discipline, turning his scholars into stone-throwers or runaways, as well as affecting their health.

In 1834, he was replaced by Dr Edward Hawtrey, who was no less opposed to the railway. Although Hawtrey failed in his endeavours to have the planned branch line scrapped, it was re-routed in a loop that avoided the Eton enclave by some distance. This delayed the project for some years, and ensured the neighbourhood of the school would never get a station to call its own. The hold-up caused consternation for Great Western, who knew rivals were also heading into Windsor and were likewise hoping for the associated royal patronage. South Western Railway had built tracks from Waterloo, and was making fine progress towards the royal town until one of its bridges wobbled. Ultimately, Great Western Railways won the race, with a wrought-iron 'bow and string' bridge designed by Brunel across the River Thames that's still holding fast today. Windsor & Eton Central Station opened on 8 October 1849, with the

Queen passing through it within a month. There was a sense of defeat in the air when South Western Railways' Windsor & Eton Riverside station, with its gabled front, arched entrances and beautifully appointed royal waiting room, opened on 1 December the same year, becoming the town's second terminus.

Railways bought the advantages of timely travel to everyone. But for Queen Victoria, there were a multitude of other advantages that transformed her life.

For a start, a railway carriage afforded a good deal more privacy than any horse-drawn vehicle, and train travel was much more comfortable, especially for those who travelled in specially built royal trains. Inside, there were luxuriously appointed sofas rather than seats. Walls were quilted satin, curtains – which could be drawn to exclude prying eyes – were made from the finest silks, and twenty-three-carat gold paint was used for some of the fixtures and fittings. There were beds so the Queen could travel overnight in comfort. At the touch of a button, she could call her dresser or a lady-in-waiting, who would be travelling further down the same train. As soon as technology permitted, the royal train was quick to install electric lighting. It came into its own not on short hops between Slough and Windsor, but when Queen Victoria made trips to her Scottish home at Balmoral. Thanks to the studied opulence, it was like travelling in a palace on wheels – and she could take her favourite books, clothes, furniture, jewels and servants with her for the holidays. The royal train was always a double-header – that is, two locomotives, each individually operated, so that if there was a breakdown, the towed carriages wouldn't be left stranded. A third engine went ahead to ensure the line was clear of obstructions.

However, when the royal train was on the move around the railway network, there was a knock-on effect for other travellers. Trains transporting royalty were given priority above everything else. Not for them the dreary business of waiting at signals. But the Queen insisted her train travelled at strict speed limits: no more than forty miles per hour during daylight, or thirty miles per hour at night. As her reign wore on, intercity trains were achieving far greater speeds than that, and passengers might have expected some sixty miles per hour or more from the most capable locomotives. Getting stuck behind the royal transport must have had its frustrations. More than that, although her royal train was equipped with a lavatory, Queen Victoria preferred land-based amenities and insisted on stopping every two hours or so in order to visit the toilet. She also had the train stopped at mealtimes and so she could change carriages, as she declined to walk between carriages when the train was moving.

It generally fell to railway companies to provide royal trains, which comprised numerous carriages, with the Queen's accommodation at the centre, for fear of shunts. In 1869, the Queen commissioned a pair of coaches with the London & North Western Railway at a cost of £1,800 (about £167,000 in today's values). It proves how invested she was by then in trains as a mode of transport.

Trains were much safer than a horse and carriage, as the Queen discovered on 2 March 1882 during a failed assassination attempt. It happened as she travelled from Buckingham Palace to Windsor in the company of her daughter, Princess Beatrice, by train. Crowds had gathered to cheer her as the Queen made her way from Windsor's Central station, through her specially-appointed waiting room across a carpeted floor, and to a carriage. Through the hubbub of the crowd a shot rang out, fired by aspiring poet Roderick Maclean. At the time, the Queen was greatly revered by the population, having come out of a long period of self-imposed isolation following the death of her husband. Maclean, aged twenty-eight, had already been committed to an asylum in the West Country but had escaped in order to take revenge for what he deemed a curt response from the royals to a poem he had sent.

Thankfully, the shot went awry. Two Eton schoolboys on the scene tackled him with their umbrellas before police arrived. Facing a charge of high treason, Maclean was found insane rather than guilty and dispatched to Broadmoor Asylum, where he died forty years later. Dismayed that the verdict on Maclean effectively pronounced him 'innocent', Queen Victoria pressed for a change in the law, so that felons might be found guilty but insane.

In 1897, Windsor's Central station was completely rebuilt to mark her Diamond Jubilee, benefitting from an impressive arch at the front and a comfortable royal waiting room. She travelled through the new-look station on 21 June 1897 on the day of the celebration, as her diary recalls: 'At quarter to twelve we drove to the station to start for London. The town was very prettily decorated, and there were great crowds, who cheered very much.'

Since then, the station has lost five of its original six platforms, and the remaining one has been so truncated it can only accommodate a three-coach train. However, a replica of the train that carried Queen Victoria to London on the day of the celebration still stands in the station, as a reminder of those glory years.

View from the train

The six-minute journey between Windsor & Eton Central and Slough is dominated by views of the town's castle, initially built by William the Conqueror, but reconstructed as it's seen today by Edward III. 'No Briton can view unmoved the stately towers of Windsor's castle keep', *Bradshaw's Guide* insists. 'Its history is the history of our country, and some of its brightest and blackest pages are inseparably linked with the towers that arrest the eye of the traveller as he approaches the station.'

Navan to Mullingar

Series 8, Episode 3

Distance: 55 miles

Michael Portillo: 'The barracks still stand. The British built this huge military compound in the early nineteenth century. Irish military services took it over and used it until 2012.'

They are two of the great engineering achievements that made modern Ireland. From the mid-eighteenth century, first the Royal Canal and then the Midland Great Western Railway became the arterial links that allowed much of the remote north and west to access the prosperity of Dublin and the south east. They are intertwined through a common history, geography and ownership; iconic structures, side-by-side, embedded in Irish folklore and literature, touched by conflict, tragedy, politics and even the supernatural.

Perhaps the most poignant literary reference comes in Brendan Behan's 1954 play *The Quare Fellow*, in which he attacks the barbarity of capital punishment and Irish piety towards sexuality, crime and religion. The plot is based on Behan's own experience of Dublin's Mountjoy Prison (as an IRA volunteer, he was arrested and detained there). A song featured in the play, 'The Old Triangle', describes the metal triangle that was beaten with a hammer to wake prisoners. It begins with the famous lines:

> A hungry feeling, came o'er me stealing
> And the mice were squealing in my prison cell
> And the old triangle went jingle jangle
> All along the banks of the Royal Canal.

The Royal Canal has been a part of Dublin's landscape since 1790, when work began to link the city's busy quays on the River Liffey with the River Shannon in County Longford, ninety miles away. This project operated in competition with the Grand Canal, which had a more southerly route to the same connection, and the hope was that, together, they would spread trade and industrial development into Ireland's heartland. In fact, the bitter rivalry of the two companies – they refused possible cooperation on at least two sections – hampered profitability. By the time the Royal Canal reached the Shannon in 1817, the project had cost £1,421,954 and was laden with debt for the taxpayer.

For the first twenty-five years, business gradually grew. The Royal Canal's route opened up a swathe of the Midlands, running from the suburbs of north Dublin, through Castleknock, Leixlip and Maynooth, then on through the pasturelands of Kildare and Westmeath to Mullingar, terminating at Richmond Harbour in Clondra, on the Shannon. By 1833, barges were shipping 134,000 tons of freight each year, while annual passenger numbers reached 46,000 in 1837. But the Grand Canal was proving more profitable. Attempts to boost business on the Royal included an extension to Longford, new hotels at Broadstone in Dublin and Moyvalley in County Kildare, and the use of lighter, so-called 'fly' boats, which cut passenger journeys between Mullingar and the capital from twelve to eight hours. But it was not enough. The railways were coming. Canal services could never compete.

Yet, just as there was competition between the canal companies, so there was between rival railways. In 1842, the fledgling

Great Southern & Western Railway considered a line linking
Dublin and the west coast, but then decided against it, leading to a boardroom split. Several directors, led by the Quaker
businessman James Perry, left to form the Midland Great
Western Railway and pursue the project themselves. In 1845,
they won parliamentary approval to raise £1 million worth of
investment capital for a main line between Dublin and Galway,
via Mullingar and Athlone. There would also be a branch line
between Mullingar and Longford in order to link up with river
traffic from the Shannon. This suited the British government,
which maintained a huge military barracks at Mullingar. The
potential for moving troops quickly by rail around an increasingly rebellious Ireland was not lost on ministers.

In a flash of entrepreneurial genius, Perry and his Midland
Great Western Railway directors realised that, if they bought
the struggling Royal Canal – and specifically the land on either
side of it – the first stretch of the track to Mullingar could
simply be laid alongside the water. A deal was done, with the
condition that the railway was legally committed to maintain
the waterway's business – but this was of little concern to Perry.
He had snapped up the entire property at the knockdown price
of £40 for every £100-worth of canal company shares, spending
a total of £289,059. This was a fraction of the cash required to
buy individual parcels of farmland across the seventy-five miles
between Dublin and Longford. Besides, Perry knew the canal's
days were numbered.

But then things got complicated. No sooner had the Midland
Great Western Railway published its proposals when the Great
Southern & Western Railway decided that, on reflection, it too
wanted a line to Galway. It pursued this by backing the plans of
another competitor, the Irish Great Western Railway, which in
1845 had poached Midland Great Western Railway's consulting
engineer, Sir John MacNeill, for a similar position. MacNeill

was now effectively chief engineer to both the Great Southern & Western Railway and the Irish Great Western Railway. From the former's perspective, this was great news: a key player had jumped ship from their bitter rivals, and now he was arranging for Irish Great Western trains to run along Great Southern & Western track, thus increasing their revenues from western traffic. Despite this, the Midland Great Western Railway plan continued at pace under MacNeill's former pupil, George Hemens. He supervised track construction between Dublin and Mullingar, devising innovative strategies to overcome the problem of building on deep bog (which was necessary to avoid severe curves on the Royal Canal). Indeed, Hemens' designs literally laid the foundations for all future rail- and road-building across the Irish bogs of the Midlands and the west.

By December 1847, the new line was open as far as Kinnegad. Within nine months, a service had started to Mullingar. Here, the line split: one section wound south-west to Galway, opening in 1851, while the north-western route reached Longford four years later. The speed and convenience of the railway abruptly ended canal passenger traffic between Dublin and the Midlands, while freight also suffered, falling to 30,000 tons annually by the early 1880s, and to 10,000 tons by 1920.

Successful it may have been, but for many poor farmers and labourers a train ticket was beyond their means. Expansion of the Midland Great Western Railway coincided with the years of the Great Famine (1845–49) and much of the countryside was on its knees. Here the railway's place in history is controversial; on the one hand, it provided work for the jobless poor (1,900 navvies were employed on the Dublin–Mullingar line); yet on the other, its managers showed an embarrassing indifference to the gathering crisis. On the day construction began, 12 January 1846, a sumptuous banquet was thrown by the directors for 'an assemblage of fashionable society'.

Meanwhile, Irish workhouses, which offered pittance wages and appalling accommodation, were seeing their inmate population increase from 135,000 in February 1848 to 215,000 by June of the following year. Overcrowding was horrific, malnutrition was rife and the situation was worsened when the government passed a law denying relief to anyone owning more than a quarter-acre of land. That increased pressure on poor families to emigrate, a result welcomed by many landlords, who did not want their private wealth supporting tenants. On many estates, landowners engaged in 'clearances': paying for their tenants' passage to America to dodge any moral responsibilities.

Not all landlords were so ruthless. The Earl of Kingston spent half his annual rental income on relieving starvation, while the Earl of Shannon ran up massive debts to create employment and distribute food. But some tenants, like those of Major Denis Mahon at Strokestown House, Roscommon, were less fortunate. In 1847, Mahon presented them with three unenviable options: 'assisted passage' migration; remaining in hovels to starve; or life in the workhouse. In May that year, 1,432 took up his emigration offer and set off for Dublin, walking along the Royal Canal towpath past navvies building the new railway to Mullingar. They were put on boats to Liverpool, where they transferred to four 'coffin' ships carrying grain to Quebec. It is thought a quarter of them died en route.

When the news filtered home, Mahon's remaining tenants refused to take his migrant money. He hit back by evicting some 3,000 people, and was promptly accused of being 'worse than Cromwell' by the local parish priest, Father Michael McDermott. On the evening of 2 November 1847, Mahon was shot and killed as he returned home from a Board of Guardians meeting in Roscommon town. The news was greeted with wild celebrations and the lighting of beacons, prompting Queen Victoria to note that the Irish 'really . . . are a terrible people'. Her view was not shared by her reforming prime minister, Lord John Russell, but his weak government proved unable to push through meaningful measures to relieve starvation.

Travelling between Dublin and Mullingar today, it is not difficult to imagine ghosts of the famine years still haunting the land. The old Midland Great Western Railway line boasts one particularly spine-chilling story linked to Deey Bridge, between Leixlip and Maynooth, and the Royal Canal's fabled Thirteenth Lock. Canal workers always claimed the lock was dug through a graveyard, and subsequently was haunted by disturbed spirits. The tale is recounted in the well-known poem 'The Spooks of the Thirteenth Lock', by the writer and founder of Sinn Fein, Arthur Griffith.

Griffith tells how a 'gallant' ship's captain sees ghosts sitting beside the lock as he waits for the water to rise. He jeers at them, ignoring warnings from his friends, but upon returning to harbour, he is afflicted by bad luck, first losing his job and then dying from a mysterious illness the same evening. The poem begins:

> Every night of the year about twelve of the clock,
> The spirits and spooks of the dread thirteenth lock,
> Sit winging their bodies a-this and that way,
> And singing in chorus: 'Ri tooril li lay' . . .
> Oh what would you think sir, and what would you say?
> If you met with a ghost singing 'Tooril li lay.'

The final lines read:

> That evening at midnight the bold captain died,
> With his poor weeping wife and his friends by his side,
> And the last words he said when they asked him to pray
> Were 'Tooril li tooril. Ri tooril li lay.'

Kendal to Windermere

Series 1, Episode 8

Distance: 10.25 miles

Michael Portillo: 'The arrival of the railways in the Lake District was hugely controversial. At the time the locals feared for their beautiful countryside.'

Many campaigns were conducted against the railway in Britain, on the basis that it would blacken the landscape, frighten the horses and/or dispossess slum dwellers with nowhere else to go. In the Lake District, objections were of a very different nature. This was the playground of the nineteenth-century literati, and it was the likely invasion of the working classes that troubled writers and poets. Naturally, their vehement opposition was eloquently expressed.

The Kendal & Windermere Railway was first proposed in 1844, sparking a flurry of objections around the concerned community. Poet Laureate William Wordsworth outlined his opposition to a rail link in the first line of a verse: 'Is then no nook of English ground secure from rash assault?' The sonnet ended with an exhortation to fellow poetry-lovers to 'protest against the wrong'.

These were just a few of the many words he wrote in a bid to obstruct the railway. Already in his seventies, the Romantic poet was certainly disturbed at the deleterious effects of advancing industrialisation on the countryside. Yet he repeatedly returned to the capacity of what he knew as the lower classes to appreciate the area as he did. With the mill workers of Preston and Manchester in his sights, he persisted with the notion that there would be armies of visitors to the area who would not benefit 'mentally or morally'.

'Go to a pantomime, a farce, or a puppet-show, if you want noisy pleasure,' he urged these nameless hordes, but he wanted others – including himself – 'to be safe from the molestation of cheap trains pouring out their hundreds at a time along the margin of Windermere'.

In October 1844, Wordsworth wrote to eminent politician William Gladstone, urging him to give special consideration to objectors, saying 'every man of taste and feeling' in the neighbourhood was concerned. As it was the same year that Gladstone, who was also President of the Board of Trade, steered the Railway Regulation Act, broadening the access to railway use for less wealthy people by limiting some fares to 'one penny per mile', it seemed unlikely the poet would get a sympathetic hearing there. Wordsworth also wrote two letters, numbering 5,500 words, to the *Morning Post*, which were published nine days apart in December. Then he gathered his campaigning rhetoric into a pamphlet directed at the railway companies, warning of the potential for ruination if working folk came to the Lakes in quantity. 'All that your railroad company can do for them is only to open taverns and skittle grounds round Grasmere, which will soon, then, be nothing but a pool of drainage, with a beach of broken ginger beer bottles; and their minds will be no more improved by contemplating the scenery of such a lake than of Blackpool.'

He related experiences he'd already had with visitors who didn't, in his view, come up to snuff:

In the midst of a small pleasure-ground immediately below my house rises a detached rock, equally remarkable for the beauty of its form, the ancient oaks that grow out of it and the flowers and shrubs which adorn it.

'What a nice place would this be,' said a Manchester tradesman, pointing to the rock, 'if that ugly lump were but out of the way.'

Most people were of this ilk, Wordsworth claimed, and 'none but the deceiver and the willingly deceived can be offended by its being stated'.

Critic and essayist John Ruskin took up the cudgels: 'I have said I take no selfish interest in this resistance to the railroad. But I do take an unselfish one. It is precisely because I passionately wish to improve the minds of the populace and because I am spending my own mind, strength, and fortune wholly on that object, that I don't want to let them see Helvellyn while they are drunk.'

It apparently never occurred to Wordsworth that, as an admired poet and the author of a Lake District guide published in 1820, he was himself fuelling tourism.

Not everyone concurred with these conservative views, and American diplomat Edward Everett, who did a six-year stint in Britain, took issue with Wordsworth's objections.

How little of rural beauty you lose, even in a country of comparatively narrow dimensions like England . . . by works of this description. You lose a little strip along the line of the road, which partially changes its character; while, as the compensation, you bring all this rural beauty . . . within the reach, not of a score of luxurious, sauntering tourists, but of the great mass of the population, who have senses and tastes as keen as the keenest. You throw it open, with all its soothing and humanizing influences, to thousands who, but for your railways and steamers, would have lived

and died without ever having breathed the life-giving air
of the mountains.

Still, Wordsworth was influential enough to garner the
support of landowners that the railway company needed onside
if they were to pursue their chosen route. To sidestep these
objections, and save money on engineering solutions for a
series of steep inclines on the proposed route, a new path was
found for the railway, which ended at Birthwaite. The station
was quickly renamed Windermere, after the lake some three-
quarters of a mile distant and a small hamlet by it, as the
railway company sought to cash in on the tourist pound and
attract more visitors. The building of the Kendal & Windermere Railway boasted a fine pedigree. The engineer was Joseph
Locke, while the contractors included Robert Stephenson and
Thomas Brassey. Wordsworth was left isolated, a lone voice
trying to hold back the tide of technology.

When the line was finally opened in 1846, a public holiday
was announced in Kendal, where residents were reportedly
dancing in the street. It's said that Wordsworth later bought
shares in the railway company. Kendal has always been more
the business end of the track, and Bradshaw's reveals the
trades that were in existence there 160 years ago: '[Residents]
are principally engaged in the carpet, woollen, linsey [cloth],
worsted, clog, comb, bobbin, fishhook, leather, rope, woollen
cord, fruit trade and marble works.'

And it was from Kendal that business interests pushed for
the rail link. Although it was the biggest town between Lancaster and Carlisle, Kendal had been by-passed when plans to link
those two cities were drawn up, primarily due to a set of tricky
inclines. Kendal thus pressed for its own branch line, stemming
from a junction at Oxenholme. (It was the start of a troubled
history between the Kendal & Windermere Railway and the

Lancaster & Carlisle Railway, resolved when the former was leased by the latter, with both eventually becoming part of the London & North Western Railway.)

With a trip on the water one of the principle attractions, the railway company's timetable and steamship boat service became integrated. Indeed, Bradshaw's told visitors: 'The lake itself should be seen from the water as well as the shores, to take in all its beauties.'

Well-to-do visitors hired a boat for the purposes of a trip, while others used the public services. But while some things in Bradshaw's remain the same, others have changed, such as the promise that the lake, 'with its beautiful islands and grassy well-wooded fells round its borders', will hove into view at the station.

Today's station was built in 1986. But even from the station's original site nearby, it is impossible to glimpse the water, as the area is now so built up. Passenger traffic on the trains gives some idea of Windermere's long-standing popularity. By 1853, there were six trains each day, with extra services in the summer, and a return ticket cost sixpence. Thirty years later, the number of visitors that came to Windermere by train on Whit Monday numbered 8,000. Meanwhile, today an estimated 10 million people visit the Lake District each year. But it's not so much the visitors who have inspired the residential expansion in the area as the wealthy merchants with commercial centres in cities, who found it an agreeable place to live. From a twenty-first century perspective, Wordsworth's objections seem inappropriate and even offensive. However, the south end of the lake has become polluted, as the Victorian sewage system that still serves households and road water runoff can no longer cope with demand. People have united to improve the lake's water quality, and the success of their efforts is regularly monitored. However, it's certain that Wordsworth, lying not too far distant in the churchyard at Grasmere, would be grimly righteous in the knowledge that a least some of his dire warnings about the arrival of tourists would be substantiated.

Hull to Scarborough

Series 9, Episode 11

Distance: 53 miles

Michael Portillo: 'The railway reached into every corner of people's lives in ways that no one could have predicted.'

Fish and chips is the nation's favourite dish. Sometimes served on plates, but mostly in newspaper, this intoxicating combination with its enticing aroma appeared across the country by the end of the nineteenth century, especially on Friday nights.

In essence, there's very little that's British in the origins of the concept. It was Belgians who brought to Britain the idea of frying potatoes, while Jewish immigrants from Spain and Portugal introduced the notion of fried fish. But it was in Britain that the pairing became high art, with competing claims for the first fish-and-chip shop being made by Bow in London in 1860 and Mossley in Lancashire, where a wooden shed had started service in 1863.

For centuries, with cumbersome transport methods and a lack of refrigeration, fish-eating had been generally restricted to coastal communities. The only safe choice for townspeople was freshwater fish. Then came fast-moving trains, which could haul the harvest of the sea around the country, providing an inexpensive option for consumption in urban areas and changing the British diet forever.

Much of the cod headed for the deep fryer came from Hull, which was, for a time, one of the biggest white-fish ports in the world.

The town had already established a sea-faring tradition, with a fleet of sixty whalers by the time the railway arrived in Hull in 1840. Hull was also seen as a resort, and that same year the railway companies began offering discounted ticket excursions: there are records of one such excursion from Leeds to Hull for 1,250 people in a train forty carriages long. But it was fishing that became the town's mainstay, as whalers became fishermen and new trawlers were added to the fleet. By 1850, twenty fish trains a day left Hull for destinations across the country.

Abundant fish arrived at the right time in mill towns and cities, where both husband and wife were labouring long hours and needed a swift and economical family meal at the end of the working day. The quantity of fish consumed in Manchester alone went up from three to eighty tons a week, while the cost of cod dropped by three quarters.

Railway lines were laid along the dockside, where the fish were unloaded. The catches grew larger after 1885, when steam trawlers began to replace fishing smacks. The men who offloaded the fish were called 'bobbers', as they constantly had to duck to avoid getting knocked over by baskets being hoisted off the ship.

With the success of the fishing industry came the Hull Fish Meal and Oil Company, which opened in 1890 to process the fish heads, tails and guts for fertiliser or animal food, so nothing was wasted. In the boom years, the trawlermen were known as 'three-day millionaires' because, when they were home, they would spend their pay in the pub and buy treats for their families. Their time ashore usually only amounted to a few days every few weeks. When they were away, their wives went to the dock office to collect their wages on what became known as 'white stocking' day, reflecting the garment they traditionally wore. During two world wars, fish wasn't rationed, so remained a popular food choice. With plenty of fish in the sea and a steady demand among fish-and-chip shops everywhere, it seemed nothing would dent the industry.

The tide changed for trawlermen in Hull in 1975 after a spat with Iceland about fishing rights. It wasn't the first 'cod war' but it became decisive after incidents of ship ramming and net-cutting. When Iceland threatened to close a NATO facility, America put pressure on the British government to acquiesce. On the near horizon there were also concerns about the viability of fish stocks. It all quickly spelled the end for fishing at Hull, seeing a fleet that was once a thousand-strong dwindle to just six vessels.

Fish wasn't the only shipborne industry centred on Hull, which had numerous docks to receive consignments of wheat and barley from Germany, for example, and timber from Scandinavia. The latter caused chaos, as giant sawn planks were dropped into the sea from visiting ships, leaving port workers to pull them out. This meant significant parts of the docks were blocked and other ships were frequently damaged. In 1850, while trains were rushing fish to markets, a new timber dock was opened with a designated pond for offloading. Later, a second pond was added, and even that was extended to accommodate the lumber. The wood was used primarily for pit props in Britain's mines.

The 1860s edition of *Bradshaw's Guide* notes the level of trade at Hull, which was by now the country's third biggest port.

All [the docks] are surrounded by large warehouses and timber yards. Upwards of 100,000 tons of shipping are owned by the port and the customs duties amount to nearly half a million [pounds]. Pottery, bricks, white lead, soap, oil cake, rope, sails, grain, timber, iron – figure among the articles of trade.

It was the number of docks around low-lying Hull and its proximity to both river and sea that inspired Bradshaw's to draw a likeness between this east coast city and Italy's jewel, Venice.

Many of those on the train from Hull in the summer months of the nineteenth century would have been heading up the coast to Scarborough for a day out or a holiday. According to Bradshaw's:

> The season may be reckoned to begin on the first of July, and terminate about the middle of October. During this period, houses and apartments can only be had at high prices; but, after the latter date, a residence may be obtained at half the amount. The Railway, as in other instances, has materially increased the influx of visitors, and now new streets are being rapidly formed, to provide additional houses for their reception.

Even before the railways reached Scarborough, it was an established spa town with visitors who probably enjoyed a private income. As the spa was perched on a rocky promontory, an elegant iron footbridge opened in 1827 to ease access issues. Furthermore, there was a twelfth-century castle to peruse as well as the purpose-built Rotunda Museum, which opened in 1829 with an enviable collection of fossils. A passion for fossil-hunting enlivened a section of British society in the first half of the nineteenth century, when the skeletons of dinosaurs were being found and assembled for the first time – in an era when the existence of these prehistoric monsters was contrary to Bible teachings.

In 1834, the 4,000-year-old skeleton of a warrior was discovered near Gristhorpe, in North Yorkshire. Much later, the man was identified as being about sixty years of age – a considerable lifespan for the Bronze Ages – and had probably suffered a brain tumour. The body, found in a hollowed-out tree along with grave goods, was put on display for visitors.

For residents in the 1860s, there were seventeen butchers, twenty-three bakers and four 'tallow chandlers', or candle-makers. In addition, Scarborough had a dozen milliners, eight blacksmiths, six clock-makers, three basket-makers, three brick-makers, a tea dealer, a nail-maker and more than seventy taverns, as well as twenty more beer houses. A gazetteer from fifty years later offers a glimpse of how Scarborough life was now slanted more towards its visitors. There was an aquar-ium, a central tramway, public baths, lawn tennis courts, the Scarborough Field Naturalists' Society, Temperance Choral and Orchestral Societies, chess, cricket, cyclists and model yacht clubs.

Other new additions to public life, as far as its 35,000-strong population was concerned, were the school attendance com-mittee, a school board, income tax commissioners and a rural sanitary authority. At that time, about 25,000 visitors arrived each year, although a gazetteer advised against hopping on the railway.

Intending visitors to Scarborough, while having plenty of facilities by rail, would do well to approach it from the sea. It has the advantage of introducing the tourist from its most attractive point of view. It has been said that travellers by rail seem to sneak into the town by the back door. Her magnificent bay is the chief glory of Scarbor-ough, and those upon whom this bright vision bursts at their first glimpse of the place, will not soon forget the pleasure of the sight.

Even if people did travel by sea, they may well have used the station clock, standing proud to remind visitors that time was ticking on their day trip.

The view from the train

For those that admire railway architecture, the stations at
Hull, Beverley, Bridlington, Filey and Scarborough all bear
the hallmarks of Victorian brickwork, iron ornamentation and
capacious glass roofs. A sense of uniformity among them exists
because they are all the work of George Townsend Andrews, a
York-based architect who was responsible for most of the buildings linked to the Yorkshire & North Midlands Railway when
it was under the control of George Hudson. In a decade when
Hudson was riding high on the railway wave, Andrews oversaw
the construction of more than sixty stations throughout East
Yorkshire. As many other examples of his work have been either
pulled down, such as the first station at York, which was built
inside the city walls, or stand by lines that no longer operate,
such as Raskelf, Haxby, Flaxton and Bolton Percy, these command a nostalgic significance now.

Keighley to Haworth

Series 5, Episode 4

Distance: 5 miles

Michael Portillo: 'I'm heading to Haworth, atop a hill in the Worth Valley where novels of passion and genius were created by three brilliant sisters. I want to know what inspired them, and whether the railway played any role in their lives.'

To the outside world, they were highly successful sisters who wrote compelling novels that took a book-reading public by storm. The Brontë sisters led a cloistered existence at Haworth in Yorkshire, yet drew vivid scenarios and created casts of characters that became imprinted through the core of the nation's very soul. At the time, few could believe three genteel young women were capable of such erudite breadth and depth.

But while the trio were a cut above most of the rest of the population in literary terms, they turned out to be just as likely as anyone else to be swept up in the Railway Mania that stalked the country in the late 1840s. The arrival of the railways was transformative and few lives were left untouched, with personal finances being just one facet of the story. In 1844, the Railway Regulation Act meant that cheap fares, equivalent to a penny per mile, had to be offered to passengers at least once a day (in covered rather than open carriages), effectively endorsing third-class travel. In fact, most working people still couldn't afford that at the time, but it signalled a government intention of expansion and that the technology was for the benefit of everyone, not just the wealthy.

But the government didn't build the railways that stretched across the British countryside: private companies did. Although each new blueprint needed parliamentary approval, the cash for the project was raised from private investors. Initially, the returns on investments had been generous, a gift that kept on giving. Everyone with some spare cash wanted to be part of the railways' success story, so finding the necessary financial backing wasn't particularly difficult for artfully drawn projects. However, the feeding frenzy that followed, as some 9,000 miles of railway were approved – that's ten times the length of Great Britain – created an illusory boom in the business, followed by a devastating bust. Not all the new lines would be a success and even the most well-established railway companies saw share prices tumble. Among those to feel the pinch were Charlotte Brontë and her sisters.

Charlotte – whose first railway trip, in 1839, was to Bridlington – had shares in the York & North Midland Railway, which had been given the go-ahead to run between Leeds and Castleford. From the outset, the project had the kudos of having George Stephenson aboard, but it was also one of the companies in the fold of railways promoter George Hudson. He resigned in 1849, when some of his sharp practices and wheeler-dealing had been laid bare. There was an element of scapegoating. Although his reputation lay in tatters, it's also true that, when it came to the railway stakes, Hudson tended to back winners. However, that didn't protect shareholders like Charlotte at the time. One of her letters revealed: 'The original price of Shares in this Railway was £50. At one time they rose to £120; and for some years gave a dividend of 10 per cent; they are now down at £20, and it is doubtful whether any dividend will be declared this half-year.'

Charlotte and her sisters were among numerous celebrities of the age who lost out during Railway Mania, with luminaries such as Charles Babbage, who invented the first mechanical computer, economist John Stuart Mill and fellow writer William Makepeace Thackeray also victims. For Charlotte, spare cash was at hand only thanks to the unexpected income from an inheritance and, later, the sales of her first novel, *Jane Eyre*.

Money had not conspicuously featured in the upbringing of the Brontë sisters, whose father Patrick was an Anglican clergyman. Their youth was haunted by tragedy, as their mother Maria died of cancer in 1821, not long after the family arrived at Haworth Parsonage. Charlotte was aged just six, Emily, three, and Anne, two. In response, their aunt, Elizabeth Branwell, came to live with the family. School was a fleeting experience, especially after the two eldest Brontë sisters, named Maria and Elizabeth after their mother and aunt, died after apparently contracting tuberculosis at the Clergy Daughters' School at Cowan Bridge. Charlotte and Emily were promptly recalled home. The privations and emotional cruelty of this school were famously recalled in *Jane Eyre*.

Alone in the parsonage, the remaining sisters – along with their brother Branwell – began writing stories and let their imaginations soar. 'What you want to ignite in others must burn inside yourself,' the fiercely intuitive Charlotte wrote. The creative bubble that flourished at the parsonage proved fertile ground, as the trio of sisters largely stayed there. (In 1842, Charlotte and Emily went to Brussels to improve their French, with a view to becoming governesses, but had to return early when their aunt died.) Their first published work, in 1846, was a volume of poetry, for which they used pseudonyms Currer, Ellis and Acton Bell. *Jane Eyre* was published in 1847 and was soon a bestseller. In the same year, a railway station was opened at the mill town of Keighley, on the Leeds & Bradford Extension Railway. In 1848, Anne's novel *The Tenant of Wildfell Hall* was in print, alongside Emily's *Wuthering Heights*. It was to Keighley station the sisters marched in a thunderstorm when they heard publishers believed a single man was behind the successful novels, taking a trip to London to prove their point.

Although the railway hadn't reached Haworth, investing in the industry had seemed an obvious option. When things began to crumble, Charlotte withheld the news from her father.

She wrote: 'The business is certainly very bad – worse than I thought, and much worse than my father has any idea of. In fact, the little railway property I possessed . . . scarcely any portion of it can with security be calculated on.'

Yet she was determined to remain sanguine, knowing that other people had been left ruined by the railways.

> However the matter may terminate, I ought perhaps to be rather thankful than dissatisfied. When I look at my own case, and compare it with that of thousands besides – I scarcely see room for a murmur. Many – very many are – by the late strange Railway System deprived almost of their daily bread; such then as have only lost provision laid up for the future should take care how they complain.

She also had many more worries that transcended those of mere money. In the autumn of 1848, Branwell and Emily both succumbed to tuberculosis. Anne died of the same disease in May 1849. Although Charlotte survived long enough to write two more novels and to marry, she suffered the same fate in 1855, aged thirty-nine. Father Patrick Brontë outlived his wife and all six children, dying in 1861.

It wasn't the only link the family had forged with the railways, however. Before he became ill, Branwell was, for a while, a clerk on the newly opened Leeds to Manchester Railway, a strategically important route spanning the Pennines, initially working at Sowerby Bridge, then Luddenden. Although he was a talented artist, his attempts to make a living as a professional portrait painter in Bradford had failed, and he'd also been sacked as a tutor, working for a family in Westmoreland. He was dismissed again in 1842 after just six months working for the railway, this time because the books didn't tally. A closer look at the book in which he was supposed to make notes of railway transactions reveals it was full of doodles, sketches of characters he encountered and a list of his favourite poets. For Branwell, after being sacked from another tutoring position, the lure of alcohol and opium consumed his existence, which in turn killed his creative light.

It was thanks to the Brontës that Haworth finally secured a station of its own. When *Jane Eyre* devotee John McLandsborough visited Haworth in 1861 to find out more about Charlotte and her family, he was surprised to discovered there was no rail link. As the area was full of textile mills, which would all benefit from a more direct form of transport, he began agitating for a line. With the help of the Midland Railway, he won backing for the Keighley & Worth Valley Railway Company. The route followed a cleavage in the hills forged years before by the River Worth. Although construction costs tripled from the £36,000 price tag promised to initial investors, the line between Keighley and Oxenhope opened on 13 April 1867, with six weekday trains and two on Sundays. Although it was only fifteen miles long, the line served Ingrow, Damens, Oakworth and Haworth. Mill traffic, as well as a tourism boost inspired by the Brontës, fuelled its success, but it survived for less than a century. In 1961, it was finally closed. However, enthusiasts were determined the line should survive and bought it from British Rail in 1968. Now the heritage line attracts some 10,000 visitors a year.

The view from the train

It's not just the link to the Brontës that makes this a stand-out line. Oakworth was the setting for the 1970 film *The Railway Children*, a fact regularly celebrated at the station, which is still lit by gas lamps. One of the story's pivotal settings, however, the Mytholmes Tunnel, was too short for the purposes of the plot, so it had to be extended by a canvas covering during filming. Although the mills that once powered prosperity in the area no longer function, their impressive shells still haunt the sides of the railway. In open countryside, dry stone walls line the tracks, keeping livestock at bay. During the summer, it acts as a commuter line for residents working in Keighley.

London King's Cross and St Pancras Stations

Series 8, Episode 1

> Michael Portillo: 'As a Londoner, I felt really excited at the restoration of St Pancras, a station that was once threatened with demolition and which has now been restored in all its glory.'

Looming above clouds of billowing ashy smoke blown from idling locomotives, the striking edifice of King's Cross station once dominated a low-rise London skyline. It was built in awe-provoking cathedral style for services operated by the Great Northern Railway, which began in the late 1840s to link important industrial cities in Yorkshire's West Riding.

At the time, all train companies wanted to send off and receive their paying customers in a grand manner and so built their London termini accordingly. The construction of King's Cross changed the neighbourhood dramatically. When the Regent's Canal reached that corner of London in 1820, there were green fields as far as the eye could see looking north. But the city was gobbling up vast quantities of coal with an appetite that wasn't about to diminish, and canal barges could not keep pace with demand. At the same time, more people than ever before were living in the metropolis. The advent of the railways was sure to mean seismic changes for London.

As services on the Liverpool & Manchester Railway were getting underway, a statue of the recently deceased King George IV was commissioned for London. Never popular, the stone likeness was removed just a dozen years later, but not before the area became known as 'King's Cross'. And it was here that Lewis Cubitt – the youngest of three brothers who were all distinguished designers and builders – drew up plans for a functional yet capacious station, distinguished by vast arches, built on the site of a former smallpox hospital. (Immunisation techniques pioneered by Edward Jenner at the end of the eighteenth century had already halted the spread of the disease around the capital.)

Before the station was completed, a temporary wooden terminus was created at Maiden Lane, used by countless people on their way to the Great Exhibition in its remarkable Crystal Palace in Hyde Park during the summer of 1851. (The Exhibition attracted more than six million visitors and this is widely seen as the advent of daily excursions.) Queen Victoria and Prince Albert also left for Balmoral from here that year.

Having already worked on the construction of London Bridge and Bricklayers Arms stations, Cubitt was thinking bigger this time and also designed a classy exterior topped by a three-faced clock built to stand the test of time. The fourth face was left blank, as no one could see it. When it was opened, King's Cross was the largest station in the country. The carriage of freight as well as passengers began in earnest, with potatoes and grain coming from East Anglia being stored in mighty goods sheds before being transported across the capital. Impressive brick and iron-built arches created coal drops, where wagons on high-level lines could be upended to pour transported coal into hoppers waiting below. The coal was subsequently loaded on to carts for delivery around the capital.

With the creation of a major railway station came the need for workers' housing, and Somers Town and Agar Town expanded to fit the bill. However, thanks to the rapid expansion of the rail network, users soon began to feel the pinch at King's Cross. Before very long there were further major changes afoot in the immediate London landscape, with the arrival of the Midland Railway and its plans for a new terminus: St Pancras.

The Midland Railway emerged as a powerful player following the amalgamation of several significant companies. It edged in a southerly direction, first from Leicester to Bedford and Hitchin, from where it paid to use the facilities at King's Cross in order to bring passengers to the capital. Like other railway companies, Midland Railway winced at the costs of sharing and, with ongoing doubts about the capacity of King's Cross, decided to invest in a major station of its own. A Royal Commission had stopped companies heading into the heart of the capital and, with an existing goods yard nearby, Midland Railway settled on a site just next door to King's Cross.

It wasn't opposition from its close competitor that nearly sank the scheme, though. The proposed route to the station site encroached on a churchyard, where bodies were buried eight deep, and also entailed the demolition of housing, which would be carried out without compensation.

The engineer in charge was William Barlow, as significant as the Stephensons in the railway story, but far less known today. Not only did Barlow help to complete the Clifton Suspension Bridge and steer the redesign of the Tay and Forth Bridges, he also designed a rail adopted by Brunel in numerous projects, and even pioneered sound recordings in the 1870s. When it came to St Pancras, he configured the lines as best he could, building raised platforms on 850 iron pillars to bridge the nearby Regent's Canal, and in doing so creating a storage area beneath designed expressly with Burton-on-Trent's beer brewers in mind, as they would be ferrying freight on the line. One indisputable triumph was the station's impressive arched cast-iron canopy. At 73 metres (240 feet) wide, it was the largest in the world.

But his achievements counted for little in London, as an enduring animosity lingered. In 1878 – a dozen years after work on St Pancras began – the book *Old and New London* revealed just how deeply resentments lay.

> . . . the desecration of the St. Pancras churchyard . . . was as nothing compared to the demolition of the hundreds of houses of the poorer working classes in Agar Town and Somers Town, occasioned by the extension of the Midland Railway. The extent of this clean sweep was, and is still, comparatively unknown, and has caused a very considerable portion of St. Pancras parish to be effaced from the map of London. Perhaps no part of London or its neighbourhood has undergone such rapid and extensive transformation. It will, perhaps, be said that in the long run the vicinity has benefited in every way; but it is to be feared that in the process of improvement the weakest have been thrust rather rudely to the wall.

Opened without ceremony on 1 October 1868, St Pancras station had five platforms, with sufficient space for cabs to draw alongside carriages to collect wealthy passengers.

In the long term, the city was also rewarded with a Gothic gem in the shape of the Midland Hotel, which wrapped around the station entrance. Its design was the subject of a competition, and winner Sir George Gilbert Scott's ambitious blueprint wasn't completed until 1876, after the country's economy hit the buffers in the late 1860s. 'My own belief is that it is possibly too good for its purpose,' Scott said, after the hotel was built. This arresting façade and spacious station created by Midland Railway now overshadowed King's Cross, run by Great Northern Railway. A century later, it was this imposing red brick frontage that saved the station from demolition after poet John

Betjeman spiked British Rail's plans by securing it a protective Grade One listing.

Only a short distance from King's Cross and St Pancras, there was Euston station, opened in 1838 for the London & Birmingham Railway, with trains being hauled up the final incline into the station on cables until 1844. Euston was the subject of major expansion as early as 1846 for the London & North Western Railway and had two railway hotels, yet was always playing catch up in terms of capacity. Despite its Doric Arch, Euston struggled to create an ambience to rival its neighbours as it was perpetually subjected to piecemeal development.

The stations, all in close proximity, brought more than just passengers to the area. Not least because of the way railway works pushed through the outskirts of the capital, the spectre of destitution continued to haunt the people of London for the rest of the century. Liverpudlian ship owner Charles Booth felt convinced that stories of hapless paupers on the capital's streets were hopelessly exaggerated until he set out to investigate. In fact, he determined the situation was far bleaker than he'd imagined. He conducted a monumental survey of the city that revealed more than one third of people lived in poverty, explaining: 'day to day, hand to mouth, they get by'.

Booth wasn't the only campaigner for social justice, but he is recalled for mapping the issue at the turn of the twentieth century, colouring in roads to illustrate how people there lived. Among the colours used, amber denoted the wealthiest neighbourhoods, red was middle class, grey indicated 'chronic want' and black 'vicious semi-criminal'. While the neighbourhoods along the Euston Road featured all colours, strips of black and shades of grey proliferated around the stations. Moreover, King's Cross developed a reputation for being a centre of prostitution, where Booth noted that 'the old & ugly' woman did as good a business as younger, better looking rivals.

During the twentieth century, Booth has been criticised for revealing some unacceptable personal prejudices during the project, and when he talks about the women who earned a living on the streets around King's Cross, he shows that, despite concerted efforts, he still understands little about the stark lack of choices faced by the poor.

> The plain and simple truth is, that for the most part, they have no desire at all to be rescued. Perhaps the most painful part of the whole work lies in the fact that so many of these women do not, and will not, regard prostitution as a sin. As one sits down and enters a conversation with these girls, nicely and neatly dressed, well-behaved, and sometimes even with serious thoughts as to the results of the life they lead, it seems incredible that they can be content to go on persistently in the same course.

The wretched poverty evident in the shadows of London's great stations would remain for decades, until the city was redrawn after the Second World War.

Paddington Station

> Michael Portillo: 'Even to twenty-first century commut-
> ers, Paddington's grandiose roof spans are awe-inspiring,
> but when the station was built in the nineteenth century,
> recent advances made it possible to construct from iron and
> glass buildings whose like had never been seen before.

As a company of such stature, the Great Western Railway
sought to make a statement about its prowess and prestige with
its London terminus. Who better to provide the necessary grand
concept than their busy talisman, Isambard Kingdom Brunel?

There had been plans to use the newly-built Euston station
as a terminus, with the main line from Bristol intersecting
with the London & Birmingham Railway at Kensal Green. But
Euston had been built with insufficient ambition, having just
two platforms, for arrivals and departures. Relations between
railway companies were rarely cordial, especially when it came
to sharing limited space with both vying for pre-eminence. Paddington, for all its shortcomings, would be the answer for the
Great Western Railway, although it was no quick fix.

The majesty of Paddington Station, with its glass roof and
corrugated iron arches, is still evident today, testament to the
fact that Brunel was clearly a man of prodigious talents.

But that's not how Paddington first appeared to early
travellers. It was a temporary station perched between bridge
arches and primarily made of wood. It was in operation from
4 June 1838, the day that the twenty-two-mile line between

London and Maidenhead first opened. Like Euston, there were just two platforms, separated by a broad avenue for horse-drawn carriages. Despite its obvious shortcomings, it was this station that Queen Victoria came to on her first train ride in 1842, and she was collected on the concourse for the last leg of her journey to Buckingham Palace. Indirectly, the Royals played a part in the design of Paddington Station. Prince Albert was the driving force behind the Great Exhibition of 1851, famous for showcasing the best of British to a huge audience drawn from overseas and the UK. Memorably, the Exhibition was characterised by the Crystal Palace, an elaborate and capacious space that awed visitors as they toured the wares of 13,000 exhibitors. Built in just nine months, it contained 84,000 square metres (900,000 square feet) of glass and covered nineteen acres.

Brunel had been on the committee that advised its designer, Joseph Paxton, and structural engineer, Charles Fox. Now Brunel wanted to emulate the same splendour for those destined to travel westward on the Great Western Railway. It wasn't something he could do alone. Brunel's reputation for control issues isn't without foundation but, with projects raining down on him, he learned how to delegate as a matter of urgency. With limited skills as a mechanical engineer, Brunel relied on Daniel Gooch to oversee locomotives on the Great Western Railway. Gooch had trained in engineering at both the Tredegar Ironworks in South Wales, and later at Robert Stephenson and Company in Newcastle, before being recruited by Brunel. Now Brunel turned to eminent architect Matthew Digby Wyatt, whose specialist area was decoration. Wyatt came from a dynasty of architects and the pair had crossed paths at the Great Exhibition, where Wyatt also served as an advisor.

A letter written by Brunel about his aspirations for Paddington in 1851 sheds light on his extraordinary self-belief, which ran in tandem with a willingness to call in help when he perceived it was needed:

> I am going to design, in a great hurry, and I believe to build,
> a station after my own fancy. [Paddington Station] will be
> entirely metal as to all the general forms, arrangements
> and design . . . [I] believe myself to be fully competent for
> [the work], but for detail of ornamentation I neither have
> time nor knowledge, and with all my confidence in my own
> ability I have never any objection to advice and assistance
> even in the department which I keep to myself, namely the
> general design.

Brunel promised Wyatt it would be one of the largest buildings ever made, but insisted all the effort was to be channelled into its interior, because the extensive roofing would deny it the opportunity of a spectacular outside aspect in the manner of King's Cross, for example. The builders were Fox Henderson & Company – that's the same Fox who was involved with the Great Exhibition, so an established master at dealing with metal and glass. Once again, Brunel was demonstrating a level of personal compromise in order to achieve the best results: Fox was an outspoken critic of broad gauge.

By now the team was very similar in profile to that behind the Great Exhibition, but didn't include Paxton, who was a director of the Midland Railway. The main station building, which included offices and the new boardroom for the Great Western Railway, was constructed along Eastbourne Terrace, with station access on to Praed Street. The project was dogged by delays, not least because Brunel, and particularly Fox, were both overcommitted on other projects. A series of written threats by the Great Western Railway board appeared to have some effect. By 8 October 1853, the *Illustrated London News* reported how work was progressing:

The new shed for the outgoing trains, being entirely roofed
with glass, presents a light and handsome appearance
with separate entrance and reception rooms for the Queen
and the Royal Family and all the other requisite accommodation for the general public, which are of the most
appropriate and complete character, are finished and the
foundation of the arrival sheds, with extensive offices, is
now proceeding with great rapidity.

The Great Western Hotel was built along Praed Street in
'Second Empire' style and was hailed as 'the largest and most
sumptuous hotel in England' when it opened in 1854. There
were 112 bedrooms, fifteen private sitting rooms and an opu-
lent two-storey coffee bar with marble pillars that set a high
standard for subsequent station hotel builders to imitate. Work
continued on the station until 1857. By the end of the year,
the Great Western Railway accounts revealed £668,790 had
been spent on the station, hotel, goods depot and associated
works – something like £62 million by today's standards. The
more cautious on the board would have groaned again, even if
they were by now accustomed to the colossal overspends that
were symptomatic of Brunel's projects. However, with its dozen
commodious platforms and ample daylight, Paddington would
be worth the money.

When it opened, it had the largest train shed roof in the
world, held up by huge iron arches in three spans. The largest
span was an impressive 31 metres (102 feet) wide, with the
others measuring 21.5 metres (70 feet) and 21 metres (68 feet).
Most importantly, the roof was robust, while the one at Charing
Cross station, built after Paddington to the design of Sir John
Hawkshaw, the engineer who built the Severn Tunnel, was not.
In 1905, the vaulted roof at Charing Cross collapsed, killing
six people and reducing stationary railway carriages to match-

wood. The station was closed for three months while rebuilding took place, giving the navvies constructing the Northern Line a greater opportunity for excavations in the station area.

Paddington Station included elements of railway travel then considered a necessity that we might not recognise today, including separate waiting rooms for first-class and second-class passengers, as well as a ladies' waiting room and a royal waiting room. There was also a horse arch, a lawn and stables.

Despite huge growth in Great Western Railway, it was a full fifty years before Paddington Station needed significant expansion, a tribute to Brunel's planning. Acknowledged as the country's holiday station, it was also where transatlantic travellers would unload enormous trunks after a stay in the States and await the arrival of their horse-drawn carriages, which were parked in anticipation down the centre of the concourse. P. G. Wodehouse later spoke of the 'very soothing . . . refined calm' of Paddington, at a time when Waterloo was 'all hustle and bustle'.

A war memorial commemorating 2,524 Great Western Railway workers who died in the First World War stands next to today's platform one. The sculpture, of a Tommy reading a letter, was by Charles Sargent Jagger, himself an old soldier. He was commissioned to create something that reflected 'pride, sadness and fondness'. Jagger had wanted the figure to stand on the ground, thus mingling with commuters, but station operators insisted on a plinth, inside which there is a list containing the names of all those who died. When it was first unveiled on Armistice Day in 1922, the statue stood by the station's main entrance.

During the Second World War, a falling bomb created a need for some remodelling and, of course, changes have been made down the decades to better serve a modern railway. But although it's not exactly as he would have known it, there's plenty that Brunel would recognise today about Paddington Station – and, if he lifted his gaze from ground level, he would still see the roof and decorated column tops that became signatures of both himself and the less-remembered Wyatt.

Stratford to Highbury and Islington

Series 3, Episode 4

Distance: 4 miles

Michael Portillo: 'From the earliest days, trains were popular with commuters, but the railways struggled to convince nervous passengers that they were really safe. Then in 1864 . . . a heinous event occurred in a railway carriage that shook the confidence of the nation.'

By the 1860s, fears about train travel had largely subsided as a new generation who had grown up alongside the meandering rail network were taking to the rails without a second thought. But one terrible incident ignited a new wave of terror that ended up changing the way trains were made.

Railway police had existed almost as long as the railway itself, introduced to control wayward behaviour by track-laying navvies, and to deter the pickpockets and con artists who later took to the rails. This low-level criminality was expected and accepted by the ticket-purchasing public. However, the apparently random murder of a passenger by a stranger on a London suburban line left travellers traumatised. The victim had been trapped inside a carriage with a bloody-thirsty killer, without any means of escape, before being tossed out of a moving train. At the time, compartments had two doors at either side, but no linking corridor – and no means of communication with the train guard.

The drama began to unfold when the 10.11 p.m. train from Fenchurch Street to Chalk Farm pulled in to Hackney station on Saturday, 9 July 1864. Two men jumped into an empty first-class compartment in high spirits, only to find sticky fresh blood on their hands after they sat down. Not only was there blood on the seat cushions, but also on the window glass and the carriage handle. A walking stick, apparently abandoned on the floor, had clearly been used as a weapon.

In an instant, the shocked pair leapt out the carriage and alerted the guard. The carriage was duly locked and the search for a body began. Before long, a train driver spotted the dark shape of a man at the side of the railway between Hackney and Bow stations, his feet pointing towards London. Railway staff carried him into a nearby pub, at the time called the Mitford Castle, and called the police. Despite every effort to treat his injuries, Thomas Briggs died the following night without regaining consciousness.

The sixty-nine-year-old banker, who was chief clerk at a city bank, was returning to his townhouse home in Hackney after enjoying dinner with friends in Peckham. A regular user of the railway, he was on good terms with the ticket collector at Fenchurch Street station. The ticket collector had seen the black-suited commuter that night, making his way home. No one knows exactly what happened next, but it seemed robbery was a motive for the attack, although £5 was found still in Mr Briggs's jacket pocket. Detectives believed Mr Briggs had been dozing in the corner of the carriage when the violence against him was unleashed. His bag was left in the carriage, with his stick and a hat. But the unusual beaver-skin hat didn't belong to the victim, and of Brigg's own top hat, there was no sign. A gold pocket watch and gold-rimmed eyeglasses were also missing. A £300 reward was offered for information.

An initial clue to the murder came via the appropriately named jeweller John Death, who confirmed that he had exchanged a gold watch chain with a value of £3 10s for another chain and a ring at his Cheapside premises two days after the killing. The man who brought in the chain was, he said, about thirty years old, with a sallow complexion and a German accent.

A full week later, a cabbie called Jonathan Matthews contacted police after a casual conversation with a fellow driver about the murder case drew his attention to the jeweller's highly noticeable name. Matthews recalled that he had seen a box with 'Death' marked on it at his own home, given to his daughter by a young German called Franz Müller. For a while, Müller had been engaged to one of his girls, Matthews explained, but the man's unreasonable jealousy brought an end to the relationship.

Aged twenty-five, Müller had been a gunsmith in his native Germany, but ended up working as a tailor in London for two years and intended to head for America to seek his fortune there. Cabman Matthews identified the mystery hat found in the railway carriage as one he had bought for Müller, and supplied police with a photograph.

Although they rushed to Müller's lodgings, police were too late to arrest him. He'd already set off for New York on the sailing ship *Victoria*. Armed with a warrant for his arrest, the police made a railway dash to Liverpool to catch a steamship, *City of Manchester*, which would outrun the *Victoria* by some margin. When Müller finally arrived, they were on the New York dockside to greet him – and found him in possession of what seemed to be a re-modelled version of Mr Briggs's hat. The band where Mr Briggs's name might have been found had been cut out.

After extradition proceedings were concluded, Müller maintained his innocence as he sailed back with his captors on the steamship *Etna*. There followed a trial at the Old Bailey, with

Müller insisting he had bought the incriminating watch and hat
on the dockside in Britain. It took the jury just fifteen minutes
to find him guilty.

Müller was hanged outside Newgate Prison in front of a
crowd of thousands (capital punishment wasn't undertaken
behind closed doors until 1868). Although Müller had insisted
he was innocent, a Lutheran pastor who visited him before his
execution said he had finally confessed.

As a result of the murder, new legislation was introduced in
the UK to prevent a repeat of the horror. The Regulation of Railways Act 1868 declared that all trains travelling for distances of
more than twenty miles without stopping had to have a means
of communication between passenger and train staff. Initially,
this amounted to a cord running down the length of the train
at roof level that would ring a bell in the locomotive if pulled.
Twenty years later, the rudimentary system was enhanced to
include automatic braking at the pull of the cord.

It's no longer possible to travel the four-mile stretch from
Fenchurch Street to Chalk Farm by overground train as Mr
Briggs did. Most people aiming to reach Hackney would probably choose to intersect with the North London Line, which
distinguished itself by being built around the capital rather
than radiating from it. Built in sections, it took no less than
twenty-five years to construct, ultimately linking Richmond in
the west with Stratford in the east. Bradshaw's remarked on
the way it had changed the horizons of Londoners, even before
it was completed.

> Such a facility was provided for them by the opening in
> 1851 of the Camden Town, or North London Railway, which
> traverses the eastern and northern suburbs of the metrop-
> olis and enables the Londoner to make the journey from
> Fenchurch Street, City, to Primrose Hill and the Regent's

Park (the latter attractive at all seasons, on account of its 'Zoological Gardens') at a very trifling expenditure of time and money.

In Bradshaw's time, a traveller would have found himself in Stratford if he travelled to the end of the North London Line, but it would have looked very different to how it does today. After a station opened in Stratford in 1839, it was quickly joined by an engine shed and was soon identified by Eastern Counties Railway as the ideal site for a general works. By the time the Eastern Counties Railway was absorbed by the Great Eastern Railway in 1862, business was booming and even greater space was needed in which to expand. In the last three decades of the nineteenth century, some 960 engines were turned out at the Stratford works – with one in 1891 being completed in just nine hours and forty-seven minutes.

Engine shop workers needed homes and the area developed rapidly. At first it was called Hudson Town, after the promotor George Hudson, but once his dodgy dealings were revealed, it became known as Stratford New Town.

The First World War saw the opening of a new locomotive shop and the carriage works became focused on turning out ambulance trains. By the 1920s, some 6,500 people were employed there.

But after the majority of railways were grouped together into four major companies, in an attempt to replicate the better fortunes the railway network experienced during the conflict, the locomotive works was closed. The site then suffered extensive bomb damage in the Second World War during the London Blitz, and barely recovered before 1963, when the majority of the general works was shut down.

By 1997, everything was not only closed but cleared, in order to make way for Stratford International Station. The surrounding area was transformed to host the Olympics in 2012, leaving no trace standing of the impressive railway history associated with Stratford. Statistics provide the only epitaph for the site now: it was where 1,682 locomotives, 5,500 passenger coaches and 33,000 goods wagons were built.

Dundalk to Portadown

Series 3, Episode 3

Distance: 18 miles

Michael Portillo: 'What a beautiful station, Dundalk: wonderfully preserved and beautifully kept, just looking great on a summer's day.'

By the 1880s, the Dublin–Belfast line was being run by the Great Northern Railway, an amalgamation of three companies, and had turned Newry into an important rail hub. Apart from services between the two cities, there was a busy section of track serving Armagh to the north-west, as well as the seaside resort of Warrenpoint, and Carlingford Lough to the southeast. This was the line that, in 1889, barely three miles outside Armagh, became the scene of Ireland's worst rail disaster. More than eighty people died, among them twenty children, and the lessons learned in the subsequent Board of Trade inquiry ushered in a new age of rail safety regulation across Europe.

Seaside day excursions were a lucrative source of business for the railways, and the one arranged by Armagh's Methodist Sunday School for 12 June 1889 created a predictable clamour for tickets. Many of the passengers were from poor families eager to take advantage of a subsidised fare, and the Sunday School organising committee advised the Great Northern Railway's Dundalk engine house that some 800 would be travelling. On the morning of the trip, parents and excited children, spickand-span in their Sunday best, were led by the band of the

Royal Irish Fusiliers in a procession from the school to Armagh Station.

Managers at Dundalk had originally assigned thirteen carriages for the 'special' and scheduled a four-coupled locomotive (i.e. one with four powered wheels) to pull them. But on the day, the engine house decided to add two extra carriages. These were apparently being repositioned, and driver Thomas McGrath was told they should not form part of the excursion. However, when McGrath pulled in to Armagh Station, he instantly realised that thirteen carriages would never be enough. Instead of 800, fine weather had swelled the expectant crowd of trippers to 940 (or 1,200, according to some reports).

There followed a heated debate between McGrath and stationmaster John Foster. Later, they would give their versions of this, with Foster insisting he wanted more carriages, and McGrath and his fireman concerned that Engine No. 86 was already under-powered and that, anyway, their instructions stipulated thirteen coaches only. In all likelihood, McGrath did not realise quite *how* inadequate No. 86 would be. He had never driven the line and could not have fully appreciated the steep hill climb (at a gradient of 1 in 82, or 1.22 per cent) from Armagh to Dobbin's Bridge. Regardless, Foster had started issuing tickets for the extra carriages and was not inclined to order passengers off the train. 'I did not write those instructions,' he retorted, '. . . any driver that comes here does not grumble about taking an excursion train with him.'

McGrath was furious, asking: 'Why did you not send proper word to Dundalk, and I should have a proper six-wheel coupled engine with me?'

At this point, the Great Northern Railway's chief clerk, James Elliot, who had accompanied the special up from Dundalk, had an idea. A scheduled service was due to run fifteen minutes behind the special. Why not allow it to help the day trippers up the hill? Alternatively, some carriages could be left at Armagh, picked up by the following train and then reattached down the line. But neither plan was accepted, and McGrath stomped off to get underway, twenty minutes late.

Initially all went well. No. 86 set off at full throttle and for the first three miles made steady progress. But as it passed Mount Pleasant and Mullyloughran Hill, it was clear the labouring locomotive was in trouble. At Derry's Crossing, still 685 metres (750 yards) from the incline's summit at Dobbin's Bridge, the wheels screeched to a halt and McGrath applied what were known as 'continuous brakes', which depended on a vacuum created by the engine. This system meant every linked carriage on the train was individually braked, but it was disliked by the Board of Trade because if power was lost, all brakes would be instantly released. Their preferred design was known as 'automatic continuous braking', in which a vacuum kept the brakes *off* while the train was moving. This was a fail-safe system. If the engine malfunctioned or the vacuum was lost, the brakes would slam on immediately.

As an extra precaution, the guards in brake vans at the front and back of the train applied their handbrakes and 'scotched' carriage wheels by wedging stones beneath them. There was then a crew conference led by James Elliot, who ordered McGrath to split the train, taking the front five coaches on to the next station at Hamilton Bawn before returning to retrieve the remaining ten. It was a baffling – and, indeed, fatal – plan. The scheduled 10.35 would soon have arrived at the scene and could have been flagged down to assist. It was a powerful engine with a light passenger load and could easily have pushed the special up the hill. But Elliot had made his decision. The fifth and sixth carriages were decoupled and, moments later, the continuous brakes came off the entire rear section of the train. The enormous weight of the ten overcrowded carriages now rested on a few crumbling stones and a single handbrake. It was an utterly hopeless situation. When McGrath rolled back slightly as he tried to move away, he shunted the sixth carriage, crushing its stone wedges and creating sufficient momentum to overcome the handbrake. The special began moving back down the hill, gathering speed, its runaway carriages hurtling straight for the oncoming 10.35. For those on board, the dream day trip was about to become a terrifying nightmare.

In later years, all railways would adopt 'block signalling', which prevented a train from entering another section of track unless that section was clear. But Armagh to Newry services were then operated on the 'time interval' system. A full fifteen minutes had elapsed since Thomas McGrath had pulled out of Armagh station, and so the 10.35's driver, Patrick Murphy, was cleared to depart. As he approached the incline, he was confronted with coaches careering towards him at forty miles per hour, the passengers escaping through windows and jumping from running boards. Children were being thrown out by their parents – a completely justifiable action, as this actually allowed many of them to survive the disaster – but too many were trapped in the packed carriages, doors locked in accordance with the practice at the time. The horror of it all is impossible to imagine. Patrick Murphy somehow managed to slow his engine to just five miles per hour, but the carnage was inevitable. The last three carriages were smashed to matchwood. More than 250 people were injured, and of the eighty who died, a third were children, and most of the rest were women.

The Board of Trade's inquiry was swift and uncompromising. It exposed that the way railway companies had been too busy expanding to give much thought to passenger safety. Signalling systems were unacceptable while, in the whole of Ireland, it was established that only one locomotive and six carriages were equipped with automatic continuous brakes. The

Board brushed aside the companies' claims that they couldn't afford better standards, and within two months of the disaster, Parliament had passed the Regulation of Railways Act 1889, making block signalling and automatic continuous brakes compulsory on all passenger lines.

The partition of Ireland following the 1919–21 War of Independence hit the railways hard, and in 1933 the Great Northern Railway closed the section of line between Armagh and Markethill where the disaster occurred. Meanwhile, Dundalk had become a customs clearance station for cross border services, leading to a market in smuggled goods. Shoppers would travel into Northern Ireland to buy goods at lower customs duty, or because they were no longer on sale in the south. Particular favourites over the years included butter, Mars bars, Tide washing powder and the *News of the World* newspaper. Items would be hung out of windows on string to try to fox the excise officers, and there were stories of women wearing their newly-bought clothes underneath the ones they had travelled north in. The end of the Troubles in the 1990s, and the European Union's opening of internal borders, meant custom controls later became unnecessary. However, at the time of writing, the United Kingdom's departure from the EU has cast doubt on whether free movement will continue.

The view from the train

The journey north from Dundalk on the Dublin–Belfast main line is a ticket to view both the natural and the man-made beauty of Northern Ireland's landscape. To the east lie the Mountains of Mourne, their 850-metre (2,000-foot) peaks massed into an impossibly tight fifteen by eight square miles of the County Down coast. Then, minutes after crossing the border near Newry, trains cross the gently curving Craigmore Viaduct, with its stone arches rising majestically from the Camlough River valley: the 'brilliant little river', as Irish Liberal politician James Richardson called it.

The viaduct, designed by Sir John MacNeill for the Dublin & Belfast Junction Railway and built by the indefatigable construction engineer William Dargan, opened in 1852. The work took three years, cost £50,000, and, together with the Boyne Viaduct, was among the most challenging railway projects of Victorian times. There was no room for error in MacNeill's mathematical calculations, and no computer models, earth-moving equipment or machinery. The eighteen arches – the highest of which rises to 38 metres (126 feet), making this Ireland's tallest viaduct – simply had to fit together perfectly along the curve, and Dargan made sure that they did. Today the structure, with its distinctive grey Mourne granite blocks, remains as serviceable as ever: a much-loved landmark dominating the south-east border country.

Paddington Station's Great Western Royal Hotel was one of the first luxury hotels to be built beside a major London terminus.

King's Cross has undergone a futuristic overhaul for the twenty-first century.

Queen Victoria and Albert, her Prince Consort, preparing to board the
Royal Train with their children in London.

The 'Jacobite Express' is a modern tourist invention of the mid-1980s, but the line
itself was opened in 1901 to support the rural highland communities.

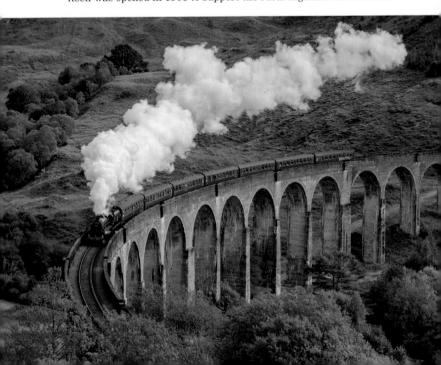

The Laigh Milton Viaduct was first operational as far back as 1812.

The opening of the Stockton and Darlington Railway Line,
27 September 1825.

J. R. Brown

The official opening of the Liverpool and Manchester Railway on 13 September 1830.

The '18 Arches' make the Craigmore Viaduct the tallest viaduct in Ireland, connecting Belfast to Dublin from 1852.

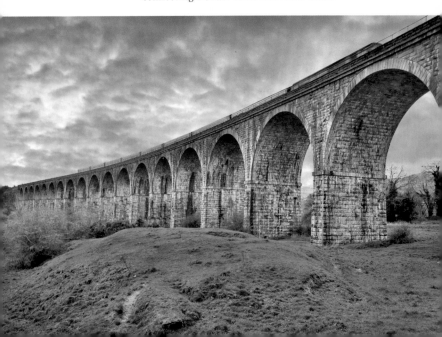

William Dargan was at the forefront of railway construction in Ireland in the nineteenth century.

The 'Father of Railways' George Stephenson was a pioneering engineer of the Victorian period.

The Flying Scotsman crosses the Royal Border Bridge at Berwick upon Tweed.

Despite a difficult birth in terms of planning and construction, the Clifton Suspension Bridge is now an iconic site for Bristolians.

Newton Abbot station was originally constructed by the South Devon Railway Company in 1846.

H. F. Stephens would pioneer the construction of light railways for rural communities in England and Wales.

The Torbay Express special approaching Splash Point, Teignmouth.

The beauty of the Old Royal Naval College ensures Greenwich remains a World Heritage site.

The Waverley Steam Express train crosses the Ribblehead Viaduct in North Yorkshire.

At 1.33 miles in length, Southend Pier is the longest pleasure pier in the world. The railway line measures 1.25 miles and began operation in 1890.

A steam train passing Ongar signal box on the heritage Epping Ongar Railway.

Preston to Blackpool

Series 1, Episode 6

Distance: 15 miles

Michael Portillo: 'The size of the station at Preston reminds us that this was a huge industrial town, but even today it is the hub of railways spreading out throughout Lancashire. Preston was a place where the early problems of the Industrial Revolution emerged, and a place where those problems were first tackled.'

For some, industrialisation brought a life of comfort and certainty. The owners of factories, which were manufacturing goods faster than ever before thanks to improving technology, reaped huge benefits, as the railway could deliver their goods far and wide. Others knew a different experience, working long hours for paltry pay. With no hope of escaping the treadmill of poverty, they saw nothing emerging that would improve their circumstances. It's the plight of lowly paid working people that perhaps explains twin facets of Preston's history: temperance and day trips.

According to Bradshaw, Preston was one of the country's principle manufacturing towns, with more than fifty cotton mills in the vicinity in the 1860s. Housing was often inadequate or even deplorable, permitting insidious diseases to thrive. Preston endured two outbreaks of cholera, in 1832 and 1848. With work in the mills a grind and life at home a challenge, it was perhaps understandable that men broke the monotony of their existence with beer. As a response to what he perceived to be the evils of drink, Joseph Livesey, a weaver turned cheese merchant, established the temperance movement there, urging people in Preston to 'take the pledge', meaning they would never drink alcohol again.

A gifted orator, he found audiences mushroomed after eight different railway lines arrived in Preston within a decade, able to transport supporters of the temperance movement to rallies. The word 'teetotal' is thought to have started with one of his lieutenants. In a speech in 1833, Richard Turner, who suffered with a stammer, called for 'tee-tee-tee-total abstinence' – and the term stuck. Livesey was a keen publisher too, not just to spread his anti-alcohol message but also to report on the problems faced by working people in the town.

His magazine, *The Struggle*, was in print in 1842 when there was a riot by workers protesting about the conditions in Preston's mills, which resulted in four deaths after armed troops opened fire. These were part of the so-called 'Plug Riots' that spread across the north of England, the East Midlands, South Wales and the Staffordshire Potteries. The riots got their name from the way the workers removed the bungs from machinery in order to bring it to a halt. Livesey was in sympathy with the Chartists, who had helped to coordinate the strikes. The Chartists were a broad movement for working people which demanded votes for working men aged over twenty-one and an overhaul of the parliamentary system. While the commonly held demand was 'a fair day's pay for a fair day's labour', many workers were seeing their wages fall in times of economic difficulty. With the Corn Laws keeping bread prices buoyant, people were struggling.

Two years after these deadly riots, Livesey started a newspaper called the *Preston Guardian*, which continued to monitor public life in the town, and he was still campaigning against

the perils of drink aged eighty-eight, even though the number
of public houses in Preston now exceeded 460.

> If only the dirty, idle, drinking men who now disgrace our
> streets on Mondays would have spent the weekends with
> their families in sobriety . . . What a blessing if all the
> working men would take their wages home for the good of
> their families instead of spending them upon drink!
>
> What happy homes we should have if mothers would
> cease sending their jugs for beer; if none of our females
> would ever call at the dram shop or beer shop, mothers and
> daughters setting a good example of sobriety, cleanliness
> and good household management.

Despite his indefatigable energy and commitment, the
impact of the temperance movement was limited, and concern
about public drunkenness continued – not least because factory owners everywhere were invested in a sober and reliable
workforce. In 1901, *The Times* newspaper claimed drunkenness
was 'the most pressing of all the social questions of the day'. By
then, some action had been taken against heavy drinkers with
a court record in the form of the 1898 Inebriates Act, which
offered treatment either privately or at state-run reformatories,
where freedoms were curbed and family visits barred for up to
three years. Women were particularly targeted. By 1904, women
accounted for ninety-one per cent of reformatory inmates, while
accounting for just twenty per cent of convictions for drunkenness. Two years later, nine of the eleven reformatories in
England were exclusively for women. Out of 3,636 compulsory
admissions between 1899 and 1910, eighty-four per cent were
women. By the end of the Edwardian era, reformatories were
replaced by lunatic asylums, with committed drinkers now
viewed as feeble-minded.

Of course, not every worker in Preston was a drinker and, although known agitators and trade union organisers were blacklisted by employers for a long while as factory owners doubled down against their workforce, pay and conditions did gradually improve as the century wore on. And with some hard-won spare cash in their pockets, people found a different way of passing the time: taking day trips to nearby Blackpool, which was linked to Preston by rail from 1846.

Bradshaw's reveals a new pier was opened in Blackpool in 1863, forming 'a most pleasant promenade'. But that was just the start. The Winter Gardens complex was opened in 1878, followed by the Opera House a decade later. A giant Ferris wheel put up in 1896 was taken down thirty years later to make way for a temporary circus. There were more piers, additional theatres, countless boarding houses and some grand hotels. Blackpool Tower was constructed in 1894, as a tribute to France's Eiffel Tower.

But for most people, the main attraction down the decades has been the illuminations. They were immediately popular when the concept got underway in 1879, when eight arc lights on 18-metre (60-foot) poles were dubbed 'artificial sunshine' by 80,000 sightseers. When the tide came in, the lamps went out, as water seeped into the cast-iron wiring pipes of the era.

However, for visitors it was a first glimpse at electricity. For at least a century, scientists had been pondering how to harness electricity, its power apparent to all during fierce lightning storms. Those who flocked to Blackpool would have been dazzled by the sight of the promenade's luminosity, equivalent to 48,000 candles, but there was nothing straightforward about getting the carbon bulbs to shine. Sixteen steam engines were needed to power eight electric dynamos which yielded the necessary charge. At the time, people were more used to the dim glow of gas or oil lighting, or even candles. The same year that Blackpool unveiled its first rudimentary illuminations, Thomas Edison invented a light bulb that would soon make its appearance in the seaside town. For now, the electric lights were a quirky draw.

Local authorities returned to the idea in 1912 when the town was garlanded with 10,000 lights to mark the visit by Princess Louise, Queen Victoria's fourth daughter. After a wartime blackout, the lights returned, with the piers being lit up alongside animated tableaux. After a second darkness during the Second World War, the lights returned in 1949 for an unbroken run. Today, the six-mile display costs about £1.9 million and takes the workforce a combined total of 65,000 hours to put in place.

One popular part of the illuminations are the trams, which are elaborately lit as they ply the routes around the town. The first tram to operate took to the tracks in 1885, just six years after the unveiling of the electric traction process. The public admiration for the electric tram was no less than it was for a light show. However, the groove in the roadway that enabled the trams to run quickly filled with sand and water, causing the power to short. There was also a crippling reduction in power when the vehicles moved too far from the power source. Horses were on standby to tow the trams when the electricity wouldn't work. Blackpool Corporation's takeover of the tram system in 1892 signalled a programme of expansion, as well as the installation of overhead wires to eliminate the issues caused by the ground level conduit system. For thirty years after 1962, Blackpool was the only town in Britain to stick by electric trams, although the system has now won renewed favour.

With its abundant attractions, Blackpool became a favourite venue for works' outings, with bosses providing trains for workers' excursions. Soon people from much further afield than Preston were visiting Blackpool as the daily excursion evolved into a weekend away for some. By 1863, there was an express running from Manchester to Blackpool at 1.15 p.m. on Saturdays, returning at 8.15 a.m. on Monday mornings. Then came the establishment of Wakes Week, when factories agreed to an annual shutdown so employees could have a holiday. While it might not have been high art, a trip to Blackpool broadened the horizons of hordes of factory workers, making monotonous daily routines more tolerable.

Chapter Four

EXODUS

With railways came the opportunity for travel among people who had never been further than a few streets from their own homes. A raft of workers benefitting from factory wage packets had a chance to escape to the seaside with their families. For some, the need to flee was far more pressing, as hunger in Ireland and persecution in Eastern Europe escalated. In reverse, the speed of the trains provided a swift last leg on the journey home after a trip overseas. In London, the Edwardian times were marked by the growth of the underground rail network, which helped the middle classes escape central London and people its suburbs.

Ballymoney to Derry/Londonderry

Series 3, Episode 25

Distance: 20 miles

Michael Portillo: 'For all its gifts of nature, Ireland is made by its people.'

For nineteenth-century railway entrepreneurs, the speed of Ireland's network expansion brought lucrative commercial opportunities. Yet perhaps even they could not have foreseen the emigration 'dividend' caused by vast swathes of the famine-weary rural poor buying tickets to the New World. By the 1860s, an emigrant family from the north of Ireland could walk into any convenient station and book a rail ticket to Derry that included both their boat fare to North America and onward travel to their chosen destination. This would often be an area already colonised by their relatives.

The figures are mind-blowing. There had long been migrations by the so-called Scotch-Irish (or Ulster-Scots, as they're known in Canada and the US), both across the Atlantic and to the British mainland. Between 1815 and 1845, statistics suggest that at least 1 million, and possibly 1.5 million, left the country. Over the next twenty-five years, a period when Ireland was in the grip of Railway Mania, a further 3 million from all cultural backgrounds departed. By 1890, more than a third of all Irish-born people were living overseas. Between 1848 and 1867, an astonishing £34 million was wired from North America to the

British Isles, forty per cent of which was in the form of prepaid rail and boat fares. Most of the money went to Ireland.

The underlying causes of this diaspora – grinding poverty, famine, religious and political persecution and a sense of hopelessness – had little to do with trains, of course. But the railway companies certainly facilitated and encouraged the exodus by offering fast, cheap and easy transport to key ports of departure, such as Derry, while guaranteeing travel connections on the other side of the Atlantic. The Belfast & Ballymena Railway (opened 1848), the Londonderry & Coleraine Railway (1852), and the Ballymena, Ballymoney, Coleraine & Portrush Junction Railway (1855) all became conduits for isolated communities to access international travel. These three railway companies were soon amalgamated to become part of the Belfast & Northern Counties Railway, which, by the turn of the century, had extended its reach across much of the rural north.

The toughest engineering challenge had fallen to the Londonderry & Coleraine Railway. A huge embankment was required at Magilligan, where some 22,000 acres of ground was reclaimed from the sea, while the creation of two tunnels at Downhill and Castlerock required over 1.5 tons of gunpowder. Blasting attracted a crowd of around 12,000 people, and when construction work finally ended, a banquet was laid on for 500 locals inside one of the tunnels. Inevitably, Ulster wags dubbed it The Great Blast.

By the 1860s, the exponential growth in migration saw the Belfast & North Counties Railway – in common with other Irish railway companies – link up with steamship lines to promote seamless journeys for America-bound customers. Brokers, agents and subagents all wriggled their way into this new market, while advertisements highlighted limitless opportunities in the New World and tugged at heartstrings with references to loved ones far away. An old chestnut for railway poster artists was the 'reading of the emigrant letter', but there were plenty of other themes aimed at the unemployed or subsistence farmers. One poster showing a healthy, suntanned young man rolling up his sleeves, promised 'agricultural settlement opportunities' across Canada.

Today, passengers travelling west through County Londonderry, between Ballymoney and Derry, follow a route taken by thousands of nineteenth-century migrants; first through the ancient settlement of Coleraine, then along the banks of the River Bann to Castlerock and past the beach at Magilligan Strand. From there, the line heads south-west to the shores of the starkly beautiful Lough Foyle with views across to the hills of the Inishowen Peninsula, County Donegal, and the fishing port of Moville. The final stretch runs alongside the south bank of the River Foyle before entering Derry.

On arrival at the city's station, emigrants would be met by shipping agents and directed to the harbour to board tenders. As many as 400 passengers would cram into these exposed boats for the eighteen-mile trip downstream to Moville, where transatlantic liners waited in deep-water moorings. It became a tradition, as the liners slipped anchor, for beacons to be lit on the Inishowen hills – an emotional farewell for those catching a final glimpse of the Emerald Isle. Passenger lists illustrate the importance of the emigrant trade to railways and the shipping lines. Regular visitors to Moville included J & J Cooke ships. Between 1847 and 1867, J & J Cooke carried 22,199 emigrants to Canadian ports such as Saint John and Quebec, together with some destined for the US. Cooke's vessels would usually return laden with timber, ensuring the voyage maximised profitability.

From the 1850s onwards, Derry was by no means the main point of departure. In Ireland's far south-west, Cork had

dispatched 425,000 migrants by 1891 – higher than any
other county. The ports of Belfast and Dublin were also busy,
while some transatlantic travellers headed first to Liverpool
or Glasgow, where passage was sometimes cheaper. But the
number leaving the north of Ireland is telling. Between 1851
and 1871, County Londonderry lost almost a quarter of its
people – perhaps 50,000 – while in County Antrim the position
was even worse, with more than half the population – 120,000-
plus – heading overseas.

The intensity of this migration was not lost on thinking
Irish and British politicians, yet the Westminster Parliament
seemed unable or unwilling to act. On 3 May 1860, *The Times*
lived up to its nickname 'the Thunderer' with a leader article
that was particularly scathing of the railways:

> The Irish emigration still continues at a rate which threat-
> ens results far beyond the calculations of the economist,
> perhaps even the wishes of the statesman. It is no longer
> the overflow of a vessel full to repletion, but the opera-
> tion of a syphon which drains to the very bottom. If that
> syphon may be regarded in any visible form, it is the rail-
> way system, which in the eyes of every Irishman appears
> to have one common terminus across the Atlantic. He
> sees trains of hopeful, if not happy, faces going off to the
> Land of Promise, from which relations and friends have
> sent not only invitations but the means of accepting them.
> A train starts to catch an emigrant vessel as regularly as
> in England to catch a steamer across the Channel. The
> emigrant-ships have no longer to peep into every little port
> to pick up their passengers. They assemble at Cork, and
> pass in a continuous stream, if it may be so called, across
> that ocean, which, wide as it be, is easier to an Irishman
> than the gulf which divides him from England.

The piece warned that Ireland's smallholdings were being bought and amalgamated into larger farms on the 'English scale', leaving young farmers 'unable to get holdings that will require little or no capital'. It concluded: 'If this goes on long, as it is likely to go on, Ireland will become very English and the United States very Irish.'

None of which seemed to matter to Irish businessmen and technologists keen to exploit every new innovation. When the German company Siemens demonstrated a railway electrification system at the 1879 Berlin Trade Fair, two Ulster brothers, William and Anthony Traill, set about raising funds for an electric tramway from Portrush to the Giant's Causeway – a natural spectacle much loved by Victorian tourists. After winning approval from the British Parliament in 1880, William, a geologist, began work on a hydroelectric power station near Bushmills and appointed engineer Edward Price to construct the nine-and-a-quarter-mile line. The Portrush to Bushmills section opened in 1883, with an extension to the Giant's Causeway itself in 1887.

Before trams could officially enter service, William had to convince both the Board of Trade and the public that a 250-volt, 100-amp conductor rail was safe. The story goes that on the day of his meeting with inspectors, he arrived in rubber boots, pulled down his trousers and sat on the rail. The Board granted him a licence, but what they *didn't* know was that staff had been instructed to run trams on other sections of the line, literally taking the heat off William's behind. He later admitted to his daughter that it still 'hurt like blazes'. His sleight of hand was tragically exposed in 1895 when a cyclist came into contact with the conductor rail and died of an electric shock. An inquiry found that the voltage could at times reach 360 volts, and Traill was ordered to cut this to 250, limiting the number of services. Four years later, overhead cables replaced the conductor.

The tramway ran for sixty-five years, but eventually the
tourist trade couldn't sustain it. Today, only the last two miles
of the track route is in use, given a new life since 2002 by the
steam-powered Giant's Causeway & Bushmills Railway.

Hull to Leeds

Series 9, Episode 11

Distance: 62 miles

Michael Portillo: 'Migrants from Europe were attracted to land at Hull because of its particularly good railway connections, that had originally been laid to transport goods and fish all over Great Britain.'

When Russia's Alexander II was assassinated in 1881, the backlash against his Jewish subjects was swift and brutal. Vengeful mobs took to the streets to loot, rape and murder. As only one in the group of revolutionaries responsible for the Tsar's death was Jewish – with the rest being professed atheists – it seemed the age-old scapegoating scourge of anti-Semitism was once again haunting the streets of designated Jewish areas.

The word 'pogrom' stems from a Russian word meaning 'to destroy, to wreak havoc, to demolish violently'. With pogroms occurring regularly in Jewish quarters, many Jews looked for a place of safety and somewhere new they could call home. For most, it would mean an arduous journey lasting days or even weeks. At the time, the Russian empire included the Ukraine, Finland, Moldova, Belarus, parts of Poland and the Baltic republics, with the number of Jews who lived in its bounds numbering in the millions.

They became part of a momentous mass migration, with many being funnelled through the ports of Hull and nearby Grimsby. While most had bought a passage from their homeland

to America, meaning they were only on British soil for a matter
of hours, there were a minority who stayed, bringing aspects of
a new culture to northern towns.

In the hundred years leading up to 1914, it's estimated
2.2 million made their way to and through Hull. Not all the
emigrants were Jewish; those escaping poverty in Denmark,
Finland, Germany, Norway and Sweden also made their way
across the North Sea. However, it's likely all travellers shared a
lengthy and uncomfortable railway journey from their erstwhile
homes and, at best, a choppy crossing.

The Continental Railway Guide issued by Bradshaw's in
1913 shows that ships from Rotterdam arrived in Hull every
weekday, along with a twice-weekly service from Harlingen,
also in The Netherlands. There was a summertime service that
linked Hull and Zeebrugge in Belgium. But only the wealthiest
would have had the option of a passenger ship. Most came on
cargo ships from Bremen and Hamburg in Germany or Libau
(now Liepāj) in Latvia.

One man, whose father helped manage the influx at Hull,
put a spotlight on the plight of those involved:

> The emigrants came across to Hull in the most deplorable
> conditions. The Russians and the Poles were the majority
> of the emigrant trade. It was pitiful to see the state they
> arrived in, and they were herded over here in ships that
> never should have been allowed to carry passengers. They
> slept on straw pallets which the crew threw overboard as
> they were steaming up the Humber River. They were very
> frightened people.'

And the incomers weren't the only ones experiencing fear.
After a cholera epidemic in Hull in 1849, which claimed the
lives of 1,800 people and was thought to have been introduced
by emigrants, townsfolk lobbied to keep them off the streets.

North Eastern Railway began transferring those who arrived at Victoria Dock by rail to Hull's Paragon Station, a journey they would previously have made on foot. It not only reduced the chances of a disease transmission, but kept weary travellers out of the hands of racketeers poised to prey on them. In 1871, North Eastern Railway built an emigrant waiting room near Paragon station, providing much-needed facilities for those on the move. It housed a ticket agency and offered washing facilities, toilets and shelter for people who had no money. Emigrants were duly fed and vetted before the next part of the journey was explained to them. After the Tsar's assassination, the waiting room was doubled in size to deal with increased numbers. At the same time, about twenty boarding houses were licensed to accommodate anything between twenty and eighty people who wanted to linger there, perhaps to try to earn enough money for the next leg of their journey.

Inevitably, some travellers put down roots in Hull – 'Britain's cheapest port' – and the first Jewish school opened there as early as 1826, when any exodus wasn't necessarily driven by hostility but a desire for new opportunity. Although their faith was different, Jews assimilated successfully into life in Hull, and notably stepped up to help when more waves of immigrants arrived, providing a kosher meal as people disembarked. According to Hull newspaperman Arthur Tidman: 'There is no town or city in the UK where the Jews have been more closely identified with public life or where their natural abilities have been more freely exercised to the advantage of a community.'

In 1885, the Hull & Barnsley Railway Company ran trains across the newly opened Alexandra Dock. Here was a deep water dock to accommodate bigger steamships, with a longer-than-usual platform to run alongside. Trains heading for Liverpool were some seventeen carriages long, with the final four being devoted to baggage. Leaving Hull at about 11 a.m., those heading for the United States would arrive in Liverpool in the middle of the afternoon, with another lengthy crossing to endure before beginning their new life.

But not everyone made it to Liverpool. Some left the train at Leeds, perhaps to find relatives or friends who had previously made the trek, with 'Leeds' being the only word of English they knew. The Jewish community in the city grew from fifty-six in 1841 to 8,000 in 1891. Among the attractions was a rapidly expanding clothing industry that began in the 1850s and accounted for the incomes of seventy-two per cent of Jews living there at time of the 1891 census. Both wages and working conditions here proved superior to those in similar industries in London or Manchester.

An area called the Leylands became the destination for newly arrived Jews in Leeds: a maze of dark courtyards, narrow streets and rundown housing. Although just a square mile in size, it contained small factories, a brewery, a tannery, a church and a school. Existing tenants moved out as soon as they could in search of better lodgings, making way for the new arrivals, and by the turn of the twentieth century, it was an almost exclusively Jewish neighbourhood.

One man, Louis Teeman, has given an account of his father's experience on arrival in the Yorkshire city, having left Russia to avoid an army conscription that lasted a quarter of a century. At the station, his father met Irishman Jimmy Gilmour, who loaded up newcomers' belongings on a cart and led a shabby procession, with the men from Russia recognisable by their peaked caps, long boots and coats that reached the floor. As they moved through the streets, the Christian population would look on askance. Gilmour, known for fighting lamp posts with his bare fists when he was drunk, announced the new arrivals loudly in Yiddish, and curious families would fill the streets, scrutinising faces in case a friend or relative had turned up. Few Jews could find employment outside the Leylands, with job advertisements in the broader community often stating: 'No Jews need apply'. As late as 1909, a vicar in Leeds admitted that 'there is hardly a Christian firm in Leeds that will employ Jews'. Those Jews who had arrived years before to make a success in a particular industry often extended the necessary helping hand. Teeman explains:

> My father got a job as a slipper maker, which was his trade. They couldn't find him accommodation so, like many others, he slept under his bench, beneath the treadle machines. People typically lived in tiny houses, many of the rooms were no more than 12 or 14 feet square. They crowded in as many people as possible. They not only let out rooms, they let corners of rooms and in some rooms, there were four couples each, with a blanket spread over the corner.

In 1888, a report about the textile sweat shops of Leeds by a parliamentary select committee on immigration observed there had been a steady influx of Polish-Russian Jews into the city, with many coming from Kovno in the Russian Empire. Although they worked fewer hours than their counterparts in London's East End, they also received less money in their wage packets. Those in the Leeds tailoring industry were threatening to strike in 1888, seeking to reduce their working week from sixty-two hours to fifty-eight while receiving the same pay.

There were some success stories for the Jewish population in Leeds to fall back on, however. Michael Marks began a penny bazaar there that later led to the creation of Marks & Spencer. Sir Montague Burton, the founder of the tailoring group that shared his name, was also a Jewish immigrant who established a manufacturing base in Leeds.

Edgehill to Liverpool

Series 9, Episode 14

Distance: 1.5 miles

Michael Portillo: 'In the nineteenth century, millions of emigrants passed through Liverpool, leaving a mark on the city that is instantly recognisable: the Liverpool accent.'

As the railways brought emigrants to Liverpool's docks from the east, there was another influx surging across the city from the west to meet it. Emigration from Ireland had long been a feature of Liverpool life, but it accelerated after the famine of the late 1840s. Being part of the British Empire, no records were kept that would identify travellers from Ireland until they boarded ships to the New World.

Furthermore, there was a sizeable number of English, Scottish and Welsh people struggling in industrial Britain who likewise used Liverpool as their escape route. Tin miners from Cornwall, for example, were trying their luck elsewhere after seeing their jobs disappear. Liverpool's streets were alive with accents from across northern Europe. In the hundred years leading up to 1930, an estimated nine million emigrants passed through Liverpool, heading for the US, Canada, Australia or South Africa. A sailing ship would take about thirty-five days to cross the Atlantic, although it wasn't the only option. In 1840, Samuel Cunard introduced regular steamship sailings to the United States and Canada, a trip that took between seven and ten days.

The station that most travellers passed through was at Lime Street in Liverpool, which started to take shape after 1833. A tunnel between Liverpool's first terminus in Edge Hill and the new station further down the hill was built earlier still. It meant that gravity propelled the first passengers, who descended the incline into Liverpool city centre through the tunnel in carriages operated by brakemen. The carriages were then hauled back up to Edge Hill by steam engine. In 1983, one of the wheels used in the winding process was uncovered during one of many revamps of Lime Street station, beneath platform four.

Bradshaw's was impressed by the engineering involved in creating the deep tunnel that stretched under the city. What he called 'a dark, yawning aperture' led into the tunnel, 'which literally pierces into the very heart of Liverpool, burrowing beneath streets thickly tenanted by the suburban population and constantly conducting trains freighted with hundreds of travellers'. He urged passengers to give pause and consider the engineering skill that made it possible in the early days of railway history. After it finally opened in 1836, Lime Street station was one of the first to send mail by rail, significant for those sending a final message to loved ones before setting sail for the New World.

As Liverpool's port continued to expand, railway services increased many times over. The monopoly initially held by the London & North Western Railway could never endure. By 1849, when the number of emigrants was stepping up to match the volume of freight, a stylish curved iron roof was completed at the station, at a cost of £15,000. Five years later, the impressive St George's Hall was opened opposite the station, with its splendid pillars and porticoes. But the wave of humanity that was crashing on Liverpool in the final half of the nineteenth century was focused on the docks rather than architectural gems around the railway station. A policy of integration between railway services and the various docks, bringing emigrants almost to their gangplanks, continued. A *Bradshaw's Guide* published in the early 1860s revealed that, at the time, 'the 21 docks [had] 15 miles of quay room, will hold 1,500 sail [ships] and enclose[d] 200 acres of water.'

The docks had largely been built by Irish labour. There had always been labourers attracted to England from Ireland by the prospect of work in a company suffering a shortage of manpower. From their standpoint, not only was there plenty of construction work available, but they remained in relatively close proximity to family in Ireland, just a short sea passage away. Thus, there's a clear distinction to be drawn here between the seasonal workers who arrived before the famine, looking for new opportunities, and those who arrived afterwards, having been made destitute.

While there may have been a sense of triumph for emigrants across the board at reaching Liverpool's port, those with tickets in their pockets and luggage in hand often found the worst was yet to come. Typically, journeys were torrid and even dangerous for those travelling in steerage, the cheapest class of accommodation. In January 1853, the *South Australian Register* reported the arrival of the clipper *Shackamaxon,* which arrived after an eighty-day voyage having suffered fifty-seven deaths among a total of 780 aboard, with some being newborns, writing: 'we fear that there may have been insufficient ventilation or an incompleteness in the arrangements and special supplies necessary for the well-being of an unusually large body of emigrants undertaking so long a voyage.' The 'special supplies' presumably included food.

Concerned, the newspaper noted a sustained rise in the mortality rate aboard recent emigrant ships and declared that 'such a succession of evil tidings will doubtless lead to serious inquiry by H. M. Commissioners in England as to the propriety and expediency of sending so large a number of families and individuals in one ship.'

Given the costs, there were those left behind, like so much flotsam and jetsam when the tide receded, who couldn't raise the money for a passage. In just five months in 1847, 300,000 emaciated Irish people landed on Liverpool's shores, unable to find the costs of a meal, let alone a ticket. That year, the *Liverpool Mercury* reported that:

in the cold and gloom of a severe winter, thousands of hungry and half naked wretches are wandering about, not knowing how to obtain a sufficiency of the commonest food nor shelter from the piercing cold. The numbers of starving Irish men, women and children—daily landed on our quays is appalling; and the Parish of Liverpool has at present, the painful and most costly task to encounter, of keeping them alive, if possible.

There were workhouses ready to house some of the poor. A *Liverpool Journal* report in 1849 recalled the fate of one would-be emigrant from Ireland.

He had come with a view to emigrating to America and on his passage showed he was quite mad. He was conveyed to [the workhouse] in a straitjacket and strapped.

One of the keepers rose at 2 a.m. on hearing a noise and found the fellow had completely freed himself. He was standing in the middle of the room completely naked, leather straps in hand ready to lash out at anyone who entered.

The torment of perpetual hunger, homesickness and having his dreams dismantled surely pushed him into the realms of insanity.

Even without penniless emigrants, Liverpool had slum areas for the indigenous population who found daily existence a struggle. In 1842, a sanitation report described the area like this:

> More filth, worse physical suffering and moral disorder than [prison reformer John] Howard describes as affecting the prisons, are to be found among the cellar population of the working people of Liverpool.

Although many had no choice but to stay in Liverpool, some caught the train to Manchester to find work in the cotton mills there. The 1871 census shows that just under ten per cent of Manchester's population was of Irish stock, compared to more than fifteen per cent in Liverpool.

Statistics also reveal that eighty-two per cent of Irish people then in Liverpool were unskilled manual labourers. Indeed, four-fifths of Irish emigrants leaving Ireland in the era were either labourers or domestic servants. In buoyant economies, it meant they had plenty of scope for getting work. When times were hard – as they were in Britain following the Railway Mania in the late 1840s, and after another railway-induced crisis twenty years after that – they were vulnerable to the worst effects of poverty.

The Irish were far from alone in making a home there. Being a port, Liverpool became used to welcoming people from across the globe. From the 1850s, a Chinatown was established, not least thanks to Blue Funnel Shipping, which employed numerous Chinese seamen.

From a public health perspective, the arrival of sailors from around the world sometimes caused mighty challenges. For example, the Egyptian steamship *Scheah Gehald* in 1861 brought with it dysentery and typhus, not only to hospital staff who treated those who were ill, but also to users of a public baths frequented by the ship's men. It was the poor health of immigrants arriving from the UK via Liverpool that finally pushed the United States government into regulating newcomers with the Immigration Act of 1882.

London Waterloo to Woking

Series 7, Episode 18

Distance: 23 miles

Michael Portillo: '[London's middle classes] added to the pressure on space, as reflected by the desperate search for places to bury the dead. Cremation was the obvious answer, but it required the overthrow of two millennia of Christian theology.'

London's booming population in the nineteenth century caused numerous unforeseen concerns, such as how to house people, what to feed them – and where to put their bodies when they died. The arrival of the railways exacerbated the first problem, with housing demolished to accommodate expansion. But trains did much of the heavy lifting with the next two, bringing fresh produce into the city, which at least helped to fend off diseases, and exporting dead bodies out of it to a new, commodious cemetery.

In 1801, there were fewer than one million people living in the capital. But within fifty years, that number had exceeded two and a half million, with cemetery space for them limited to a mere 300 acres. Old bodies were dug up to make way for new ones, and soon even relatively fresh graves were being disturbed so as to squeeze in another corpse. Bones, maggoty remains and fragments of coffins that had been smashed to sell as firewood to the poor were strewn around churchyards in the process.

Disease was rife in the city, with frequent epidemics of cholera, smallpox, measles and typhoid, and at the time, science held that noxious fumes from dead bodies were a cause of infection. (It wasn't until the 1880s that the existence of germs became known.) People felt threatened by the very presence of dead bodies and burial grounds. A cholera epidemic in the late 1840s that claimed the lives of more than 14,000 people in London brought the system to breaking point, and a law was finally passed in 1851 to stop any further burials in the city's graveyards. Various outer London sites had already been suggested as appropriate for the dead, including Highgate, West Norwood and Brompton, which became part of what became known as 'the Magnificent Seven' cemeteries. Other enterprising churches found their own fields away from London in which to bury their congregation. But two men, Sir Richard Broun and Richard Sprye, had a more radical solution: a cemetery miles away in Brookwood, Surrey, linked to London by train.

The London Necropolis and National Mausoleum Society was formed in 1854, and bought a 500-acre swathe of Woking Common on which to create Europe's largest cemetery. It installed two railway stations: one serving an area for Anglicans and another for the section designated for Nonconformists or non-believers. The company offices were close to London's Waterloo Bridge station, as it was then known, where the chill railway arches proved ideal mortuaries. Funeral trains, containing coffins (on a one-way ticket) and mourners (who had returns), ran on London & South Western lines from a dedicated platform, with a short branch line heading off to the cemetery. A wall protected funeral parties from the gaze of other station users. After the cemetery opened for business, the first burial was of stillborn twins.

For Londoners, this would prove a cheaper alternative, as other cemeteries required costly horse-drawn hearses for transport. Plus, any lingering threat of disease was firmly dispatched outside the city boundary. It seemed like the perfect antidote, but inevitably there were objections. Many of these centred around the spectre of desperate illness spreading from the dead in storage or transit, but there were also concerns linked to the deeply rooted British class system, with some alarmed at the thought of a goodly citizen's coffin butting up against that of a low-born ruffian.

For that, the company had an answer. Funerals came in three classes, with each segregated at the station, on the train and in the cemetery itself. Choosing a first-class funeral, costing £2 10s, offered a broad choice of plot. Second-class funerals cost just £1, but if a permanent memorial was not erected, the ground might be used again. Third-class or pauper's funerals were paid for by local authorities, and the plot rarely carried a marker. Mass graves were not permitted, although Sunday funeral services were, which made it a popular option for those who couldn't afford to take a day off to attend a funeral, and also for actors, as theatres were shut that day. Of course, funeral services could still take place in parish churches, much as they always had. But failing that, a waiting room at the company offices could be pressed into service before the coffin and the mourners took their places on the train. The journey to Necropolis Junction, which took about fifty minutes through lush countryside, was outlined in a feature in the *Illustrated London News* in 1856.

> By and by, the scene becomes wilder and more solitary. The dun heath reaches us on either hand and we seem, whether so or not, to toil up a rugged ascent, to break speed, make pauses; and then on, on our difficult way. The sense of ascent adds inconceivably to the coming effect.

By then, more than 2,000 people a year were taking their final journey by train. One of the largest funerals the company conducted was for Charles Bradlaugh, who died in 1891. A

Liberal MP, founder of the Secular Society, and an advocate of trade unions and universal suffrage, his funeral attracted 3,000 mourners, demanding a far longer train than usual. Among those paying their respects was a twenty-one-year-old Mohandas Gandhi. Enormous efforts were taken to ensure the cemetery surroundings were agreeably planted and well kept.

In the wake of the London Necropolis Company's great success, another change in Britain's rituals was starting to take shape. Burial was the accepted Christian funereal practice, while cremation was taboo. Christians believed they needed their body intact for the promised resurrection. But in 1874, the Queen's physician Sir Henry Thompson found there were compelling arguments for burning bodies, as happened in colonial India, being in favour of 'purification rather than putrefaction'. He was convinced that cremation would cost less, spare dutiful mourners the risks of illness after winter funerals and save grave monuments from vandalism. When it became clear the procedure was frowned upon by the government, the Cremation Society was duly formed to help sway public thinking.

The Society purchased some land owned by the London Necropolis Company that bordered the cemetery at Brookwood and had a crematorium built. At a loss to know how to express themselves with this new genre of building, architects fell back on what they knew and created a building with a religious feel, although it would not be consecrated. A newly wrought cremator was installed, with Victorian engineers proving their prowess once again by building a furnace that reduced remains to ashes within two hours. The body of a horse was cremated to illustrate the efficiencies of the system.

Once again, there were objections, this time from people in Woking. They appealed to the Home Secretary Sir Richard Cross for support, and – with his misgivings based on the perils of destroying a murdered body before proper examination rather

than rampant Paganism – Cross stopped the future use of the
Woking crematorium. Bizarrely, it was a court case in 1884,
involving eighty-three-year-old Dr William Price, a self-pro-
claimed Druid, that changed things. Price had attempted to
cremate the body of his five-month-old baby, named Jesus
Christ. Mr Justice Stephen, at South Glamorgan Assizes, ruled
that cremation was legal providing it didn't cause a nuisance
to others.

Even before any corresponding bill was agreed in Parliament, the first official cremation took place at Woking on 26
March 1885, that of painter Jeanette Pickersgill. Hers was one
of three to take place that year. By 1901, six crematoria had
been built nationwide, but only 427 cremations took place out
of more than 551,500 deaths, a figure representing less than one
tenth of one per cent. The following year, Parliament legislated
on the use of crematoria, clarifying matters, and gradually the
idea gained traction as the century progressed. In 1928, author
Thomas Hardy was cremated at Woking, before his ashes were
taken to Westminster Abbey.

There was an uptick in business for the London Necropolis
Company at the turn of the century, and it was given new premises by the London & South Western Railway when expansion
plans at Waterloo got underway. But motorised vehicles were
soon cashing in on funerals, offering flexibility and privacy. The
company, though, met its end in much more dramatic style than
merely falling into insolvency. On Friday, 11 April 1941, the body
of seventy-three-year-old Chelsea Pensioner Edward Irish was
ferried to Brookwood from Waterloo, earning a place in the history books as the company's last burial. Five days later, London
suffered one of the Blitz's most damaging air raids, during which
the company's trains, rolling stock and platform were destroyed.
The offices, by now in Westminster Bridge Road, remained
intact, but there was little hope for the company of rising from

the ashes, and the Necropolis railway duly closed. But thanks to evolving attitudes towards death, the sombre railway could now safely be consigned to history. The crematorium that had been built there for a revised version of an ancient practice ended up offering an answer to the same problem that the out-of-town cemetery had been intended to resolve. Although it wasn't until 1968 that the number of cremations began to exceed burials, by the turn of the twenty-first century, more than 240 crematoria accounted for seventy per cent of funerals nationwide.

Amersham to Regent's Park

Series 6, Episode 6

Distance: 22 miles

Michael Portillo: 'From the start of the nineteenth century until my *Bradshaw's Guide* was published, the population of London grew from one million to three million. But it was still a city without extended suburbs. They came with the trains. And as the Metropolitan Line was pushed into green fields, it created Metro-land.'

Take a journey into central London along the Metropolitan line and you become part of living history. The section between Baker Street and Farringdon, familiar to hundreds of millions of travellers over 150 years, follows the route of the world's first underground passenger railway: a concept that changed the face of life in the capital. Within a few years, it led to the creation of so-called 'Metro-land', set a template for the London suburbs and spread wealth generated in the commercial heartland of the City far into the Home Counties and beyond. It also helped ensure that the streets of one of the world's greatest cities stayed largely free from disfiguring overground rail infrastructure.

By the mid-nineteenth century, travelling *to* London was reasonably straightforward but travelling *through* it was another matter entirely. The urban core was served by seven rail termini: King's Cross and Euston to the north, Waterloo and London Bridge to the south, Paddington to the west and Fenchurch Street and Shoreditch to the east. But for workers

heading into the City, only Fenchurch Street offered a convenient destination. Those arriving at other stations had to make
their way via a heaving, eclectic mass of horse-drawn carriages,
carts, gigs, cabs and omnibuses, all vying for position on the
roads. On top of which, some 200,000 people a day entered the
City on foot.

In 1846 Charles Pearson, solicitor to the City of London
and an enthusiastic social reformer, put forward plans for a
central London station at Farringdon to be shared by various
companies. This was rejected by the 1846 Royal Commission on
Metropolitan Railway Termini, which ruled that there could be
no new track, or stations, anywhere within the urban centre.
But Pearson was undeterred. His dream was for City workers
to be able to live outside the capital in affordable, quality suburban homes while commuting in at reasonable cost.

In 1854 he tried again, proposing a railway that would connect all the main-line stations. He commissioned a survey to
show the rocketing levels of road traffic congestion, telling a
House of Commons Select Committee on Metropolitan Communications that it was caused 'first by the natural increase in the
population and area of the surrounding district; secondly, by
the influx of provincial passengers by the great railways North
of London, and the obstruction experienced in the streets by
omnibuses and cabs coming from their distant stations, to bring
the provincial travellers to and from the heart of the city'. These
were the 'migratory population, the population of the city who
now oscillate between the country and the city, who leave the
City of London every afternoon and return every morning'.

After a number of false starts, Pearson's plan materialised
in August 1854, when Parliament approved the building of the
North Metropolitan Railway (the 'North' was later dropped) at a
cost of £1 million. Britain was by now committed to the Crimean
War and investors were twitchy about pumping capital into an

expensive and untested project. However, two major players, the Great Northern Railway at King's Cross and the Great Western at Paddington, both of which would benefit from cross-city connections, eventually pledged around £175,000 apiece. Even so, it was not until 1860 that construction began, using a 'cut-and-cover' technique in which a trench was dug, fitted out with rails, walls and platforms, and topped with a pre-cast concrete roof. Three years later, the Metropolitan Railway (known as 'the Met') opened between Bishop's Road (now Paddington) in the west and Farringdon Street (now Farringdon) in the east, via Edgware Road, Baker Street, Portland Road (now Great Portland Street), Gower Street (now Euston Square) and King's Cross. Some 38,000 passengers used it on the first day.

The success of the Met brought a blizzard of applications for new cross-London lines, and companies such as the Midland, the London, Chatham & Dover Railway and the Hammersmith & City became household names. The Met itself applied for, and got, extensions to Tower Hill and South Kensington, and then collaborated in a separate company – the Metropolitan District Railway – linking Kensington and the City. The network grew, but the ever-rising cost of land purchases and tunnelling took its toll on profitability. This sowed the seeds of scandal, and during the early 1870s, the High Court ordered several Met directors to repay excessive dividends and expenses drawn from the company. In 1874, to calm nerves, the board appointed one of Britain's most experienced and ambitious railwaymen, the MP Sir Edward Watkin, as its new chairman.

Watkin nurtured a dream to connect the Met to the Manchester, Sheffield & Lincolnshire Railway (where he was also director) using a 100-mile route via Aylesbury in Buckinghamshire. In the process, he planned to open up vast rural swathes of both that county and Middlesex, attracting a new breed of rail commuter into London from the north-west at a fraction of the cost of building new lines in the city. Although relations between the Met and the Manchester, Sheffield & Lincolnshire Railway soured over the latter's decision to construct its own terminus at Marylebone, the London end of Watkin's grand plan proceeded apace. Harrow was reached in 1880, then Verney Junction, and by 1891, Watkin's had taken over the Aylesbury & Buckingham Railway, allowing a direct link from Aylesbury into central London. This line became the Met's single most important service, especially after a deal was struck to share tracks with the Manchester, Sheffield & Lincolnshire Railway – now renamed the Great Central Railway – in 1897.

As the twentieth century dawned, most railway companies were looking to electrification to drive profits and deflect passenger complaints about the smoke and dirt generated by underground steam trains. More advanced tunnelling techniques had opened new opportunities and deeper lines were being constructed, among them the Bakerloo, which linked the Met at Baker Street to Waterloo, via Regent's Park. The Met began running electric locomotives out to Harrow in 1905. But it was also eyeing a lucrative new sideline in property development: specifically, the development of Metro-land.

Throughout the nineteenth century, railway companies were banned by law from holding on to unused land; once construction had finished, they were required to offer such areas back to the original landowner. But the Met got round this by lobbying for separate parliamentary powers to permit the purchase and development of residential land. Although Sir Edward would not live to see it – he died in 1901 – the initiative allowed his vision of a super-connected, middle-class suburban London to become reality.

In the summer of 1915, the Met began promoting ten housing estates owned by a subsidiary company close to its stations. So successful was the result that, during the 1920s, the company banked twice as much per third-class seat as any of the country's three largest main-line railways. Equally impressive was the performance of Metropolitan Railway Country Estates, which gave investors a comforting eight per cent dividend at the height of the 1920–21 economic depression. Much of the credit for all this goes to the Met's marketing department and its use of the Metro-land slogan, reportedly coined by an executive while he was in bed with flu; he is said to have leapt from his sick bed and headed straight to the office to share his inspiration.

Metro-land was promoted as a rural idyll springing from the doorstep of London. An annual *Guide to the Extension Line* booklet, priced at one penny, carried illustrations of quaint cottages and neatly tended gardens set amid rolling countryside and peaceful villages. The copy verged on the poetic, describing 'a land where the wild flowers grow' and suggesting that 'each lover of Metro-land may well have his own favourite wood beech and coppice – all tremulous green loveliness in Spring and russet and gold in October'. The reality was somewhat different, as farmland was transformed into long avenues of mock-Tudor 'villas' and semis characterised by ubiquitous bay windows, half-timbered gables and steeply pitched roofs. Here, so the marketing message ran, white-collar workers weary of their day's labours in the grime of the city could quickly commute home by train and find fresh air amid England's green pastures. As with all the best marketing campaigns, it had a simple message. And it delivered – in some cases literally – in spades.

Within a couple of decades, Harrow, unofficial capital of Metro-land, was leading Britain's housing boom. In a single year, construction companies such as F&C Costin, T. F. Nash and E. S. Reid built a total of 1,000 semis on just one estate, grouped around the town's Northwick Park station. To some,

this was the inevitable result of faster, better rail links –
H. G. Wells had predicted the emergence of suburbia in his
1901 non-fiction book *Anticipations* – yet not everyone was
impressed. The novelist Anthony Trollope wryly observed that
the railway companies had 'brought the city to the countryside'.

Southend Pier

Series 3, Episode 3

Distance: 1.5 miles

Michael Portillo: 'The Victorians invented the seaside holiday and bequeathed it to us – and another part of their legacy is this magnificent pier.'

As the concept of tourism took giant strides, trippers could visit Southend to unite two of their greatest pleasures: a day trip to the seaside on the railway, followed by a train ride suspended above the waves. The proud possessor of the longest pier in the world, the Essex resort became a focal point for everything that made a British seaside holiday memorable: shellfish shacks, boat rides, ice cream parlours and Punch and Judy shows. There was plenty of scope, too, for those who wanted to put on their Sunday best to promenade among other holidaymakers flocking to pier-end entertainments. Accordingly, Southend Pier, with its elegant ironwork, became an emblem of the era. It has survived arson, electrical fires, enemy action and unscheduled bumps by assorted sea-going craft, not to mention the effects of time, tide and weather, and remains a popular destination for visitors today.

A wooden pier was built in Southend in 1830, just 182 metres (600 feet) long and with a charge of 2d. There followed a succession of extensions, making the pier so substantial it was incorporated on to the Admiralty charts for the area by 1835. Initially, the aim wasn't to have a world-beating seaside structure, but to compete with nearby Margate for visitors. Low tides at Southend left the town devoid of a landing stage above the damp mud at a time when people were compelled to make their seaside trips by boat. A decade later, Southend's Central station opened, operated by South Eastern Railway.

An entry in *Bradshaw's Guide* from the early 1860s reveals what visitors would have found. Southend was, it said:

> a picturesque village . . . situated at the mouth of the Thames, nearly opposite Sheerness. It has lately become known as a watering-place [resort].
>
> Several handsome rows of houses have been erected and bathing machines established. The company that assemble here in the season will be found more select than at Margate but it suffers severely in its climate when an easterly wind prevails. There are assembly rooms, theatre, library, a wooden terrace pier 1,500 ft long with a causeway 4,000 ft by 14 ft, which enables passengers to land at low water and forms besides a pleasant promenade for those who love to enjoy the salubrity of the sea breeze and several places of worship. The view of the Thames from Southend is very pleasant and the town is gradually rising in importance.

To put its early popularity into context, a temperance excursion, which ran from London to Southend in September 1875, involved six trains in order to bring 4,200 people into the resort. (Unfortunately, there was a crash on the return journey in which one passenger was killed. It was found the guard of one train was so drunk he'd been sent to the guard's van to sober up.)

For a while, there were horses drawing trams for reluctant walkers who still had aspirations of visiting the end of the pier. That was stopped in 1881, as horses kept putting their hooves into holes in the planking – which might give an indication as to why there were calls for the pier's replacement. Building work on an all-new version started in September 1888, although the final extension to it wasn't installed until 1929. The new pier featured an electric railway.

The engineer behind it delighted in the name of Colonel Rookes Evelyn Bell Crompton, an inventor and industrialist who was one of the first to begin manufacturing electrical equipment in quantity. His autobiography told how he was inspired at the 1851 Great Exhibition by the locomotives on display there 'with their brilliantly polished piston rods and brasses burnished like gold'. After schooling, he spent some time at Doncaster in 'the Plant', where the Great Northern Railway had its locomotives made. For a while, he chose a military life above one in industry, but when he came out of the army, he realised the potential of electricity after designing an arc-lighting system for his brother's factory.

In 1887, he designed and installed one of the world's first domestic electricity supplies in west London, and at his death in 1940 he was remembered as someone who not only pioneered lighting and electric trains, but also experimented with improving steam cars, bicycles and even squash balls.

In fact, Southend was not the first resort to have an electric railway as a lure for holidaymakers. At Brighton, an electric train installed by Magnus Volk had been operating since 1883: the first to be ridden by the public and a popular attraction.

Still, the success of the railway at Southend was immediate and impressive. At its inaugural run on Saturday, 3 August 1890, 800 people clambered aboard within a three-hour window. Two days later, during its first full day in operation, some 3,000 ticket holders made the trip. Paddle steamers brought trippers from the capital who caught the electric train into town, while railway-borne visitors made the journey in reverse, to see the view from the pier's end.

Standing proud in the sea, the pier encountered a number of unexpected difficulties with seafaring craft. It suffered substantial damage three years running, with a hay barge hitting it in December 1907, followed by a Thames Conservancy hulk the following year, then another barge in 1909 – the same year the Royal Navy's Home and Atlantic Fleets gathered in the vicinity for their annual review. The crowd could see the pride of the British Navy better than ever before, thanks to a newly added upper deck on the pier.

In 1928, there was a train crash on the pier at the loop where services normally slid by one another. While there was substantial damage to the carriages, there were no serious injuries. However, three years later, there was a fatality after thirty-eight-year-old visitor Ernest Tucker fell on the lines. A brewer's drayman, he was one of more than 500 on a works outing from Ansell's Brewery in Birmingham. He had travelled to the pier by boat from London. An inquest held two days later determined that it was an accidental death.

During the Second World War, the pier played a pivotal role. Rather than destroy it to hinder invasion forces, it became HMS *Leigh*, a naval site that kitted out convoy ships. Before the conflict ended, more than 3,300 convoys had departed from it, having taken aboard fresh water and supplies. The pier was protected from above by barrage balloons, used to stop low-flying attacks by the Luftwaffe.

In 1944, HMS *Leigh* was responsible for dispatching shipping to support D-Day, the Allied attack on German-occupied France. There's a sinister mark of the work undertaken there that still exists today.

Florida-built Liberty ship SS *Richard Montgomery*, carrying 7,000 tons of explosives to Britain for the war effort, was directed by HMS *Leigh* to anchor off sandbanks near Sheerness, in what's known as the Great Nore. On 20 August 1944, the SS

Richard Montgomery dragged her anchor and grounded. Salvage operations were hampered when a crack appeared in her hull and were eventually abandoned with about half the cargo still aboard. The masts of the wrecked ship still poke above the water, even at high tide.

In May 1980, there were two near misses in a week, with one passing ship coming within just fifteen metres of the wreck. The second vessel, a chemical tanker, diverted from it with only minutes to spare. There are fears that, as the ship deteriorates further, the ammunition that remains aboard will be triggered, with catastrophic results.

After the Second World War, there was another golden age for the pier, with its rolling stock – made in the likeness of London Underground trains, but bearing cream and green livery – completing the four-minute journey from one end of the pier to the other at a speed of eighteen miles per hour. In the post-war period, the railway carried 55,000 people in one day. Although electric railways then disappeared from Southend, it wasn't the end of the line for the pier railway. Its replacement – powered by diesel engines – opened in 1986.

Belfast to Whitehead

Series 1, Episode 6

Distance: 16 miles

Michael Portillo: '[Belfast's] huge industrial development began in the Victorian era. It was the centre for linen and, by 1873, produced more of it than anywhere in the world, employing thousands of workers and earning itself the moniker "Linenopolis". But another industry also gave Belfast global renown. It was the water and the railways that made Belfast great.'

The line from Belfast's Great Victoria Street station to the seaside resort of Whitehead provides one of Northern Ireland's most beautiful day excursions, yet its popularity among Victorian tourists lay not only in the glorious sea views across Belfast Lough. Early railway entrepreneurs recognised that to really drive passenger numbers, they needed additional lures. In Berkeley Deane Wise, they found just the man to create them.

Wise began his civil engineering career in 1872 as a pupil with the Midland Great Western Railway. Over the next sixteen years, he secured promotions by moving to other companies: first the Dublin, Wicklow & Wexford Railway, and later the Belfast & County Down Railway. His final job, which he held for eighteen years until his retirement on health grounds, came in 1888, when he was hired as Chief Engineer to the Belfast & Northern Counties Railway. His boss was General Manager Edward John Cotton, and together they turned the company

into the most profitable in Ireland through a shared vision of
rail tourism. Wise designed not only stations and railway lines,
but also golf courses, tearooms, bandstands, bridges, walkways
and promenades, right across the network. Whitehead – with
its extraordinary cliff-face path, known as The Gobbins – would
become his career-defining achievement.

The context underpinning Wise's innovations was rooted in
the prosperity of Belfast itself. To flourish in the Victorian age,
tourism required four key factors: a large population, spare
time, disposable income (even among the lower classes) and a
reliable, cheap means of leisure travel. All these ingredients
emerged from a Belfast economy turbocharged by the railways
during the second half of the nineteenth century.

By the time the railways arrived in Ireland, Belfast was
already one of Europe's great trading cities. Traditional produce,
such as beef, butter, linen and corn, had an insatiable market
in Britain, while imports included coal, wine, timber and paper.
But the Industrial Revolution took trade to a new level. There
was a huge expansion in manufacturing during the early nineteenth century, and steam technology meant linen workers
– once part of a countryside cottage industry – now operated
power looms in urban factories.

As the 1850s dawned, Belfast was enjoying an unprece-
dented boom, taking full advantage of its proximity to Belfast
Lough and the River Lagan to service commercial shipping. The
mechanised flax-spinning industry alone meant 250,000 tons of
coal had to be imported from Britain by sea, while one-fifth of
all Irish linen was exported through the port. Plentiful employment was reflected in a population explosion: Belfast was barely
a third the size of Dublin according to the 1841 census, but
within half a century it had overtaken its southern neighbour,
with 276,114 citizens to Dublin's 269,716.

Instrumental in the north's growth was the expansion of rail links. Industrialists, such as the textile tycoon Andrew Mulholland, had seen the transformative effect of the railways in Britain. When Ireland's first railway, the Dublin & Kingstown line, opened in 1834, the northern businessmen were determined not to be left behind. Mulholland was among lead promoters of a parliamentary bill to authorise the Ulster Railway Company: 'a railway from the town of Belfast to the city of Armagh in the Province of Ulster . . . which will prove of great public advantage by the opening of cheap, certain and expeditious communication between the port of Belfast and the city of Armagh.'

Construction work began in 1837, although progress was slow as navvies dug their way through the Bog Meadows and then found themselves shovelling claggy clay soils around Dunmurry. There were further delays when powers granted under the Ulster Railway Act expired and Presbyterian ministers launched a campaign against Sunday rail travel or, as one put it, 'sending souls to the Devil at sixpence apiece'. Not until 1848 did the tracks finally reach Armagh, allowing the Ulster Railway to become fully operational. It fought the fights that gave later railways a freer hand, a good example being the introduction of third-class tickets for the working classes. This was a notion frowned upon in the upper echelons of society, even though the 'unwashed' third-class traveller was consigned to freight wagons. By standing firm, the Ulster Railway gave Belfast's economy a further fillip. A large, cheap labour force could now commute to fill new factory jobs.

The railway revolution had not been lost on the harbour authorities. In 1837, the Corporation for Preserving and Improving the Port and Harbour of Belfast, better known as 'the Ballast Board', obtained powers to straighten and deepen the Lagan. During the 1840s, work overseen by the Father of Irish Railways, William Dargan, ensured vessels no longer had to partially offload heavy cargo at Garmoyle before navigating shallower water into the main docks. Now they could sail straight along the new Victoria Channel into the heart of the city.

An added bonus was that spoil from the channel could be used to build Queen's Island, which, in 1858, became the site of Edward Harland and Gustav Wolff's new shipyard. Their innovative designs, such as iron rather than wooden decks, and flatter bottoms for increased cargo capacity, saw business flourish. But the harbour commissioners also played a key role, providing state-of-the-art heavy lifting gear and three industrial railway wagons, each capable of carrying 150-ton loads. These were hauled by teams of up to fifty horses, later replaced by steam locomotives, and enabled materials to be delivered directly to the Harland and Wolff yard. By the end of the nineteenth century, Belfast boasted the largest shipyard in the world, with Harland and Wolff alone employing 12,000 workers. The company went on to build arguably the most famous ship of modern times, the ill-fated *Titanic*, and although it briefly expanded into locomotive production in the 1930s, ships would remain its core business.

It was against this background that Cotton and Wise set about tapping rail tourism for the masses. Mindful that 'getting there' was part of any day's excursion, they built stations full of character and architectural distinction, typically red brickwork topped by half-timbered gables and extended awnings in the Old English style of architect Norman Shaw. That said, Wise's first station for the Belfast & Northern Counties Railway, at Larne Harbour in 1890, was one of his more functional designs – essentially a transfer point for boat train passengers travelling on ferries between Ulster and Stranraer. It had a double-faced platform with a standard-gauge line to Belfast on one side and the narrow-gauge Ballymena track on the other. Its most distinctive feature was its magnificent clock, now sadly lost to history, which had two minute hands. One showed English time, the other Irish (twenty-five minutes later).

Perhaps Wise's most famous station is Portrush, which by 1891 could no longer cope with the hordes of day trippers passing through. He completely revamped the structure into a mock-Tudor building – white stucco render and black beams rising from a red-brick base – and incorporated a 250-cover restaurant, complete with a balcony overlooking the Atlantic. The station itself had a 15-metre (50-foot) high clock tower and three 180-metre (600-foot) platforms, each one-third covered with a canopy. This canopy was supported by a so-called 'Belfast truss', a framework of girders shipped in from the city. But it was at Whitehead that Wise earned his place in the annals of the engineering greats – and he didn't need a railway to do it.

Wise had first designed cliff-mounted paths and walkways at Glenariff, said to be the most beautiful of the nine Glens of Antrim, after the Belfast & Northern Counties Railway acquired a lease for the higher ground in 1889. Tourists would travel by narrow-gauge railway to Parkmore, then transfer to horse-drawn carriages and be driven down to negotiate the footpaths, some of which were cantilevered off precipitous rock faces. Here they could view three spectacular waterfalls or rest in Wise's strategically placed Arts-and-Crafts-style shelters. Later, he built a tearoom equipped with its own darkroom – a surefire attraction for nature photographers – at the foot of the glen.

Wise then focused on Whitehead, first creating a promenade with railway sleepers, then a beach using sand from Portrush. In 1892, he built a mile-long path to the Black Head promontory, again employing cantilevered platforms for the cliff sections, and followed this with what would be his fantastical engineering masterpiece: the Gobbins. This path, following a breathtaking two-mile route, comprises a series of tunnels and walkways cut into 76-metre (250-foot) cliffs and supported by reinforced concrete using, of course, old sleepers. There were also two tubular iron bridges linking the Man O' War sea stack, and these allowed Victorian visitors, who loved nothing better than bracing sea air and a dramatic landscape, to gaze down on a heaving swell 21 metres (70 feet) below. They flocked to the Gobbins by the thousand.

In a final nod to railway tourism, Wise arranged for a small boy to sit on steps at the path's entrance to collect sixpence-per-head, a not inconsiderable charge. However, train passengers were admitted for free, on production of a valid ticket.

The Cornish Riviera Express
(Paddington to Penzance)

Series 9, Episode 10

Distance: 253 miles

> Michael Portillo: 'Railways and steamships had vanquished
> distance, but the self-confidence of this golden age of travel
> was soon to be dented.'

Nothing says 'bucket and spade' holiday like a train service
called the *Cornish Riviera Express*. That wasn't always the
case: when it became established in 1904, the line was used
mainly by wealthy people, who boarded the train with their
own servants in tow. So the services of a travelling valet – there
to shine shoes – and the maid dressed in a nurse's uniform –
whose job it was to patrol the corridors, with a special brief to
watch over women passengers without escorts – were for those
who didn't have a first-class ticket.

At the time, the *Railway Magazine* held a competition to
find a name for the popular service, with the winner being
promised three guineas and 'immortality' for coming up with
the best suggestion. As it turned out J. R. Shelley and F. Hynan,
both from London, have been entirely forgotten by ensuing generations of train travellers for their prize-winning suggestion
of 'The Riviera Express', picked from 1,286 entries. Perhaps
it's because their chosen name soon morphed into the *Cornish
Riviera Express*. In its heyday, the locomotive steamed out of
Paddington bearing the name proudly on its nose. Among rail

workers, it was known as 'the Limited'. This was a term used years ago to imply that all seats had to be booked in advance, a notion that failed to gain traction in the UK.

This train service out of Paddington, with its chocolate and cream livery, quickly became the best route to access all the popular holiday destinations of the South West. It was non-stop until Plymouth, then visited a variety of stations before it reached Penzance, the biggest town in the foot of Cornwall. However, it also towed 'slip carriages', which could be deposited in named stations, to be taken on to resorts in north and south Devon and north Cornwall, at a time when connecting lines were far more widespread in the South West than they are today.

Timetables reveal it took seven hours to complete the entire journey in 1904, six hours and forty-five minutes in 1920, and six-and-a-half hours in 1939. Times were cut as better locomotives pulled the train, capable of faster speeds than ever before. Today, modern, fast diesels cover the distance in just over five hours.

But the *Cornish Riviera Express* wasn't the first train to achieve fame heading west. The *Flying Dutchman*, named for a famous racehorse who won the Derby and the St Ledger, ran to Exeter over much of the same track from 1862. Its era ended when the broad-gauge tracks so familiar to passengers on the Great Western Railway were ripped up in 1892, to be replaced by standard gauge.

In the age of Atlantic cruise ships, passengers in the know – and in a hurry – disembarked at Plymouth to catch the *Express* as it made its way back to London, in far better time than any ship could achieve. In the early years of the twentieth century, liners were competing for the Blue Riband, an award for the fastest crossing. Every year brought new record-breakers. *Lusitania* was dominant between 1907 and 1909, with what was then a fastest-ever time of four days, sixteen hours and forty minutes timed between Cork and New York. But its speed – of more than twenty-six knots – was equivalent to less than thirty miles per hour at a time when the train went a more direct route, at least twice as fast.

Plymouth is famous for its connections to the sea in general, and the Royal Navy in particular. It's less known as one of the cities linked to the doomed RMS *Titanic*, which sank in 1912 with the loss of some 1,500 lives. *Titanic* was built in Belfast, registered in Liverpool and set sail on its ill-fated voyage from Southampton. It was the largest ship in the world and bore four funnels when other ships had three, as a bold statement of its potential. In its first-class smoking room hung the painting *Plymouth Harbour* by maritime artist Norman Wilkinson, who was also a poster artist for Southern Railway, London & North Western Railway, and London Midland & Scottish Railway.

The story of the catastrophe is often told: keen to achieve a speedy crossing, the *Titanic* was going a-pace when it found itself among icebergs, one of which fatally holed the ship shortly before midnight on 14 April 1912. The iceberg was colossal and reached the height of the bridge as the ship scraped along its side.

One woman who survived, Vera Dick, told a newspaper there was a 'perceptible jar' from the collision, but that some passengers slept through it.

All of us felt that there was no danger, having full confidence in the staunchness of the vessel. The officers, however, summoned the women to enter the [life] boats, telling us that it was simply a measure of precaution. There was no sign whatever of a panic.

She was one of the lucky ones, escaping in a lifeboat when there were only enough spaces for half of those aboard.

There was ice all round us, but it was not so cold as to make us ill. As soon as we reached water we pulled strongly away from the *Titanic*, for we did not want to be caught in the suction.

It was a clear, starlit night and, with other survivors scattered across the cold ocean, she watched in horror as the ship nose-dived.

Titanic's lights were still burning, and it was their disappearance that told us it all was over. First we saw one row of port lights along the side go out, then another, and then others, and then we saw the great black mass make a final plunge and disappear. We were told afterwards that the wreck broke in two and that the boilers exploded as she sank, but we did not see this, nor did we hear any explosion.

Along with other survivors, Mrs Dick was taken to New York, where an inquiry began. Plymouth's role in the disaster occurred shortly afterwards, when surviving crew were landed there two weeks later. Of the 903 crew aboard the *Titanic,* 549 were lost. Even after this awful ordeal, the men and women were only offered third-class accommodation on SS *Lapland*, a Red Star Line ship hired to make the crossing, which anchored in Cawsands Bay. Unlike paying passengers like Mrs Dick, they were unable to share their stories of the night, by order of their employer. As the 167 surviving crew members waited for tenders to take them to shore, the air on the *Lapland* was ringing with shouts as White Star Line officials competed with Board of Trade interviewers and British Seafarers' Union representatives to get their attention. *Titanic* historian Nigel Voisey takes up the disturbing story.

Despite the best efforts of the Union, the crew was not released straight away but locked up in the docks behind iron gates and guarded by the Port's own police force. Warned by officials not to talk to the press, and denied access to visitors the crew was initially treated like suspects in a criminal investigation. The male crew members were quartered on makeshift bunks in the dock's waiting room; the twenty stewardesses fared much better, being booked into the Duke of Cornwall Hotel in the town.

One of the female stewards was Violet Jessop, who had already had a close call at sea when the SS *Olympic* collided with HMS *Hawke* in 1911. The *Olympic*, a sister ship to *Titanic*, stayed afloat because two watertight compartments in the hull weren't breached. In 1916, Violet was a nurse aboard HMHS *Britannic*, which was sunk by a German mine, at the cost of thirty lives. This time, Violet found herself in the water, perilously close to the crippled ship's propeller. Happily, she lived until she was eighty-three.

A few of the *Titanic* crew's survivors were Devon-born and had relations who'd rushed to the harbour on hearing about the return of their loved ones. Most went to the station after their uncomfortable night, to catch a train to Southampton, where many crew members lived.

One other rail line in the region does hard yards for the economy in Cornwall, but with far less fanfare. The tracks that link Lostwithiel to Fowey Harbour carry china clay, extracted throughout the county and exported by ship to customers all over the globe. The passenger service that once used the line was stopped in 1965.

An 1860s Bradshaw's certainly takes the shine off Cornwall with its entry, calling it 'the least inviting' of the English counties. 'A ridge of bare and rugged hills, intermixed with bleak moors, runs through the midst of the whole length and exhibits the appearance of a dreary waste'. This landscape has been considerably changed by the excavations for china clay.

View from the train

Shortly before reaching Plymouth, the train climbs upwards on the South Devon Banks, the rocky uplands of Dartmoor that caused early line surveyors some issues and initially limited the size of the *Cornish Riviera Express*. Demand for more seats led to the introduction of a pilot engine – running behind the train engine – from 1911. Today's travellers will be less aware of the haul, thanks to the power of diesel engines. But they won't fail to notice St Michael's Mount near Marazion, a castle and chapel isolated by tides twice a day. Beneath the rocky escarpments of the island, there's an underground railway, built by miners on a steep gradient and used for years by the island's small population to replace pack horses in the delivery of goods.

Chapter Five

TRAINS AT WAR

Historian A. J. P. Taylor famously declared that the First World War was 'imposed on the statesmen of Europe by railway time-tables'. In Britain, troops, trains and supplies were locked into such a hectic schedule that the network was jam-packed with traffic. Sometimes that acute pressure led to accidents, with civilian jobs having front-line hazards. But the First World War was not the only conflict affected by the development of railways. The progress of the Crimean War in the mid-nineteenth century was quickened by the arrival of tracks and trains. Meanwhile, in Ireland – where locomotives were held to be a symbol of the British Empire – the railway system became integral to a fight for independence.

Ballina to Westport via Manulla Junction

Series 8, Episode 15

Distance: 36 miles

Michael Portillo: 'Colonial repression and a terrible hunger
. . . at the time of my *Bradshaw's Guide*, Ireland was
approaching boiling point.'

The Great Famine, thought to have killed more than a million
people in Ireland in the late 1840s, drove mass emigration to
North America. But for the subsistence farmers of County Mayo,
in Ireland's remote north-west, such desperation was nothing
new: crippling rents and crop failures had forced families off
their ancestral lands since at least the early 1800s. Nor did
starvation end in the mid-nineteenth century. Crop failures
and unscrupulous landlords continued to undermine the rural
economy, and simmering anger at the apparent indifference – at
best, incompetence – of the British government to address the
ongoing crisis led to an upsurge in support for Home Rule and
an Irish free state. By the 1870s, the political temperature of
Ireland, then still part of Britain, was rising fast.

The rapid growth of Ireland's railway network played a key
role in the unravelling of events. Whereas once farmers and
labourers had felt isolated and abandoned, a train ticket meant
they could now more easily attend mass meetings and hear calls
to organise. Demand for land reforms became intertwined with
Irish nationalism, and Mayo towns connected to Dublin by rail

during the 1860s – Claremorris, Castlebar, Westport, Foxford, Ballina – became hotbeds of agitation.

On 20 April 1879, around 15,000 tenant farmers converged on Irishtown, just outside Foxford, for the first so-called 'monster meeting'. Among the speakers that day were well-known nationalists, or 'Fenians', such as James Daly, John O'Connor Power, John Ferguson and Thomas Brennan. But it was not until 1 June that the land reform movement really picked up momentum with a rally in Westport addressed by Charles Stewart Parnell.

It is hard to understate Parnell's contribution to the cause of an independent Ireland. His Irish Parliamentary Party became Britain's first truly disciplined, focused political party. He showed the Irish peasantry the power that came with democracy and persuaded wealthy Irish Americans to finance his cause. Most importantly, he played the balance of power in Westminster with consummate skill, eventually convincing Liberal prime minister William Gladstone to back Home Rule.

Travelling by train today between Ballina and Westport, the landscape is breath-taking. Fertile fields along the banks of the River Moy, haunting boglands to its west, the wild, windswept beauty of Lough Cullin – all are scenes which rightly contribute to Mayo's image as a rural idyll. But in the late 1870s, death from fever and famine stalked these lands just as surely as they had during the Great Famine, when Mayo's excess annual death rates hit seventy-two per 1,000, the highest recorded anywhere in the country. Ireland was now facing an agricultural crisis, which, however tragic, arguably sped her towards statehood.

In the decade leading up to 1876, agricultural production and profitability had generally expanded. But over the following two years, heavy rain and crop blight produced first a disastrous harvest and then an inadequate recovery. The situation was made worse by a fuel shortage in the west and further rain and cold during the summer of 1879. Ireland was now facing a perfect storm in terms of food production, as imported American grain and beef had arrived on the British market, hitting domestic prices and particularly affecting the smaller farms, which reared beef cattle to sell on to large-scale graziers for 'finishing'. To make matters worse, the potato crop failed again – it was down by around three-quarters. Banks and shops began calling in credit, and rent defaulters faced imminent eviction.

It was amidst this febrile economic atmosphere that Parnell stood before his Westport audience and urged them to stand united against rapacious landlords. Tenants should pay only rents that were appropriate 'according to the times' and 'keep a firm grip of your homesteads and lands'. By August, the National Land League of Mayo had been formed and, encouraged by a campaign which had secured twenty per cent rent reductions and a freeze on evictions, it quickly evolved into a national organisation, the Irish National Land League.

The Land League's founding meeting, held on 21 October 1879 at the Imperial Hotel, Castlebar, saw Parnell become president, with Brennan as joint honorary secretary alongside land campaigner Andrew Kettle and, tellingly, the Fenian Michael Davitt. Davitt was a key organiser of the secret Irish Republican Brotherhood, a group committed to physical force in pursuit of Home Rule. He had served seven years in Dartmoor Prison in Devon for arms trafficking, and his partnership with Parnell was inevitably seen by some as a formal pact between the land reformers and militant Fenians. In fact, there is no clear evidence of this. More likely, Davitt was signalling to fellow Irish Republican Brotherhood members that the Land League's two main aims sat well with their own. They set a clear goal – aimed at both the British government and the landlord class – to 'first, bring about a reduction of rack rents [unreasonably high rents];

second, to facilitate the obtaining of the ownership of the soil by the occupiers'.

Although Ireland was now locked in a 'Land War', as it was popularly known, Parnell cautioned against any campaign of violence and instead argued for legal and constitutional reform. This did not stop rank-and-file tenants ostracising those who *did* pay their rent on time, nor did it prevent many landlords receiving threatening letters. Crimes supposedly linked to the Land War rose, from accounting for twenty-eight per cent of all Irish crime in 1879, to fifty-eight per cent in 1881. However, serious crimes, such as murders, were rare, and few involved landlords or land agents. One notable exception was the unsolved murder of Lord Mountmorres in September 1880, shot six times as he drove his horse and trap near Clonbur on the Mayo–Galway border. Mountmorres did not have particularly large holdings; nor was he known for evicting tenants, of which he had only eleven. Michael Davitt would later claim the peer was assassinated for doing 'spy's work' for Dublin Castle, the seat of British governance in Ireland.

Despite the gathering rebellion in rural Ireland, expansion of the railway continued at pace. Mayo had enjoyed a direct link to Dublin since 1861, when the Midland & Great Western Railway extended track from Castlerea, County Roscommon, to Ballyhaunis. The following year, the route reached Claremorris and Castlebar, and by 1866 had linked to Westport, then pushing to become a major new seaport for inbound freight. In 1874, a further extension to Westport Harbour was completed.

The success of the railways in boosting economic activity led to the creation of Balfour Lines, named after the Conservative politician and future prime minister Lord Balfour. As Chief Secretary of Ireland, Balfour introduced an act which provided state aid to build light railways in deprived areas. A branch line from Westport to Achill was among the first proposed. It would serve an archipelago of islands in Clew Bay, with islanders from Achill crossing to the station on the mainland via a short road bridge, and those from smaller islands arriving by boat. This route initially proved a great success: around 1,000 construction and maintenance jobs were created, local towns and villages prospered, and goods such as fish, eggs and even turf were transported directly to Dublin. But the boom didn't last. By 1937, the line had closed, taking with it one of the saddest histories of any Irish country railway.

For decades, Achill islanders had been forced to eke out a living by travelling to Scotland or the British mainland for seasonal agricultural work. On 14 June 1894, more than 400 excited young people, most of them teenage girls, assembled at Darby's Point to await the four ferry boats or 'hookers' hired to carry them across Clew Bay to Westport. There they were to transfer to the SS *Elm*, a Laird line steamer bound for Scotland and a summer's work picking potatoes.

Most of these youngsters had never even set foot on the Irish mainland, let alone Scotland, and had bid farewell to their families in something of a festival atmosphere. As one of the hookers, the *Victory*, came within sight of Westport Quay, they crowded to the starboard side in order to catch their first glimpse of the *Elm*. Others who had been seated below in the hold clambered up to join them, and the boat's skipper, Pat Healy, realised his vessel was dangerously top-heavy. He shouted for everyone to sit down, but it was too late. The boat capsized and thirty-four young people drowned. Two days later, the very first Midland & Great Western Railway train from Westport to Achill carried their bodies home to the island as mourners lined the twenty-five-mile route. The *Mayo News* described the scene as 'a mighty steam hearse moving quietly along through mountain and bogland' as surrounding hills become 'black with people who kneel and pray as the train comes into sight'.

It would not be the last time an Achill train carried home
coffins from a dreadful accident. In September 1937, ten boys
and young men from the island who had been working as
'tattie-hokers' (potato pickers) at Kirkintilloch, near Glasgow,
died when fire swept through the barn where they slept. The
bodies were brought to Dublin by steamer and transferred to
a special train for the journey back to Achill. Contemporary
reports tell of people lining stations, bridges and level crossings along the route, while in Castlebar and Westport crowds
dropped to their knees on the platforms. More than 3,000 Achill
islanders – half the population – turned out to see them home.
It was among the last train journeys ever made on the Westport
to Achill line: two weeks later, on 30 September, the line was
closed for good. For many, the tragedy fulfilled a prophecy made
by the seventeenth-century Erris seer Brian Rua Uí Cearbháin,
of 'carriages on iron wheels, blowing smoke and fire, which on
their first and last journeys would carry corpses'.

Netley to Aldershot

Series 5, Episode 11

Distance: Netley to Southampton – 5 miles;
Southampton to Aldershot – 50 miles

> Michael Portillo: 'Upset by the poor standards of care she saw in Chatham on a visit to soldiers injured in the Crimean War, Queen Victoria spearheaded the development of an institution that would revolutionise the treatment of injured troops.'

From fashionable spa resort to main embarkation point for luxury transatlantic liners, Southampton was a key nineteenth-century destination for wealthy travellers. The arrival of London trains in 1840 – when London & South Western Railway locomotives set out from Nine Elms – and the completion of the docks two years later meant it became a chic tourism hub, with a popular pier and a promenade that, for a while, rivalled Brighton. Initially consisting of two platforms and an engine shed, Southampton's dockside terminus station soon expanded, followed by a slow spiderwebbing of train lines across the dockside.

However, when conflicts came during the last half of the nineteenth century, its long-established links to better-dressed society were pushed to one side as the city and its railways and docks became a pivotal location for fulfilling the requirements of war. Southampton was the last glimpse of home for millions of men dispatched in defence of the British Empire.

This is why the country's first dedicated military hospital was built just five miles to the east, at Netley, in the grounds of a tumbledown abbey. The trigger was the Crimean War, which started in 1853 and lasted for three years. At its end, the profile of casualties was troubling, for while nearly 3,000 men had been killed in action, with a slightly smaller number dying from wounds, a mighty 16,500 perished through disease. Better care was seen as critical in the battle to save Britain's fighting men.

Thanks to the campaigning work of Florence Nightingale in the Crimea, there was great emphasis on the provision of a dedicated military hospital. Queen Victoria herself was an advocate and laid the granite foundation stone in 1856 on a twenty-seven-acre site flanking Southampton Water. Beneath the mighty stone was a time capsule; a copper box containing coins, hospital plans and the first Victoria Cross, awarded for outstanding gallantry. The hospital's magnificent structure, designed by a War Department architect, was under construction for seven years. Behind a grand red-brick façade, measuring a record-breaking quarter of a mile in length and three storeys high, it had 138 wards, with beds for 1,000 injured men. A pet project, it was here in 1863 that Queen Victoria made her first public appearance following the death of her husband two years earlier.

When the Royal Victoria Hospital finally opened, it was a new base for the Royal Army Medical School and became the destination for sick soldiers who had previously been sent to what newspapers described as 'the invalid depot' in Chatham, Kent. At the time, a report in the *Army and Navy Gazette* described the hospital in glowing terms and told how ambulance ships used a pier to offload injured men.

These invalid soldiers, all of whom have served their country faithfully and many of whom have added to its glory in having taken part in many hard-fought battles in various climates, were quickly and expeditiously landed and were immediately received into well-aired and well-ventilated wards with all their diseases attended to and all their wants amply supplied.

Unfortunately, Florence Nightingale did not concur. With style getting the edge on substance, she was horrified by the fundamentals of the design, which offered little ventilation, and fearful that cramped conditions would lead to unnecessary infections. While the long corridors that served the wards had the benefit of a magnificent south-westerly view over Southampton Water, along with the administrative block, the wards themselves looked out over outhouses and coal bunkers, feeling the brunt of any chilly north-easterlies.

She had the ear of the prime minister, Lord Palmerston, who tried to halt the £350,000 scheme and branded it a vanity project 'whose sole object [is to] make a building that should cut a dash when looked at from Southampton Water'. Both were placated with some modifications, but one element that could not be rectified were plans to bring wounded men to the pier end, so they would enjoy a psychological boost from the magnificent edifice as they were being wheeled inside. The depth of the water at the end of the pier was usually insufficient to accommodate ships used by the navy at the time. Three years after the hospital opened, a connecting railway line was built between Netley village and Southampton. By 1900, when the Boer War was raging, railway lines came virtually straight to the hospital door with specially designated ambulance trains.

Men from numerous conflicts were treated here as violent spats around the Empire flared up regularly. Private Frederick Hitch, who won a Victoria Cross fighting at Rorke's Drift during the Anglo-Zulu War in 1879, was presented with his medal by the Queen while he was recovering from severe inju-

ries. Two other patients, Piper George Findlater of the Gordon
Highlanders and Private Samuel Vickery of the Dorsetshire
Regiment, received the same distinction for bravery in the
Indian Frontier skirmishes of 1897. From 1900, there was an-
other influx of patients from South Africa. By now the London &
South Western Railway had purchased the docks, which helped
to integrate troop movements.

But it was during the First World War that the hospital
finally reached capacity. Over the course of the war, it treated
as many as 50,000 men, who had survived one of the onslaughts
of shells that defined trench warfare, or been cut down by a
sniper's bullet. Men were brought here 500 at a time, stacked
in triple bunks on ambulance trains. Crisp linen on the beds
was quickly turned ditch-coloured with smears of trench mud.

Among the raft of injuries there were burns, amputations,
blindness, deafness, respiratory problems and gangrene. Being
run by the Red Cross as army doctors headed overseas, the hospital established isolation units, a centre for limbless soldiers
and one for those with head injuries. With hutted wards built
behind the hospital, the number of beds was doubled to more
than 2,000. For some men, it was a place of rest, recuperation
and hope for a future back in civvy street. For those consigned to
D block it was a different story.

D block was a sixty-bed asylum used during the conflict
to treat soldiers with neuroses or combat stress. Apart from
bodily injuries, there was an epidemic of shell shock, a condition
unseen until the age of industrial warfare.

At first, doctors were baffled by shell shock, and even sus-
pected men who were displaying symptoms of cowardice. Its
symptoms were wide-ranging, from perpetual tremors to unac-
countable deafness, hysteria, dizziness, amnesia and paralysis.
One of the soldiers treated for shell shock at Netley was poet

Wilfred Owen. Doctors administered anaesthesia, such as ether or chloroform, or used electric shock therapy (at this time, the cruelty of the treatment was ignored) before the men were returned to their padded cells. While medics may have scored some successes, the more effective treatment of psychotherapy came later.

Royal Victoria Hospital was used in the Second World War, but its design flaws loomed large in a post-war era when modern hospitals were being built. It was finally abandoned in 1958 and partially destroyed by a fire five years later. Demolition crews moved in during 1966, sparing only the chapel at the centre of the complex, which still stands today at the heart of a country park. After dry spells, visitors can see the outline of the original building picked out in the grass.

Footfall at Netley was high during the First World War, but it was as nothing compared to military traffic at Southampton, which was Military Embarkation Port No. 1. Packed troop trains arrived at the docks every twelve minutes during the course of a fourteen-hour day immediately after the outbreak of war. Within four weeks, some 118,000 men had sailed for France from there, along with 37,000 horses and 52,000 vehicles. Over four years, an estimated eight million soldiers passed through the city on their way to the Western Front.

Patients at the hospital who managed to glimpse Southampton Sound would have seen it teeming with ships. Able-bodied men were shipped back to the killing fields of Flanders, while boatloads of wounded, including prisoners of war and dominion troops, returned via the port. By April 1919, the number of sick and wounded soldiers returned from the conflict was estimated at 2,680,000. Injured servicemen funnelled through Southampton went not only to Netley, but by railway to centres across the country.

Some of those men heading in the opposite direction came
from Aldershot, some fifty miles to the north-east of Southampton and the home of the British Army since the middle of
the nineteenth century. Previously, the army lacked a beating
heart, with men and machines spread across the country in
long-established garrison towns. As the top brass cast around
for a centre, Aldershot seemed an obvious choice as it was surrounded by inexpensive heathland that could not be farmed,
but was ideal for hosting military exercises. From 1854, some
25,000 acres were bought up at a price of £12 per acre. Initially,
1,200 huts were built for accommodation. Brick-built centres
followed as two distinct camps emerged, north and south of the
Basingstoke canal, with North Camp station opening in 1858.
For a while, there was even an eighteen-inch suspended narrow-
gauge train to carry men and military machinery around the
mushrooming army site. Aldershot had its own top-flight medical facility from 1879: the Cambridge Military Hospital. Thanks
to the railway, the hospital received casualties directly from the
Western Front and became known as the birthplace of plastic
surgery. Although it closed in 1996, the hospital building is still
a familiar landmark. Even in Bradshaw's time, when lines were
more plentiful, the journey between Southampton and North
Camp entailed a change of trains.

Manchester Piccadilly Station

Series 8, Episode 6

Michael Portillo: 'The railways attracted a particular sort of man: tough, resourceful and duty bound. From among their ranks stepped forward some of the most effective volunteers for the First World War. Britain owes them a debt.'

The shortest platforms at Manchester Piccadilly are mostly used by local trains serving the south and east of the city: routes largely unchanged since early twentieth century Lancashire railwaymen commuted to work at what was then London Road Station. When these workers were called to fight in the First World War, most would have bid a tearful farewell to loved ones from this same station. Fitting, then, that a memorial to the eighty-seven who never returned now stands solemnly between Platforms 10 and 11, short platforms flanking a tribute to tragically shortened lives.

Some 580 employees of the London & North Western Railway joined the colours during the First World War. These men all worked in and around the London Road goods yards and they were among 100,000 other UK railwaymen who signed up as raw recruits. At the outbreak of hostilities in August 1914, train companies were collectively one of Britain's biggest employers – with some 700,000 on their pay rolls – and they ran a vast network comprising 23,000 miles of track and 4,000 stations.

But the loss of so many workers inevitably took its toll on efficiency. Apart from normal civilian and goods traffic, train

companies were having to deal with insatiable demands from
the military. As the London & North Western Railway's general
manager Robert Turnbull put it in a notice to staff : 'The Government has decided to take over the control of the Railways of
Great Britain in connection with the Mobilization of the Troops
and general movements in connection with Naval and Military
requirements.'

In his 1963 book *The First World War*, the British historian
A. J. P. Taylor observes that the course of the conflict had been
'imposed on the statesmen of Europe by railway timetables'. He
expanded on this in later works, pointing out that all the great
European powers had vast conscripted armies which could not
be maintained in peacetime. They had to be mobilised and 'all
mobilisation plans depended on railways'. The problem was
that timetables had to be precise and immovable. This meant
that 'modification in one direction would ruin them in every
other direction. Any attempt for instance by the Austrians to
mobilise against Serbia would mean that they could not then
mobilise against Russia because two lots of trains would be
running against each other.'

Hardly surprising, then, that the British State seized control
of its railway network, although in practical terms, the management remained in the hands of railway general managers. They
comprised the Railway Executive Committee, officially chaired
by the new President of the Board of Trade, Walter Runciman,
but effectively led by the head of the London & South Western
Railway, Herbert Walker. Because of its size and links to the
army's Salisbury Plain heartland, the London & South Western
Railway was critical to the deployment of the British Expedi-
tionary Force, along with its arms, rations, water, ammunition
and equipment.

Over the last three weeks of August, together with the Great
Western Railway, the London & South Western Railway ran

some 670 special troops trains to embarkation ports. By the end of the conflict, it would carry more than 20 million military passengers and almost 1.5 million horses. Other companies also weighed in: the Great Eastern Railway, for instance, ran 870 military trains supported by 20,000 vehicles (many horse-drawn) between August and September 1914.

Nor was the role of the train companies confined to logistics. In October 1914, Runciman asked the London & North Western Railway if rail engineering depots could adapt their skills to produce shells and other ammunition. This was a big ask – outside the army's Woolwich Arsenal, there was no real understanding of the manufacturing processes – but the company's Locomotive Superintendent, Charles Bowen-Cooke, was an acquaintance of Sir Frederick Donaldson, head of the Royal Ordnance Factories, and together they thrashed out a plan. Technical drawings were circulated to the railways' chief mechanical engineers and, within weeks, major plants at Crewe, Swindon, Derby and Doncaster were studying shopping lists from both the War Office and Admiralty. The demands were many and varied – shells, fuses, shell cases (which were recycled and repaired), gun carriages and carts, ammunition stores, artillery mountings, anchors, ship fittings, mines and, in the case of Swindon, an extraordinary 'mobile pillbox' armoured train, complete with artillery pieces and machine-gun posts.

The public response to a declaration of war verged on euphoria. The official recruiting slogan – 'Your King and Country Need You' – encouraged over a million men to enlist inside six months and *Railway Magazine* proudly observed that, by the end of 1914, some 20,000 railway workers had answered the call. But for the train companies, this presented a problem. They found it hard to either attract or retain workers and there was a real risk that Britain's key transport infrastructure would become dysfunctional – with all the unthinkable implications that held for the military. In November, recruiting officers were ordered to request an employer's certificate from railwaymen, confirming that they had permission to enlist.

Soon even that fell by the wayside as demand for troops rose. In March 1915, the Secretary of State for War, Lord Kitchener, asked the Railway Executive Committee to establish the minimum number of workers needed to run the network safely. He had long believed (unlike his political masters) that a long war lay ahead, which would require British manpower 'to the last million'. Nine months later, conscription was introduced for all fit men aged between eighteen and forty-one, although train drivers, crews and other key railway personnel were classed as exempt. Their employers issued them with lapel badges bearing words such as 'Railway Service' to help them avoid accusations of cowardice.

The rail companies were also mindful of anti-German sentiments; early in the war, *Railway Magazine* reported that the name of London & North Western Railway's 460 passenger locomotive had been changed from *Germanic* to *Belgique*. However, perhaps in the frenzy of a war footing, managers neglected to expunge *Germanic* completely. It could still be seen, crossed out but readable, on the engine's driving wheels. Curiously, the railway insisted there had never been any vindictiveness in the name change.

What of those London Road goods yard men who paid the ultimate price? The fact that their stories can be properly told is largely down to two Virgin Trains managers at Manchester Piccadilly, Andy Partington and Wayne McDonald, who were determined to give them a station memorial and end what they called a 'stain on the railway'. The original bronze plaque bearing the eighty-seven names went missing in the 1960s during renovation work, but a photograph of it remained and this, together with records provided by the Railway Heritage

Trust and the Commonwealth Graves Commission, was enough to create biographies of the men – all of whom were locals. In each case the brutal, unforgiving reality of war shines through.

No more so than in the service record of Private Robert Birtles. He was a van-setter, responsible for moving drays or carts into place along platforms so that goods trains could be quickly unloaded, ready for carters to take out on delivery. Robert was one of the first London & North Western Railway workers to enlist and his regiment, the 2nd Battalion of the Lancashire Fusiliers, was plunged straight into action on the Western Front. A little over three weeks after landing in Boulogne on 20 August he was killed in the First Battle of the Aisne in September 1914. His body was never found. It was a similar, sad story for twenty-six-year-old Private Harry Pickup of Ancoats, Manchester, a carter in the goods yard, who joined the 1st Battalion of the King's Royal Rifle Corps. He fell on 20 September 1914, a week after Robert, in the aftermath of the main Aisne engagement.

Sergeant Joseph Daly, a goods truck 'caller-off' (equivalent to a dispatcher today), joined the 9th Battalion of the Loyal North Lancashire Regiment in 1915. He died in June 1917, aged twenty, during the British victory at the Battle of Messines. Goods yard telephone attendant Alfred Bearder, aged nineteen, of Gorton, Manchester, fought with the 19th Battalion of the Manchester Regiment at Passchendaele, but died following the second battle in December 1917. Goods porter Corporal Albert Isherwood, of the 1st/8th Battalion of the Lancashire Fusiliers, was wounded at Gallipoli and listed as 'injured' in the November 1915 edition of the *London & North Western Railway Gazette*. The following month, the same journal recorded he had 'Died of Wounds'.

Most of the London & North Western Railway workers were recruited by infantry regiments, but at least one, a young clerk

called Richard Tetlock, signed up for the Royal Naval Volunteer
Reserve. He joined HMS *Vanguard*, one of the navy's fast St
Vincent-class dreadnought battleships, as a signaller and saw
action during the Battle of Jutland in May 2016. But just over
a year later, the *Vanguard* suffered a catastrophic magazine
explosion, probably caused by degraded and unstable cordite,
while anchored at Scapa Flow. She sank almost instantly, killing all but two of the 845 men aboard.

By the end of the war, the London Road eighty-seven were
among an estimated 20,000 railway workers who had lost their
lives. For those of us passing through Manchester Piccadilly
today, taking a few, quiet moments beside that grey marble
memorial on Platform 10 is a way to remember them.

Gretna Green to Glasgow

Series 1, Episode 9

Distance: 86 miles

Michael Portillo: 'The factory was built at Gretna because it was remote, but also it had a fast rail link to deliver shells and bombs to the Western Front. Another internal railway carried the munitions around the vast site.'

For most people, Gretna Green evokes images of reckless romance and youthful passion, with star-crossed lovers set to defy the establishment with speedy matrimony on a heady whim. But for those with a passing interest in railway history, it brings to mind a far darker topic, as this was the site of Britain's worst rail disaster. At least 227 people died in the conflagration at nearby Quintinshill after three moving trains collided. Most of the dead came from Leith, where barely a family was left untouched by the tragedy. It happened early on Saturday, 22 May 1915, with most victims being soldiers from the 1/7th Battalion of the Royal Scots. They'd been ordered to board a ship at Liverpool that would take them to fight at Gallipoli in the Ottoman Empire.

Historically, railways had always seemed perilous in the thinking of the travelling public, with overarching hazards like exploding engines, broken rails, inadequate brakes, and much more besides. Of course, railway workers faced far greater danger, but it was passenger safety that occupied the minds of travellers and the multitude of railway companies at the time.

For author Charles Dickens, it was a nightmare that came to life, after he was involved in the 1865 crash at Staplehurst in Kent. In a letter afterwards, he wrote: 'No imagination can conceive the ruin of the carriages or the extraordinary weights under which the people were lying or the complications into which they were twisted up among iron and wood and mud and water.'

Six years after that, the Regulation of Railways Act gave an inspectorate the power to investigate train accidents, pushing safety standards up for passengers and railway workers alike. By the twentieth century, the number of crashes had diminished, and those travelling on the day of the Quintinshill disaster would not have been haunted by anxiety.

But in terms of railway management, war had changed matters. The government was now in control of the network through the Railway Executive Committee, although rail companies were still trying to make a profit from running services. The lines were far busier than ever before. Quintinshill lies about a mile outside Gretna and there were some passing loops there, which allowed fast trains to overtake slow services on the busy West Coast Main Line. On this ill-fated morning, those sidings were blocked by freight wagons, leaving a local stopping service parked on one of the main lines.

Responding to a positive signal, the troops train, with almost 500 men aboard, flashed past the signal box, only to plough into the stationary local train at some eighty miles per hour. Moments later, there was a sharp whistle and the sound of hard braking before an express train heading for Glasgow smashed into the wreckage of the other two trains. As the disaster unfolded, signalmen James Tinsley and George Meakin, in charge of directing rail traffic that morning, watched in horror from the lofty heights of the nearby signal box. The long-established system of section alerts, used to indicate whether tracks were clear, had broken down when the men failed to contact the next signal box up the line. Distracted during a shift change, the men seemed woefully unprepared for the two oncoming trains and appeared to have forgotten all about the local train – but their inadequate responses were not the sole issue.

Redundant rolling stock had been hurried back into service during the war years, and it was into such insubstantial carriages that the troops had been packed. The carriages concertinaed on impact. Beneath them were gas cannisters used to power lighting, which exploded, so many of the men trapped in the wreckage burned to death. (Years later, one survivor said he had seen soldiers being shot by officers to spare them this agony.) Some of those who tried to flee the scene across adjacent tracks went straight into the path of the oncoming express.

With records of those soldiers who boarded the train lost in the fire, the army resorted to guesswork when it came to listing fatalities, as only eighty-three men's bodies could be identified. However, the youngest recorded victim was Bugler John Malone, aged just sixteen. Soldiers who died of their injuries after being ferried to Carlisle were not included in this figure. Later that day, a roll call revealed that just fifty-eight men and seven officers had escaped unscathed out of the 499 who set off that morning.

In addition to the soldiers, the dead included the crew of the troop train, two passengers on the local train and seven passengers of the express. Soon, more than 100 sealed coffins were lined up in the Battalion's Drill Hall in Edinburgh. Two days later, they were taken in open horse-drawn carriages to a mass grave along a route lined by 3,150 soldiers and countless citizens, mute with grief.

While the Board of Trade began investigating, an inquest opened in Carlisle three days after the tragedy quickly concluded

that signalmen Tinsley and Meakin were responsible for the
appalling loss of life. Four months later, they were jailed at the
High Court in Edinburgh after being convicted of culpable homicide arising from gross neglect of duties. Tinsley – who suffered
from epilepsy – was deemed the worst culprit of the pair and
received a three-year prison sentence with hard labour. Meakin
was jailed for eighteen months.

A Fatal Accident Inquiry held in Dumfries on 4 November
that year painstakingly recorded the cause of death for the
dozen civilians as 'injuries received in railway collision'. With
regards to the deaths of three railwaymen who had perished
in the incident, the inquiry had harsh words about some of the
Caledonian Railway Company's protocols. That the system was
under pressure because of the high priority given to military
trains was not highlighted; nor was the use of structurally weak
rolling stock.

The National Union of Railwaymen pressed for the jailed
men's sentences to be reduced. On 3 April 1916, Tinsley himself wrote to the Scottish Secretary asking for leniency. In the
letter, he admitted forgetting about the local train standing on
the main line when he signalled for the troop train to move
through. 'I would have willingly laid my life down for those
fine men that morning,' he said, saying his heart was near
broken. His words seemed to hit the mark. Tinsley and Meakin
were released, both on the same day, and were immediately
re-employed by the Caledonian Railway. Had they agreed to
shoulder the responsibility for the crash in order to save the
reputations of both government and railway company?

The same month as the crash, in distant London, a momentous decision was made that would further alter the war history
of Gretna Green. After the notorious shell shortage, when
Britain's continued progress in the war hung in the balance,
David Lloyd George became minister for munitions and arrived

in the job with some ambitious projects in mind. The biggest of these was scheduled for a site on the Solway Firth, which would become the largest cordite factory of the conflict. Some 10,000 Irish navvies were soon at work, and within nine months had transformed a peat bog some nine miles long into four large production sites and two wooden townships, ready to house 20,000 workers drawn from all over Britain and the empire. The vast majority of those employed there were women, known as 'munitionettes'.

It was an opportunity for Lloyd George to not only accelerate ammunition production, but also to provide better living conditions, with the contrived settlements having laundries, cinemas, shops and a hospital. The accommodation included cottages for couples, bungalows for groups of girls and hostels. However, it was all enclosed by high barbed-wire fences, and freedom to enjoy pubs outside the compound was severely curtailed.

When HM Factory was completed, it had 1,255 miles of military narrow-gauge track measuring 61 centimetres (2 feet) wide, with thirty-four locomotives towing wagons containing highly volatile cargo. Stackers and packers who helped dispatch high explosives on the first leg of their journey to the Western Front via these small-scale railways knew the hazards they faced, and those that survived blasts often lost limbs. At its peak, some 800 tons of cordite, which was used to propel shells, was produced every week. As a correspondent for *The Times*, Sir Arthur Conan Doyle visited the site and noted how guncotton and nitroglycerine were kneaded together in what he dubbed 'a devil's porridge':

> Those smiling khaki-clad girls who are swirling the stuff round in their hands would be blown to atoms in an instant if certain very small changes occurred . . . it is a narrow margin here between life and death.

His undisguised admiration for the cool heads kept by women workers amid the danger made it clear their place was no longer necessarily 'in the home' and this realisation bolstered women's fight for the vote at the conflict's end, although they didn't get equal terms for a further decade.

It wasn't just explosions that the workers risked, but chronic illness from the effects of the raw materials they handled. As they laboured, they were served milk in the factory to counter the effects of TNT poisoning. Still, women yielded to toxic jaundice after their skins, teeth, hair and clothes turned orangey-yellow. Using machinery in the manufacturing process instead was out of the question, because nitroglycerine was too unstable. Although the number of workers that died isn't known, it is a matter of record that more explosive was produced here than anywhere else in Britain.

View from the train

On its way from Gretna to Glasgow, the train passes through Lockerbie, the site of a terrorist outrage in 1988 when Pan Am Flight 103 was brought out of the sky by a bomb. Undulating Scottish countryside eventually gives way to Glasgow's suburbs, and the train finally pulls into the station, a stone's throw from the River Clyde. In 1863, Bradshaw's gave a long description of all the manufacturers in the city, which included hat, umbrella and glassmakers: 'These are the distinguishing characteristics of modern Glasgow and the commercial activity and restlessness of its inhabitants have caused the immense impulse its trade has received within the last 50 years.' Today, as a result of that buoyant commerce, the city has a fine array of Victorian buildings, now restored. Yet while the tenement blocks that were once a hallmark of the city have gone, social issues are still in evidence just a few steps away.

Dromod to Sligo

Series 8, Episode 14

Distance: 48 miles

Michael Portillo: 'Sligo. The high ground here is more mus-
cular, more rocky, and somehow Ireland's universal green
is even more intense here.'

The old Midland Great Western Railway line from Dromod to
Sligo winds through the Shannon River Basin, a landscape
shaped by glaciers, peppered with loughs and framed by the Ox
Mountains to the west and the peak of Killery Mountain to the
north-east. This is a place the Irish poet W. B. Yeats saw as his
childhood and spiritual home – 'the country of my heart' – and it
inspired much of his finest work. In one famous 1888 poem, 'The
Lake Isle of Innisfree', he writes of leaving behind 'pavements
grey' (he was then living in London) to find peace and solitude
on one of the Lough Gill islands in County Sligo:

I will arise and go now, and go to Innisfree,
And a small cabin build there, of clay and wattles made;
Nine bean-rows will I have there, a hive for the honey-bee,
And live alone in the bee-loud glade.

But Sligo was not always the rural idyll of his childhood. Like
much of the far west, it became a stronghold of the Sinn Fein
party's republican cause, first through intensified nineteenth-
century opposition to British rule, and later as a key battle-
ground in both the 1919–21 Irish War of Independence and the

1922–23 Irish Civil War. Throughout the long and violent birth of nationhood, the railways of County Sligo and neighbouring County Leitrim would play a vital strategic role: relied upon by government forces to move troops into remote regions; targeted by rebels as a practical and symbolic reason to stop them. Many railwaymen joined a campaign of civil disobedience by refusing to transport troops or military supplies.

By the time Sligo town station opened in 1862, creating a direct rail link to Dublin via Dromod, the push for independence was in full swing. Many in the Roman Catholic community rightly resented the so-called Ascendency, that political and social class represented by the professions, the Protestant clergy and a minority of landowners. This self-serving 'Anglo-Irish' community maintained its economic privileges by excluding outsiders from politics and higher-paid management jobs. In the west of Ireland, they were reviled by the majority Catholic population.

One story which well illustrates this comes from the annals of the Cavan & Leitrim Railway. Built in 1887, this was a fifty-mile branch line running from Dromod through Mohill and Ballinamore to Belturbet, with a second branch linking Ballinamore to the important coal-mining district of Arigna and Lough Allen. The railway's management was Anglo-Irish, while the drivers, firemen and station staff were diehard Catholic republicans. As the country moved remorselessly towards a war footing, rebellious gestures became ever more meaningful.

Among engines pulling freight on the Cavan & Leitrim Railway was a small Stephenson locomotive named *Queen Victoria*. For obvious reasons, Catholic crews were unhappy about driving it. One night they unscrewed the name plates, concealing them in a wood store at Ballinamore. The management was tipped off, recovered the plates and promptly refitted them, only for the crews to remove them once again, drive the locomotive out to Drumshanbo and deposit the plates down a deep well where, according to local folklore, they remain today. When the engine returned to Dromod, it was painted green, white and orange and rechristened the *Sinn Fein* engine.

The political background that, in 1922, saw Ireland move from a form of independence into civil war is at once tragic, complex and compelling. In essence, republicans stood implacably opposed to the treaty with Britain establishing an Irish Free State, not least because it required members of the new Free State parliament to swear an oath of allegiance to King George V. It also allowed Northern Ireland's Protestant majority to remain under British rule. Rebels saw the deal as a sell-out, a Westminster trick designed to stifle the true republic for which they had fought so hard. They had seen how disruption of the rail network had undermined British rule and hampered troop movements. Now they turned similar tactics against the fledgling Free State.

In January 1921, rebels attacked a troop train on a remote stretch of the Sligo–Dublin track near Lough Gara. In November of the following year, Sligo's signal box was destroyed and, a month later, an engine was detached from its coaches at Ballymote and sent full steam ahead down the line. One of the most notable acts of rail sabotage occurred on 11 January 1923, when armed men destroyed Sligo station by dousing it in petrol and igniting explosives. They also sent seven engines hurtling into the goods yard, one of which crashed through a concrete wall into the harbour. Ultimately, the guerrilla war failed. It was not until 1949 that southern Ireland was formally declared a republic.

Important though they were during Ireland's internal struggles, early railways in the west of Ireland were better remembered (at least in popular culture) for bad time-keeping, unreliable trains and low-quality tracks. This notion, while

undeniably true, was hammered into the Irish psyche for
decades – in no small part because of a satirical song by the
music-hall performer Percy French, 'Are Ye Right There,
Michael'. The song has been mythologised over the years, but
it is based on an actual journey made by French on the West
Clare Railway.

The West Clare was among the later lines built, purely
because investors were sceptical about turning a profit in one
of Ireland's most remote areas. However, once the 1883 Tramways Act approved the laying of narrow-gauge lines it meant
building costs could be slashed and completed faster. Work
began in 1884 between the county town of Ennis and Miltown
Malbay under a contract awarded to businessman, politician
and future newspaper tycoon William Martin Murphy. Murphy
ordered four locomotives from the English-based manufacturer
W. G. Bagnall, and these proved their worth ferrying navvies
and materials during the construction phase. But when, in
1892, they were pressed into service for passengers and freight
travelling the branch line to Kilkee, the locomotives proved
something of an embarrassment. At the railway's annual meeting in 1894, their performance was conveniently blamed on the
Board of Trade's insistence that passenger carriages and goods
wagons could not form part of the same train – a rule that
apparently caused constant delays. Whatever the reason, the
composer Percy French's lyrics were merciless.

On 10 August 1896, he had been due to perform at Moore's
Hall, Kilkee, but arrived more than four hours late. In January
of the following year, he sued the West Clare at Ennis Quarter
Sessions and was awarded £10 plus expenses for loss of earn-
ings. The railway immediately appealed – no doubt concerned
that a long line of aggrieved passengers would soon be serving
similar writs – and a hearing was fixed for March at Clare
Assizes before one of Ireland's best-known judges, the Right

Honourable Chief Baron Christopher Palles. Things looked bleak for the plaintiff when he turned up more than an hour after proceedings were due to start and Judge Palles sternly observed: 'You're late, Mr French.' The reply was succinct and decisive: 'I travelled by the West Clare Railway, your honour.' The case was dismissed.

It seems that by the time French *v* The West Clare Railway Co. reached the courts, Percy French was already thinking about writing a song to recount his ill-fated journey. When it was finally completed in 1902, it was a huge success – not only in Ireland, but in Irish communities around the world.

> You may talk of Columbus's sailing
> Across the Atlantical Sea
> But he never tried to go railing
> From Ennis as far as Kilkee
> You run for the train in the morning
> The excursion train starting at eight
> You're there when the clock gives the warnin'
> And there for an hour you'll wait
> And as you're waiting in the train
> You'll hear the guard sing this refrain:
> Are ye right there, Michael, are ye right?
> Do you think that we'll be there before the night?
> Ye've been so long in startin'
> That ye couldn't say for certain
> Still ye might now, Michael
> So ye might!

It had certainly been a bad start to the year for the West Clare's lawyers. While French's case was going through the courts, they also opted to defend a claim from a Mrs Mary Ann Butler, of Limerick, who was knocked down by a donkey while waiting for her train at Limerick. Again, the railway lost.

Although there was some criticism of French – it was argued that his song would undermine the line's viability – the West Clare survived until 1961, when annual losses of more than £23,000 per year finally forced it to close as a main-line service. It lives on today as a heritage railway, running steam trains out of Moyasta station along a three-mile track bed.

Sandwich to Folkestone

Series 2, Episode 19

Distance: 21 miles

Michael Portillo: 'The River Stour and the charming harbour of Sandwich. Difficult to believe that, a few miles from here on the same river, a massive port, on an industrial scale, was constructed in a few years for the purposes of war.'

By the end of 1915, the First World War was sucking in vast amounts of British manpower and resources and depending on the railways to deliver it. Key to the resupply of troops on the Western Front was the Port of Dover, where the Inland Waterways Transport division of the Royal Engineers had been tasked with commandeering, manning and dispatching shallow-draft barges. These could be loaded directly from railheads, towed across the channel and piloted along French waterways to army depots near the front lines.

But Dover and the other Cinque Ports were already under enormous pressure, and the Royal Engineers needed a dedicated port of their own. They chose Richborough, on the River Stour near Sandwich, where a modest nineteenth-century wharf had already been constructed to serve local coal trains and handle gravel for use in the Admiralty's Dover sea defences. Richborough was also conveniently close to the South Eastern & Chatham Railway's Minster Junction and the main rail network. With assistance from the Army Service Corps, the river

mouth was dredged, banks were widened and diverted, and
a new embarkation camp rose in marshlands on either side.
Britain's Secret Station, served by sixty miles of track, linked
to hundreds of yards of docks and eventually manned by 19,000
men, was soon in business.

As a logistics operation, Richborough made total sense.
Munitions and heavy equipment could be moved quickly and
directly to where they were needed, rather than being locked in
the rigmarole of unloading at French ports and reloading on to
battlefield-bound military trains. There were other advantages,
too: shallow barges were less vulnerable to torpedo attack.
Splitting cargos between smaller craft rather than combining
them on to a fully laden ship meant more supplies were likely to
evade German U-boats. By 1916, Richborough's value to army
commanders was incalculable. Britain was about to introduce
conscription, and its army was growing at jaw-dropping speed
– 1.2 million were now serving on the Western Front – meaning
demands on the resupply network were ever more intense. Yet
despite this cranking-up of the country's war machine, there
seemed precious little reward on the battlefield.

In June 1916, David Lloyd George succeeded the late Lord
Kitchener, whose ship had been sunk en route to talks in
Russia, as the new Secretary of State for War. One of Lloyd
George's first acts was to appoint the deputy general manager
of the North Eastern Railway, Eric Geddes, to review military
transportation in France. Geddes was one of the industrialists
dubbed 'men of push and go' by Lloyd George, brought in to
shake up the military's war effort. His report was excoriating.
Arrangements were a shambles, and around 300 more locomotives, 20,000 wagons and 1,000 miles of track – with railwaymen
to maintain it – were needed before winter set in.

There was no conscionable alternative; the army's entire
in-theatre transportation system was in the midst of melt-

down. Back home, the Railway Executive Committee responded at pace, ordering companies to pool essential rolling stock and send any surplus across the Channel. Double track lines were converted to singles to provide rails and a huge locomotive production programme eventually built 1,000 engines. With every month, the Allied railways in northern France grew, including narrow-gauge 'field' lines to link standard-gauge railheads with artillery positions and trenches. Steam locomotives and petrol tractors hauled everything from shells, poison gas canisters and barbed wire to timber, concrete and occasionally soldiers (making them important targets for enemy gunners). Many routes were in a constant state of repair, but momentum was maintained. Railways were seen as a force to revitalise Field Marshal Douglas Haig's campaign after appalling and largely fruitless losses during the four-month Battle of the Somme, in which 420,000 British and 650,000 German troops died.

The aftermath of the Somme fiasco saw Geddes appointed Director General of Military Railways and Inspector General of War Transportation in all theatres, a hugely powerful role for which he took the rank of Major-General. He reinvigorated the Richborough project, but such were his organisational skills that within six months he was redeployed, this time to tackle an underperforming Royal Navy. By July 1917, following a by-election in Cambridge, he was occupying a safe seat in the House of Commons and settling into his new role as First Lord of the Admiralty. Lloyd George later observed that Geddes was 'one of the most remarkable men which the State called to its aid'.

At the end of 1917, demand for fast resupply of the front line was reaching its peak. The administrator in overall charge of Richborough was now Sir Guy Granet, former general manager of the Midland Railway and a man who knew a good plan when it crossed his desk. The latest one was certainly ambitious: if you could uses barges to supply army depots near the front line, then you could do the same with trains. Wagons could be shunted on to ferries equipped with onboard rails and then coupled directly on to locomotives waiting at the French ports of Calais, Dunkirk and Cherbourg. The boat trains would also offer improved loads and capacity for more tanks, heavy artillery, armoured cars, lorries, ambulances and replacement locomotives. Granet and his successor, Sir Sam Fay of the Great Central Railway, were convinced. Three vessels were ordered, two to operate out of Richborough and the other from Southampton. The world's first sea-going, roll-on-roll-off ferries would carry railway wagons.

By the time the first boat train left Richborough on 10 February 1918, the Secret Station had become a remorseless distribution machine supplying all theatres of war. It had its own engineering plant to repair wagons and build barges (there were 242 of these in operation, including ten with a 1,000-ton capacity) five separate railway yards and a signalling centre controlling tracks across more than 2,000 acres. Here was a logistics operation on a gargantuan scale, capable of handling 30,000 tons of traffic a week – just as well, since America was about to enter the war. It increased supplies to the Allies at the very moment the Germans launched what they hoped would be an overwhelming spring offensive. The Secret Station's strategic role, which ultimately helped lead to the Armistice of 11 November 1918, cannot be underestimated. This was later spelled out in the House of Lords during a debate on the post-war future of Richborough. A proposed sale to an industrial development company had fallen through and the government, faced with mounting maintenance and dredging costs, became desperate to offload its responsibilities. In 1925, to make the site more attractive to industry, it drafted the Sandwich Port and Haven Bill, aimed at permitting prospective purchasers

Pearson, Dorman, Long (PDL) the right to run railways to the Kent coalfields directly across the main Sandwich to Ramsgate Road. Opening the bill's second reading on 29 July 1925, the Earl of Plymouth told his fellow peers:

> During the War the brilliant idea – and it was a most brilliant idea – occurred to the War Office of conveying its warlike goods direct without transhipment – from the manufactory almost, I believe – right away by rail to Richborough putting the trucks on to barges, taking them across to the other coast, and I believe in some cases taking them up the waterways of Flanders and France. It was a magnificent scheme, there is no question about it. Richborough Port was a magnificent asset during the War.

Not all peers were quite so eulogising in their assessment. Lord Carson, who had served as First Lord of the Admiralty during the war, commented: 'In my opinion the whole thing was constructed on the most elaborate and ridiculously expensive permanent basis at a time when it was thought that to throw away as much as possible of the money of the taxpayers of this country showed extreme patriotism.' The developers, he warned, would find the port 'a very expensive one, having regard to the amount of dredging I was acquainted with when I was First Lord'. However, he did offer one lighter anecdote. Recalling how 'the whole place was at that time cut off as being a military area', he confessed that during one of his visits a sentry had refused him entry, despite his position as political head of the Royal Navy, 'because I had not a pass'.

Much of the debate centred on whether the taxpayer should build three £18,000 railway bridges over the main Sandwich to Ramsgate road so that coal trains did not disrupt road traffic. This idea got short shift from Lord Plymouth, who sniffily commented that: 'this traffic is almost entirely of a pleasure character. There are numbers of charabancs, and the road is connected very intimately with the game of golf. The Government do not think that the interests of the development of industry in that district should be sacrificed lightly for those purposes.' The bill was eventually passed, but it could not secure Richborough's future. Although PDL obtained government grants to develop the port for coal shipments, the project was hit badly by the Wall Street Crash of 1929, fell into disrepair and was finally abandoned some years later.

Fort William to Mallaig

Series 2, Episode 25

Distance: 43 miles

Michael Portillo: 'This is the line that reaches places that are otherwise unreachable.'

With mountains and moors, red deer and golden eagles, it's been voted the most scenic railway journey in the world. The extension of the West Highland line was the last to be built in Queen Victoria's reign, opening in 1901. It had taken four years to build forty miles of track.

There was an appetite for the project after the railway reached Fort William in 1894, despite the challenging terrain, which included sharp ascents, treacherous downhills and peat bogs. But the scheme ran into difficulty, not for the number of navvies that died during the hazardous construction process, but for the amount of money it cost. Ultimately, a subsidy of public money was agreed, in the order of £260,000 – worth perhaps £17 million today – so the line could be finished. For numerous politicians, in an era where private capital had, for better or for worse, financed the railway network, it was a bitter pill.

In charge of the scheme was Robert McAlpine, a Scottish builder and civil engineer who earned the nickname 'Concrete Bob' for his preference in building materials. As a consequence, the Glenfinnan Viaduct on the route became the longest concrete bridge in Scotland, at 380 metres (1,247 feet). The railway was

in a particularly testing location for navvies, who found themselves marooned far from towns and so accommodation and
provisions – and medical help if there was an accident. A picture
of a navvy working outside London in 1904 reveals he lived in
an earth shelter, so it's likely these men lived in similar circumstances, probably using heather for bedding and campfires
for heat.

In the Second World War a special breed of men, every
bit as tough as the navvies who built the line, were using the
railway to join an elite unit being created outside the sphere of
the regular army. For the first time, Britain would be fielding
commandos in the fight against Fascism.

Winston Churchill was at the forefront of this concept. After
British troops were unceremoniously removed from Europe in
June 1940, he sought some fresh thinking in how the war would
progress. That month, in a letter to his staff officer General
Hastings Ismay, Churchill asked for the training of 'shock troops'
who were agile and ruthless, like those fighting for Hitler. It was
a radical departure for a country that prided itself on having a
professional army superior to guerrilla tactics.

> We have always set our faces against this idea, but the
> Germans certainly gained in the last war by adopting it,
> and this time it has been a leading cause of their victory.
>
> There ought to be at least twenty thousand Storm
> Troops or 'Leopards', drawn from existing units, ready to
> spring at the throat of any small landings or descents.
>
> These officers and men should be armed with the latest
> equipment, tommy guns, grenades etc., and should be given
> great facilities in motorcycles and armoured cars.

As Churchill was writing, it must have seemed only a matter
of time before Britain was invaded and he was now all for a
'butcher and bolt' philosophy, so alien to regular soldiers of the

era. While he knew the newly formed commandos were unlikely to win the war, he believed they could bring new energy to the fight. Inverailort House was duly requisitioned as the special training centre for the group. It was in an ideal location: well within marching distance of Lochailort railway station, on the West Highland line, yet still remote and beyond the bombing range of the Luftwaffe. The sea was close by, for waterborne training, while the deserted moors were ideal for mock attacks or practice demolitions.

The men who came there had been rallied from orthodox regiments to join 'an independent company', with most that volunteered suspecting a route to action at a time when the home-based British Army was inert. An American pamphlet written in 1942 explained men were selected for 'intelligence, self-reliance and . . . and independent frame of mind'. An early trial came as soldiers making their way from the railway station to the house were met with volleys of live ammunition. It was going to be no ordinary training. Among the instructors were veterans of Scott's expedition to Antarctica and men who had fought for the Empire on the North West Frontier, much older but also wise to specific survival strategies. Eric Sykes and William Fairbairn left the Shanghai Municipal Police to teach close-quarter combat methods. Both had studied Chinese martial arts and, during his time in China, the heavily scarred Fairbairn was thought to have survived about 600 non-training fights. However, the duo are best remembered for designing the double-edged Fairbairn–Sykes Fighting Knife, with its stiletto blade, used by commandos for silent throat-slitting.

There were also experts in signalling, demolitions and guns. In Edwardian Britain, the main reason to visit this isolated corner of the country had been to attend a hunting or shooting weekend on one of the large estates there. Now deer stalkers came in to share tips on tracking. Before long, the outfit was

known as Combined Operations and had Lord Louis Mount-
batten at its head. Veterans of the courses recalled both the
rain and the rigorous physical training being relentless: crossing a rope bridge under artillery fire, immediately followed by
launching an assault on a defended beach and then marching with full kit for miles. It's no surprise to hear there were
casualties, with men drowning, dying from gunshot wounds
or mortar explosions, falling in mountaineering accidents and
contracting illnesses. Those who survived but failed to impress
were 'RTU'd', or returned to unit. Eventually, commandos
would be known for their distinctive green berets, but until
1942, they simply wore the headgear appropriate to their regiment, which might include berets, forage caps, peaked caps or
Tam O'Shanters. They also wore their own regimental insignia
alongside the commando insignia.

As the number of commandos grew, the opportunities for
short, sharp raids against German-held territory grew too.
Operation Claymore was one such outing for the commandoes,
who typically hungered for action and resented long periods
penned up in Scotland. On 4 March 1941, men from No. 3
Commando and No. 4 Commando, along with a Norwegian
Independent Company and a section of Royal Engineers, landed
on the Lofoten Islands, off Norway, which had been identified as
an industrial target. Although they were expecting resistance,
the only casualty was an officer who suffered a self-inflicted
injury from his revolver. They returned with 228 German prisoners, 314 Norwegian volunteers and some collaborators, as
well as the rotor wheels and code books of an Enigma machine.
Winston Churchill lauded it as a success, but there were critics
who felt that blowing up a fish oil factory and taking prisoners
was not a cost-effective use of ships and posed an unacceptable
risk to highly trained troops. At the time, of course, the value of
the Enigma code books, which went on to help with the victory

at the Battle of the Atlantic as convoys were steered away from U-boat wolf packs, was not revealed.

Inevitably, the small raids led on to bigger ones. There was concern that the *Tirpitz*, a formidable warship, could wreak havoc on Allied shipping if she broke out of the Norwegian fjords. The only base that could accommodate the ship would be Saint-Nazaire on the estuary of the River Loire in occupied France. An audacious plan was drawn up to scuttle an old destroyer, loaded with explosives, in the mouth of the dock area in a night-time raid. A flotilla of motor launches were to accompany the ship, carrying men instructed to inflict further damage to the port. On 28 March 1942, Operation Chariot unfolded with mixed results. While the port's dry dock was destroyed, only about a third of the men who took part returned, leaving 169 dead behind. A further 215 men were taken prisoner. Still, it was a benchmark for the commandos, enhancing their reputation for stealthy approaches and deadly combat. Hitler was so enraged he issued an order that permitted the summary execution of any captured commando. Valuable lessons were learned through all the commando raids, and these lessons were taken forward for the Normandy landings. By now the training centre had moved some thirty miles to Achnacarry, with Inverailort House becoming a naval establishment.

Rightly, there's a memorial for the commandos at Spean Bridge, within sight of their training grounds at Achnacarry, that pays tribute to their courage and sacrifice. Once again, there's no memorial for the navvies who built the line in the Highlands, other than the route itself. But, by now, more were literate and a few records of their experiences were written down. Patrick MacGill was an Irish navvy, born in Donegal in 1890, who ran away to Scotland as a boy to work. He was too young to have laboured on the West Highland extension, but his book *Children of the Dead End*, focusing on the navvy experience and published in 1914, is the closest we can get to an appropriate commemoration today. In it, he talks about passing a lighted window on a snowbound night and feeling a hunger 'that was not of the belly kind': 'I was in the open country and I did not know where the road was leading to but that did not matter. I was as near home in one place as in another.' There can be little doubt that, if they'd been of a different generation, many of the men who built the railway would have instead been signing up for the commandos.

Chapter Six

THE SURVIVOR LINES

With Railway Mania, many lines were planned, built and axed in short order for want of money or customers. This treacherous economic bubble, which kept recurring, saw numerous families lose their savings, having been convinced that railways were a sure financial bet. More than a century later, more lines were lost after a review by Richard Beeching, who thereafter lent his name to swingeing cuts to the network. Yet against the odds, some quirky lines survived or have even been reinstated.

Whitland to Llanelli

Series 9, Episode 6

Distance: 22 miles

Michael Portillo: 'At the beginning of the twentieth century, Britain had 20,000 miles of railways. In South Wales, they threaded up the valleys and linked the villages. Locomotives had exceeded 100 miles per hour. But Edwardians who craved speed looked to a different technology. The motor car demanded individual skill and offered the freedom of the open road.'

The 'Father of Railways', George Stephenson, saw the future of his innovation with great clarity: trains would revolutionise communications and commerce, and supersede all other forms of transport by becoming a 'great highway'.

'The time is coming when it will be cheaper for a working man to travel on a railway than to walk on foot,' he declared before his death in 1848.

And for some five decades, he was on the money – until another disruptive technology came along, and elbowed rail-bound transport to one side.

Steam-powered cars, which appeared at the end of the eighteenth century, didn't pose a threat to the popularity of trains, but after the internal combustion engine was invented in the 1870s, the future for self-driven vehicles looked assured. Here was a form of transport that was faster than a horse-drawn carriage and more versatile than a train. The first cars that started appearing on British roads in the 1890s were imports subject to severe domestic legal restrictions, entailing each car to have a crew of three aboard as well as adhering to a two miles per hour driving limit. But, after the law was adapted in 1896, it was only a matter of time before British firms turned their attentions to manufacturing the vehicles. The arrival of King Edward VII on the throne in 1901 seemed to signal this new age. While his mother had been closely linked to railway travel, he became the first car-riding monarch, and was one of many people to fall in love with the individual endeavour of the early motoring years. Still, roads often remained in dubious condition and the speed limit was twenty miles per hour.

Those who wanted to celebrate their need for speed made their way to Whitland in Carmarthenshire where, close by, a stretch of seven miles of flat, firm sand was used to put vehicles through their paces. The first international motor rally took place there in 1909, but its heyday was in the 1920s, as two men battled for an international speed record on Pendine Sands. It was a quest that would claim the life of engineer John Parry-Thomas, while Sir Malcolm Campbell distinguished himself by becoming one of the few land speed record-breakers to die in their beds. Campbell, an English aristocrat, set the pace at Pendine Sands in 1924 in a Sunbeam car called *Blue Bird*, breaching 146 miles per hour. After that, he and Parry-Thomas vied for supremacy, with Campbell achieving 174.22 miles per hour (280.38 kilometres per hour) in February 1927.

A month later, Parry-Thomas returned with his car *Babs*, sporting an aircraft engine and a hefty chain to provide the drive between gearbox and wheels. Parry-Thomas had peaked above 170 miles per hour in *Babs* the year before. Now, having been so recently overshadowed by Campbell, the Welshman was keen to wring a bit more speed from his vehicle to gain the lead once more. But as he accelerated, it's thought the chain broke and snapped back, causing a devastating head injury. He was killed immediately and the wreckage of the car was buried in the sand dunes by respectful fans, remaining untouched until a college lecturer gained permission to excavate it in the sixties. Campbell's record was the last to be set in Europe.

Pendine hit the headlines again in 1933 when aviator Amy Johnson and husband Jim Mollison took off from there in a de Havilland plane to fly non-stop to New York. A crash landing, after thirty-nine hours in the air and having covered a distance of more than 3,300 miles, left both injured.

Those who travelled by train to the early motor rallies at Pendine would have come in to Whitland station, which was opened in 1854 on the broad-gauge South Wales Railway on a line that aimed to open a door to Ireland via established sea routes. It was changed to standard gauge in 1872 after a campaign by freighters who were weary of its sedate pace. Motor enthusiasts en route to Whitland would probably have passed through Llanelli, where an altogether different atmosphere prevailed at the time. While Pendine's visitors were adventurous and carefree, the people of Llanelli were angry and careworn. The whole country was subject to strike action by workers across the board, unhappy with their pay and conditions.

In 1910, it was miners at Tonypandy in the Rhondda Valley who confronted bosses, only to be faced down by police and soldiers. One man was beaten to death. The following year, there was something of a general transport strike centred on Liverpool, soon followed by rail workers across Britain abandoning their posts in response to the industry's first national strike. While rail companies were making record profits, some men were working at least sixty hours a week for about twenty shillings, at a time when social reformers deemed twenty-five shillings a bare minimum weekly wage. Working on the railway was also a hazardous occupation, with 5,000 deaths in ten years and a further 146,767 injuries.

At Llanelli, the station had level crossings at either end of the platform, so strikers occupied the station and severed railway traffic. Their ranks were swollen with tinplate workers, in a town known as 'Tinopolis', who were showing solidarity.

Troops had been dispatched across the country even before the strike was called: Home Secretary Winston Churchill was determined to force men back to work, and 127 men from a North Lancashire regiment were installed at Llanelli. Locally, magistrates were keen to read the Riot Act to disperse the protestors. However, fearing the law would not be sufficient in and of itself, one magistrate sent a telegram to London, reading: 'Very serious position at Llanelly [sic]. All trains held up by mob. Engine fires taken out. Soldiers unable to cope. If forces not augmented by nightfall anticipate serious results.'

More troops arrived, with the 150 men of the Worcester Regiment and 100 from the Devonshire Regiment being led by Captain Brownlow Stuart. As the Riot Act was read, defiant strikers began singing 'Sosban Fach', which served as a nationalist anthem at the time. Soldiers reopened the line by force to allow a locomotive to make its way through. Then the scene turned ugly.

With one moving train surrounded by strikers, Stuart ordered marksmen to shoot at men sitting on a nearby garden wall. Two fell dead: tinplate worker John John, a promising rugby player aged twenty-one, and Leonard Worsell, a nineteen-year-old labourer from London, who was suffering from tuberculosis. The soldiers swiftly withdrew to the shelter of the station, which duly came under attack from enraged strikers, who smashed the windows and pulled up the tracks. Then they turned their attentions to a goods shed owned by one of the magistrates and ransacked it. By now there were pitched battles on the street as the police and soldiers tried vainly to establish control. At some stage, a wagon full of explosives was ignited, killing another three people. Only after a further 350 soldiers from the Sussex Regiment arrived were the rioters dispersed.

The town was cleared of protestors by 2 a.m. on Sunday, 20 August, with an unknown number of people dragged away suffering from truncheon or bayonet injuries. Soon the national strike was over, thanks to the diplomatic skills of David Lloyd George, who was Chancellor of the Exchequer at the time. But the men remained unhappy that they hadn't won union recognition. There was another mass demonstration on Sunday, 10 September, not least because the inquests into the deaths had decided it was 'justifiable homicide'.

A quick scan of the Railway Inspectorate records for 1911 gives some idea of why feelings among railway workers were running high. First, there were the local victims.

In January that year, twenty-eight-year-old labourer Joseph Donovan had his finger amputated after it was crushed between wagon and buffer at Llanelli as he struggled to uncouple it. According to the records, he was distracted by someone shouting instructions and the cause of the accident was 'chiefly due to Donovan's inexperience'.

At Whitland, packer R. James was hit by a wagon as he put ballast on the line on 2 March. It seems he got caught between two trains running in opposite directions. Although the record includes a grudging acknowledgement that there should have been a lookout, the inspector found the cause of the accident was that James 'got so excited he forgot to lie down in accordance with Rule 273 (b)'.

Thankfully, there were no deaths locally, although there were numerous fatalities nationwide. The first two cases that appear in the 1911 record book relate to William McBeth and Peter McLeish, in Blackford, Perthshire, both of whom died when there were 'struck by an approaching train when standing clear of another'. As they were allegedly distracted by a farmer and his horse in a neighbouring field, they were found 'in breach of Rule 273 (a)'.

It was an era when death and injury could propel a whole family into abject poverty. The book records 961 incidents for 1911 alone, and 3,915 from the start of January that year to the summer of 1915. While George Stephenson had good reasons for feeling optimistic about the railways, the appalling casualty rate among workers and the high-handed approach of railway companies were unintended consequences of his life's work.

Reedham to Lowestoft

Series 3, Episode 1

Distance: 11 miles

Michael Portillo: 'Sir Samuel Morton Peto had designs on the riches of East Anglia, which required him to conquer the tough landscape. Part of the solution was a piece of Victorian engineering genius, the swing bridge, that allowed passage for traffic on both the river and the railway.'

A locomotive is a fitting emblem of the railway age. Shiny, steam-huffing engines still draw the admiration of crowds today. But, in truth, there were many heroic and unsung engineering feats that accompanied the arrival of Britain's train network, without which it would not have been able to run so prodigiously. One of them is the Reedham Swing Bridge across the River Yare. When the bridge is closed, it forms a link in the railway line between Norwich to Lowestoft, the Wherry Line, which dates back to 1847. But when it's open, river traffic can make its way out to sea, gliding past the bridge parapet untroubled by height restrictions. To open, the bridge pivots at its centre, with the bridge ends sliding off the river bank piers where they usually rest and moving a quarter turn, until the middle section of the bridge mirrors the route of the river, offering a tidal shoulder of the river for wherry boats – too tall to pass under the closed bridge – to use.

The present bridge at Reedham, and another at nearby Somerleyton, crossing the River Waveney, date back to Edwardian times. But the originals were installed in the 1840s, at a time when ships were just as important as railways. Thanks to the bridges, ships and trains could go about their business without being thwarted by the other. Behind this innovative bridge design was a man who emerged from a bizarre childhood into the railway era, which proved to be the perfect platform for his talents.

George Parker Bidder revealed his extravagant genius to his family as a child, at a time when Napoleon was romping victoriously around Europe. After being taught the numbers on a clock face, young Bidder arranged his marbles into numerical configurations, seeing links and hacks where others merely saw idle patterns. Later, the Devonshire Association wrote that he was executing taxing sums at the age of seven, 'when . . . he did not know the meaning of the word "multiplication", nor could he read the common numerical symbols'.

With an eye on income, Bidder's stonemason father William exhibited him as 'the calculating prodigy' at fairs and fetes and he became a popular sideshow, with spectators marvelling at his mental dexterity. Always genial, Bidder spent his childhood years touring Britain and performing in front of paying audiences. He even showed off some mental maths magic for Queen Charlotte in 1816. Three years later, aged thirteen, he was spotted by academics from Edinburgh University, who persuaded him to forsake an itinerant showman's life for formal study. At the university, Bidder met Robert Stephenson. In 1834, the pair teamed up again while Stephenson was building the London & Birmingham Railway.

In partnership with Stephenson, Bidder became an advisor on railway lines in Norway, Denmark, Belgium and India. He put the powers of his retentive memory to work in Parliament when rival railway projects to their own were being considered, as he was capable of seeing anomalies in the calculations on other blueprints being presented at a glance. His impact in eastern England extended beyond the swing bridges. He had garnered considerable experience in dock construction in London, where he built the impressive Royal Victoria Dock at North Woolwich, exploiting empty marshland to achieve its considerable size. The same talent was used to good effect at Lowestoft, where he built docks from which a sizeable fishing fleet emerged. With its growing prosperity, Lowestoft became not only a significant fishing port but also a centre for ship-building and engineering.

Bidder was also among those behind the Electric Telegraph Company, launched in 1846 to take advantage of a new and immediate form of communication. Exclusively used on railways in its early years, the telegraph enabled railway companies to make the most of single-track railways – like those crossing the swing bridges at the time – both safely and economically. He was also a keen supporter of training women as telegraph operators, creating a new career path in a world of work where opportunities of this ilk were lacking.

Much later in his life, in 1856, Bidder gave a lecture to the Institution of Civil Engineers that shed some light on his maths genius. In the beginning, he said, he saw numbers as shapes, which is how he remembered them. To multiply two three-digit numbers, he started with the hundreds and worked backwards, but he acknowledged that, the larger the number, the more his capacity to hold the intermediate figures achieved before he reached an end result was compromised. He also stored in his head the results of significant calculations, like the number of inches in a mile, or seconds in a year, as well as the square and cube roots of particular numbers that helped in engineering equations. Other short cuts presented themselves over the years, but his ability to retain data, like a human computer, underscored it all.

But projects like the Reedham Swing Bridge needed more than awesome brain power to get off the ground. Happily, Sir Samuel Morton Peto, entrepreneur and engineering enthusiast, was on hand to make it happen. As a local, living at Somerleyton Hall, Peto took a keen interest in the area, particularly its railways. In an area that was remote and economically moribund, he knew faster, better links would transform the neighbourhood. Peto was born in Surrey, the son of a tenant farmer, and was apprenticed to a builder uncle to learn bricklaying. As he completed his apprenticeship, his uncle died and Peto inherited the company with a cousin and became a well-known contractor. His firm put up Nelson's Column, helped to build the Houses of Parliament and became involved in numerous railway schemes. But his cousin and business partner Thomas Grissell became concerned about perceived risks Peto was taking with train company investments at a time when the country was gripped by Railway Mania, and the seventeen-year partnership was duly dissolved in 1847. Grissell took command of building projects while Peto was left in control of the railways arm of the business.

Peto turned to another relative, this time brother-in-law Edward Betts, for support in running a business that was now almost exclusively dealing in railway construction. In his memoir, Betts outlined the some of the work the partnership undertook: the loop line of the Great Northern Railway from Peterborough to Doncaster; the East Lincolnshire line connecting Boston with Louth; the Oxford & Birmingham Railway; the Oxford, Worcester & Wolverhampton Railway; and other major railway projects in Argentina, Latvia, Algeria and Norway.

For a while, Thomas Brassey linked up with the pair, bringing with him a golden touch in railway construction. By 1847, Brassey had built about one third of the railway in Britain before turning his attentions to the global market. It's estimated that, at the time of his death in 1870, he had built one in every twenty miles of railway in the world. Early in his career, Brassey met George Stephenson, who had advised him to get involved in railway construction. Despite the rush to build by some contractors, Brassey refused to compromise on standards and safety, so his alliance with Peto must be seen as a vote of confidence. Together Peto, Betts and Brassey masterminded a thirty-nine-mile-long railway in Crimea, shipping materials and navvies at their own expense. The railway was deemed a significant factor in Britain (along with allies France and Turkey) successfully breaking the siege at Sevastopol and ultimately winning the war. For his contribution, Peto received a baronetcy. Beyond that, they built lines in Australia, Canada and France.

Peto was an MP three times, as well as figuring prominently in the Baptist Church. But although he had weathered the first Railway Mania, Peto fell victim to the slump of 1866, sparked when the bank Overend, Gurney & Company collapsed owing £11 million. He was made bankrupt and, as such, was compelled to resign as an MP. When he left, political foes William Gladstone and Benjamin Disraeli united to pay tribute to his talents, with Gladstone calling him 'a man who has attained a high position in this country, by the exercise of rare talents, and who has adorned that position by his great virtues'.

Later attempts to reinvigorate his career failed and Peto died in obscurity in 1889. Bidder had died eleven years before. Both men were giants of the era, yet their names fell out of the lexicon of railway history. Their engineering prowess, however, is still in evidence, in the shape of the swing bridges and railway lines across the country and the globe: testament to their vigour, foresight and commercial courage.

Taunton to Exeter

Series 4, Episode 19

Distance: Bishop's Lydeard to Minehead – 20 miles;
Lynton to Lynmouth – 1 mile;
Woody Bay to Killington Lane – 1 mile;
Barnstaple to Exeter – 39 miles

Michael Portillo: 'I have filled my lungs with smoke and my eyes with smuts. What better place to blow them away than here on the Devon cliffs, where the romantic poets took inspiration: one of the finest views in England.'

If you're in hurry, you could travel between Taunton and Exeter using the direct train service, which takes just twenty-six minutes, and see the verdant countryside flying past the window during the thirty-five mile trip. But there's another route between the same locations in which the views from the train will be more spectacular still. Admittedly, it involves using a car for one section – even the Victorians, who might have favoured taking the long way round, would have had to resort to a carriage. But the route less travelled presents a rare opportunity to travel on four different railway systems, all dating from the nineteenth century and all in close proximity.

The first is the West Somerset Railway, first opened between Taunton and Watchet in 1862. At the time, Watchet was a significant commercial port on the Bristol Channel, from where iron ore mined in the Brendon Hills was dispatched to South Wales and its furnaces. A mineral line took the freight from mines to port, its rails finally taken up during the First World War. But Watchet, with its quaint cottages and a coastline strewn with fossils, became a destination for Victorian visitors, who came in using the Western Somerset Railway, designed by Brunel and one of his broad-gauge lines. At the outset, Watchet was the line's terminus.

Further up the coast lay Minehead, where dignitaries were concerned that they too should reap a reward from increased tourism and sought to lengthen the railway in its direction. At the time, different pockets of the country had their champions and George Fownes Luttrell was Minehead's. After he inherited nearby Dunster Castle in 1868, he instituted a redesign, which turned it from Elizabethan pile into modern home, with bathrooms, piped gas supplies, some central heating and a well-ventilated kitchen. Standing four-square behind efforts to popularise the area, he became the first director of the independent extension to the line, which was duly completed by 1874.

With better connections to London, Minehead now experienced a leap in its number of visitors. In the eighteenth century, the town had been a bathing resort strictly for the upper classes. Now it was far more accessible and, happily, the line's new terminus had been built with broad, long concourses to accommodate incoming tourists. The arrival of the railway led to the construction of new hotels and a sewerage scheme, also paid for by Luttrell. Both sections of the line were upgraded to standard-gauge tracks in 1882, and later and became part of the Great Western Railway fold. Today, the line starts five miles out of Taunton, at Bishop's Lydeard. The original route was closed down by British Rail in 1971, but stayed shut for just five years before being revived by steam enthusiasts. Now it's the longest heritage railway line in the world.

At Minehead, the turntable used to pivot locomotives is a nineteenth-century model installed in the twenty-first century to replace a more cumbersome system that existed previously. Yet still the heavy train engines, weighing 110 tons, have to be pushed around the turntable by hand until their noses face the opposite direction.

Within sight of Minehead station are the Exmoor hills behind Porlock, a natural barrier to railway construction. Brunel thought they could be overcome, but schemes to breach them came to nothing, and it is for this section of the journey that passengers must resort to a car. For up the coast, Lynton had a champion of its own, with different ideas about where the remote town's railways should be heading.

Sir George Newnes was a publisher, with *Tit-Bits*, *The Strand Magazine* and *Country Life* all in his stable, as well as an MP. He moved to Lynton in his later years, and his house was perched on top of Hollerday Hill, on the cliffs above the town. A thousand feet below, there was Lynmouth, where most goods were landed by ship, the most viable option for transport in the absence of decent roads or a railway. A steep mile separated the two small towns. Thanks to Newnes's cash backing – and some Victorian ingenuity – a cliff-side funicular railway was built to connect the two.

The steep track is almost perpendicular, with two carriages permanently attached to one another by a system of hefty hauling cables that wind through a pulley wheel, with one carriage counter-balancing the other. At the top of the line, a tank beneath the first carriage is filled with 700 gallons of water drawn from a nearby river and piped into storage tanks at the station. The second carriage, waiting at the bottom until its partner has been fully charged, is already filled with water. Then they both begin the short journey. As the top carriage begins to descend on one track, the connected bottom carriage heads upwards on the other, discharging water as it goes, being pulled by the greater weight of its opposite number. Even the brakes are hydraulic, powered by water rather than oil, and nothing about the funicular has changed since it was opened on Easter Monday 1890, backed by an Act of Parliament dating from 1888 that permits the taking of 60,000 gallons of river water each day.

Still, this transport innovation wasn't sufficient for Newnes, who now turned his attention to reaching the nearest big town, Barnstaple, by rail. The Lynton & Barnstaple Railway proved far less straightforward, though. Its construction was dogged by disputes with landowners and the bankruptcy of a contractor. By the time it opened in 1898, it had cost twice the expected amount, even though it was built with a narrow gauge to conquer some demanding and lengthy inclines along the route. It took an hour and three-quarters to cover the nineteen-mile distance between Lynton and Barnstaple – and all this when the age of cars was rapidly unfolding.

Still, it remained popular with locals, one of whom wrote to a local newspaper in 1899 about his trip to Barnstaple Fair:

The train waz zo vool es e could hold, an us waz zo thick es dress in a bed; an gawain round the cawnders us ed yessel agin wan tother. There waz a purty young umman next tu me, an her rather zimmed tu like it.

A more recognisable account of the journey comes from Londoner J. Hartnoll, who was delighted with the service's punctuality, but gave a word of warning about the hazards of smoke inhalation.

Though a small 'puffing billy' it emits an enormous quantity of black smoke and specks of soot which fills the nearest carriages with a sulphurous odour most objectionable to persons having bronchial effections [sic].

Ten years ago one would have thought it impossible to get from Barnstaple to Lynton for 1 s 7½ d but this is the fare today by all the trains, [as opposed to] 10s or more by the coach of former times. The trains per day are not numerous . . . This gives plenty of opportunity to the porters to cultivate the platform gardens and pick out the names of the stations with white 'dappy stones'.

The number of passengers travelling on the line was disappointingly low, but still, Newnes didn't lose money on it before his death in 1909. In fact, the service didn't make a loss until 1922 – but, after that, it was all downhill and it finally closed in 1935 with its five locomotives fetching just £236 at auction. In the last forty years there's been a plan to open the line again, with one stretch in operation at the moment.

The last leg of the journey to Exeter is from Barnstaple on the North Devon Line, which has been operating since 1854 and is once again a standard gauge. Today, it's known as the Tarka Line, so-called for the novel by Henry Williamson about an otter family, set in the Devon countryside. Many of the stations along the route are in settlements so small they are request stops, but the train always comes to a halt in Eggesford, itself so remote that the church there has no village from which to draw a congregation. But it was in the vicinity of a country house belonging to the incumbent Earl of Portsmouth. Championing his personal cause rather than the railway's, he permitted the line on his land only with the agreement that the train would always stop in the station to enhance the journey of his house guests. The 160-year-old constraint is still integral to the route.

The North Devon Line has sections of single track, and on second passing loop, drivers wait at the signal box for a machine-generated token. Only trains that have been issued a token can proceed, which ensures the line ahead is clear.

A rail link between Taunton and Barnstaple, the Devon & Somerset line, did not survive; nor did links heading out of

Barnstaple to Ilfracombe and Bideford. All were victims of the swathe of cuts that happened in the mid-1960s or soon afterwards. It makes it all the more worthwhile to take the time to see the survivors.

East Grinstead to Sheffield Park

Series 10, Episode 15

Distance: 11 miles

Michael Portillo: 'When my Bradshaw's guidebook was published, and for about seventy years in total, the line continued on to Lewes via a few small rural stations. After being closed in the 1950s, it was raised from the dead as one of Britain's first heritage railways with the beguiling name of the Bluebell Line.'

When it comes to heritage railways, few are more famous than the Bluebell Line, which began to salvage the age of steam in Britain even before it officially ended. The line was built in 1882, extending one of London's radial lines to Lewes in East Sussex. Sheffield Park was one of its stations, built at the behest of the Earl of Sheffield, who was one of the railway's promoters. Almost from the outset, the London, Brighton & South Coast Railway was in the driving seat, as the company that had originally proposed the line had money troubles. There were a few good years, notably when the Earl of Sheffield staged cricket matches at his estate with the visiting Austral-ian national side. One memorable game in 1896 was attended by 25,000 people, including the Prince of Wales, five years before he became King Edward VII. Yet this kind of footfall was exceptional. It was a tranquil area, with the barely used line serving hamlets rather than towns. Perhaps unsurprisingly, British Rail planned to close the line beyond East Grinstead long before the notorious Beeching cuts. A last engine puffed up the line in May 1955.

But the closure wouldn't be quite as straightforward as first supposed, thanks to the formidable opposition to closure plans of Rose Ellen Margaret Bessemer. Madge, as she was better known, was the granddaughter of Henry Bessemer, famously the originator of the steel manufacturing process, and she proved pretty steely herself in a dispute between her fellow affected villagers and the corporate suits of British Rail. She not only chaired a fighting committee to reverse the British Rail decision, but looked into the paperwork by which permission for the line had been won from Parliament. In dusty files unseen for seventy years, there was a clause that instructed the London, Brighton & South Coast Railway to provide four services a day, including Sunday. That legal obligation, she argued, had been passed to Southern Railway – which took over the line in 1923 when 'the big four' were formed – and, beyond that, to British Rail. As the associated Act of Parliament had indeed not been repealed, British Rail's actions were declared illegal. There was nothing for it. British Rail had to resume services until all procedural niceties had been sorted. In the interim, somewhat petulantly, British Rail would only run trains to the named stations in the act, so it thereafter became known as 'the sulky service' until it was finally closed, as far as British Rail were concerned, in March 1958. The response from rail enthusiasts was immediate and overwhelming. Another committee was organised, this time to launch a heritage service to replicate everything that had been lost. It was perfect timing, as British Rail were already shedding paraphernalia related to the age of steam. The first outing on the Bluebell Line was in 1960, a full eight years before the last main-line steam passenger service ran between Liverpool and Carlisle.

Today, the Bluebell line is run by 800 volunteers. It has thirty-five locomotives, rolling stock dating from the mid-1800s to the 1950s, and attracts 200,000 visitors a year. Visitors are not only encouraged to admire the sleek lines of the engines and take a ride in the liveried carriages, but also to use new technology to discover what life was like as a train driver, with a screen and sound effects. It's tempting to talk about the railway age without paying tribute to the courage of these men.

Of course, the experience of men in charge of engines on small rural lines was less challenging than those on the main lines. But at the time, all were lionised as men who tamed machines that were snorting flames and issuing billowing, smoky breath. Of all the jobs on the railways, being the locomotive driver was by far the most glamourous. Yet even with the benefit of new technology, it's difficult to get a measure of what it entailed.

Being at the controls was exciting, physically demanding and extremely stressful. Missing a signal or misjudging a junction could end in death or ignominy and no one knew what lay around the next bend. All training was on the job. In 1898, Michael Reynolds gave this advice in his book *How to Become a Model Engine Driver*:

> The foot-plate of a locomotive engine is the only place where experience can be acquired of the ways in which it is possible for an engineman or an engine to go wrong.
>
> During the time that an engine is under steam with a train, everything seen, heard, felt, and smelt is capable of affording a lesson. On the engine foot-plate the eye is trained to distinguish different colours at considerable distances. The ear learns to detect the slightest variation in the 'beats' and knocks about the machinery. The human frame learns to distinguish the shocks which are due to

a defective road from those which are due to a defective engine. The olfactory nerves become from experience very sensitive, so as to detect the generation of heat from friction before any mischief is done.

He acknowledged that drivers won the admiration of society, but insisted that observers were only seeing 'the picturesque side of the result of many years of patient observation and toil'.

It took bitter experience for railway companies to realise not all men were cut out for the task: for example, those who were colour-blind could not see the necessary signals. Certainly, men had to amass years of experience before being promoted to engine driver. Even then, some experiences never lost their ability to shock. Plunging into the obsidian black of a tunnel, where engine smog closed in on the cab, was always a test of nerves.

According to driver David Stevenson, although people became accustomed to it, 'you never went through anything more awful'.

Imagine the most utter darkness – a mighty roar beneath a vaulted roof, made by the steam, the machinery, and the action of twenty or thirty tons weight of iron rattling along at thirty miles an hour over iron rails, every joint of the rails giving out a loud sound – and then the convulsive vibration of the plate on which you stand and the rail you hold. You feel alone in the deep gloom, but yet feel that two men stand somewhere near you, and you know that all are impressed with the thought that the crack of a wheel, the fracture of a spring, a stone on the line, a loose rail, or any irregularity, would send all the iron and wood and flesh and blood and bones and fire into one wrecked heap in that dreadful place. Nothing gives me the feeling that we are helplessly in the hands of the Almighty so much as riding on an engine through a long tunnel.

As the nineteenth century progressed, there was a growing professionalism in the industry, with one Great Western Railway driver, Maurice Vaughan, advocating self-improvement classes for men when they were off duty, where they could swap ideas and problem-solve. This was while men were working long hours and often spent nights away from home. And the idea wasn't derided, but embraced by men invigorated by their revered place in society. The train drivers' union – the Associated Society of Locomotive Steam Enginemen and Firemen (ASLEF) – began in 1880, when sixteen-hour working days were not unusual. Men in the cab were also imbued with a huge sense of duty towards passengers, and one incident in 1898 underlined the self-sacrifice that might ensue.

Driver Walter Peart, forty-one, and his twenty-five-year-old fireman Harry Dean were fatally burned when a piston rod broke, piercing the boiler casing as their train raced between Windsor and Paddington. Despite their terrible injuries, they manhandled the controls until the train came to a halt, saving the lives of passengers that day. At the hospital, shortly before his death, father-of-five Peart was asked if he had jumped off the train to escape the torrent of scalding steam. He replied, 'No, I stopped my engine.' In 1892, when engine driver Samuel Watson spoke to *The Strand Magazine*, he was less taken by the notion of heroism among drivers, focusing more on what was to him, the mundane. Most drivers' experiences were similar, he felt, 'although some are unfortunate to meet with more accidents than others'.

I began life as a boy in the lamp-room at Hitchin; then I went into the cleaning-shed at King's Cross, to clean engines at 2s. 6d. a day. After three years I became fireman on a main line passenger train to Peterboro', and in another five years was promoted to driver in the 'goods' yard at

King's Cross. During the last five years I have worked express trains on the Great Northern main line; but it was my ambition to be driver of the special Scotch express, the fastest train [service] in the world.

The existence of heritage lines now pay homage to the bravery of men like him and countless others, for literally driving the railway age forward.

Ryde to Shanklin

Series 3, Episode 8

Distance: 8 miles

Michael Portillo: 'I used to take summer holidays on the Isle of Wight every year with my family and we would travel on this rail service, which in those days was steam. But now the service is provided by trains taken from London Underground.'

One nostalgic line has long given holidaymakers a sense of well-being as they trade hectic urban lives for a fortnight of sun, sea and sand on the Isle of Wight. When they step off the ferry that transported them from the mainland, they board a train that seems out of place and time. Yet this line is a battle-hardened survivor of a network decimated by cuts. Today, this small island's railway history seems to represent the rest of the country's chequered experience, in microcosm.

The history of the railway network on the Isle of Wight is piecemeal and complex. At its zenith, the population of the southerly island was well served by trains, with a web of tracks amounting to fifty-five miles, spreading across an island twenty-two-and-a-half miles wide and thirteen-and-a-half miles deep. This was in the second half of the nineteenth century, when the egalitarian nature of railways brought hope to isolated communities like this, always at risk of new technology passing them by. And it wasn't just residents who made the most of the railways, but tourists who were already coming across the

Solent to the island in numbers. Queen Victoria's delight in the location and her newly built Italianate home there, Osborne House, only served to boost numbers visiting. The main wing of Osborne House was completed in 1851, a decade before the death of Prince Albert. A year after the death of Victoria, her son King Edward gave the estate to the nation. But much later, when the government looked to economise by shutting railways considered to be performing poorly, the island's routes were not immune. First, here's a quick-fire history of the railways on the island.

A first set of tracks laid down in 1832 on the estate belonging to architect John Nash for the purposes of transporting construction materials under horsepower didn't endure. It had disappeared by the time Ordnance Survey mapping occurred in 1860. The first standard-gauge railway on the island opened in 1862, linking Cowes and Newport, and was served by two blue-painted engines called *Pioneer* and *Precursor*. Two years later, Ryde – the resort closest to Portsmouth on the mainland – was linked with Shanklin by a set of rails. After a 1,188-metre (3,898-foot) tunnel was built, the line extended to Ventnor.

Like every other part of Britain, the railway system on the Isle of Wight depended on Acts of Parliament and private capital. There were objections from landowners, who jealously guarded their private estates, and eyewatering costs that rose with every blip and hitch. There followed a slow and sometimes painful process to construct a system that would link all the major towns on the island, reflecting what was occurring all over the country at the time. But the idea of a joint committee soon presented itself as the most coherent way to function. This enhanced cooperation was a refreshing change from competing interests and helped to smooth some difficulties. Accordingly, these first two railways soon ran by joint committee.

Next on the stocks was the Isle of Wight (Newport Junction) Railway, less than ten miles long and beset with financial difficulties almost from the get-go. Although the final leg, linking Newport with the Ryde & Newport Railway with a viaduct, finally bankrupted the company, the operation went ahead in step with the same joint committee. It was also responsible for building a new pier and railway in 1880 – the one that served holidaymakers and their families so faithfully for decades afterwards.

There were other railway lines constructed as well, in areas with few inhabitants and virtually no tourists. One was sent towards the west of the island, on the promise of a railway tunnel from the mainland that never materialised. A latecomer to the fold was a stretch that went from Merstone to Ventnor, opening shortly before the death of Queen Victoria. The net result was the Isle of Wight Central Railway, formed in 1887, an amalgamation of the most viable railways that at last formalised the joint committee. In 1923, when the country's railways were pulled together into large, regional companies, Isle of Wight lines became part of Southern Railway. With eyes on the prize of tourist spending power, Southern kept faith with lines on the island.

But when railways were nationalised in 1948, some of sections were early casualties of cost-cutting measures. The picturesque section at Ventnor was shut in 1952 after a comparatively brief fifty-year history. Then there were closures at Ventnor, Bembridge, Freshwater and between Newport and Sandown. When it became clear the 1955 modernisation plan mooted for the national rail network had not borne the necessary savings, British Rail looked for a new strategy. The man they asked to deliver it was Dr Richard Beeching, a physicist and engineer who was lured from corporate firm ICI to become chair of British Rail.

He became a household name and references to the 'axe' he wielded against the railways are still made today. There's little doubt that some branch lines had outlived their usefulness in the age of private motoring. Talk of men in charge of a rural signal box with feather-light duties making money on the side by hairdressing and carrying out bicycle repairs didn't help their cause. In 1959 the M1 opened, signalling that roads were in the ascendancy and railways were on the run. At the same time, package holidays abroad were becoming more popular than rail trips to British resorts. Beeching was motivated by statistics, measuring passenger density maps with timetables as he sought to prove many railway lines should be scrapped. Although he saw a future for the major routes, his findings were stark, claiming half the country's route miles were unviable.

> Revenue does not pay for the maintenance of the track and the maintenance and operation of the signalling system, quite apart from the cost of running trains, depots, yards and stations. Also, it is found that the cost of more than half of the stations is greater than the receipts from traffic which they originate.

In his report – packed with tables and graphs – he declared that of 4,300 stations, one-third contributed only one per cent to passenger revenue, and that half of the total number contributed only two per cent. Stopping passenger services outside the major conurbations were shown in a particularly bad light. It was therefore no surprise to discover that all the railway lines that remained on the Isle of Wight had been earmarked by him for closure.

At the time, those who supported Beeching believed the surge in support for lines nominated for closure came from a well of sentimentality that would soon ebb away. Privately, Beeching believed it would be cheaper for the government to buy everyone in the country a car than to maintain railway services.

Of course, it wasn't Beeching himself that shut lines, but ministers responding to his recommendations. A total of 4,000 route miles on the national rail network were lost, leaving 13,721 miles still in existence. Yet the implied 'break-even' point for British Rail was never reached. Although Beeching had aimed to make savings of £100 million, critics said the gains from the widespread closures amounted to just £30 million. As the government rowed back on some of the suggestions and considered subsidies to keep some lines running, Beeching was scathing about its incompetence and lack of wisdom. But he also failed to recognise that statistics hid the way branch lines contributed to the success of the main lines, by bringing traffic to them. On a smaller scale, he didn't understand how small communities were reliant on humbler transport links. Although the focus of railways on the Isle of Wight was mostly passengers, there were also fresh goods, including milk and strawberries, carried by train to markets on the mainland.

The Isle of Wight closures inspired a campaign among users, just as they had done elsewhere in the country. Despite protests, the Ryde to Cowes link ended in February 1966, although its steam locomotives and Edwardian carriages had proved a great attraction for tourists. Two months later, the Shanklin to Ventnor line followed suit. However, the transport minister Barbara Castle declined to shut the Ryde to Shanklin line, despite Beeching's recommendation. It was duly electrified and furnished with redundant London Underground trains. Other lines saved at the time included remote ones serving the Scottish Highlands and Central Wales and one in Devon, where the roads were poor.

And as with other parts of the country, there was sufficient support to relaunch at least part of the closed line, and a steam railway now runs on five miles of track re-laid by enthusiasts along a route which once belonged to the Ryde & Newport Railway. Any equipment that had been mothballed rather than dismantled was brought back into use. It's left the island with a somewhat idiosyncratic network, but one that's functional, transporting the public and visitors, as well as celebrating a railway heritage from a bygone era.

Paddington to Whitechapel

Series 4, Episode 16

Distance: 6 miles

Michael Portillo: 'I'm going to visit a London railway which, as a Londoner, I've never travelled on. I have never even seen a photograph of it, it is that mysterious.'

Beneath the well-trodden streets of England's capital city, there is a maze of unseen tunnels, stacked up in layers. Somewhere down there are hundreds of miles of brick-built sewers, courtesy of civil engineer Joseph Bazalgette, a relatively unsung hero of the mid-nineteenth century, whose work to guide effluent out of the city did so much to improve public health for Londoners. Camden Market stands on catacombs, where horses and ponies that once worked on the railways were stabled, while a disused tramway disappears underground at Kingsway. There are some plague pits, used to bury the bodies of thousands who died in the seventeenth-century scourge, and deep-level shelters built in the Second World War. Eight of the ten shelters initially planned were completed, capable of accommodating 80,000 people. All were linked to underground stations. And, of course, there's a maze of underground train tunnels, some not so far below the pavements and others at a much deeper level. Hampstead is the deepest station in the network, being fifty-eight metres down. As well as brightly lit stations and the spare illuminations of the busy tunnels, there are a few locations now severed from the main arteries that stand in darkness.

Carriages flash by these gloomy stations that have now been erased from the tube map, including Down Street, St Mary's, York Road and South Kentish Town. A labyrinth that was once open to the public but now can be found abandoned next to Euston station, with defaced posters still gracing its walls.

Then, at twenty-one metres deep, there's a little known railway that once helped parcels, cards and letters get more speedily to their destinations. The London Post Office Railway was a highly successful innovation in its day, transporting mail across the capital without risking delays on the heavily congested roads. The email age spelled its end in 2003, but the diminutive railway has since been resurrected as a tourist attraction.

At its busiest, mail rail was operating for nineteen hours a day between its western terminal at the Paddington sorting office and Whitechapel in the east, with seven stations in between. Laid end-to-end, the 60-centimetre (2-foot) gauge tracks would have measured twenty-three miles. It boasted driverless trains a full sixty years before the Docklands Light Railway opened with a similar concept. But before its incarnation, several methods to deliver mail between railway stations to sorting offices were tried. The idea of subterranean mail transport wasn't new. Rowland Hill had founded a fair-for-all post office service in 1840 despite his idea of a prepaid letter being denounced as 'preposterous' and 'wild and visionary'. He looked into the notion of having a pneumatic tube to help dispatch mail from one part of London to the next, but decided costs would be too high. (When he was ousted from the Post Office in 1842 as part of a political dispute, Hill became a director and later chairman of the London & Brighton Railway. His tenure is credited with lower fares, expanded routes, timetabled excursion trains and improved train comfort for commuters.)

In 1853, the first mail 'tube' went into operation, with letters pulled along a pipe by vacuum. The London Pneumatic Despatch Company was formed in the middle of 1859 to improve on the idea, with eminent directors including Richard Temple-Grenville and the third Duke of Buckingham and Chandos, with contractor Thomas Brassey also on board. Tests proved that two or three cars carrying a total of up to fourteen tons of mail could be sent on their way by the power of vacuum created by a static steam engine. After these successful trials were carried out above ground in Battersea, a subterranean line with a 60-centimetre (2-foot) gauge inside a cast-iron tunnel was built between Euston railway station and the North West District Post Office. Although the total length of the journey was a modest third of a mile, it was completed in just one minute. The network expanded, with a line from Euston to Holborn, which then pushed on to the General Post Office. The technologically impressive line provided great kudos for the General Post Office, which found itself at the hub of a communications network including domestic and overseas destinations, and prided itself on speed. But the eyewatering costs for its continuation were put into stark relief by the collapse of the bank Overend, Gurney & Company. Although the capsule speeds were an admirable sixty miles per hour, the cars had a habit of getting stuck, and the letters sometimes got wet. Ultimately, the Post Office felt it could not justify high costs for time saved. The system closed in 1874.

By 1911, there was once again interest in a tunnel system for mail delivery, at a time when the Board of Trade discovered that sixty-four per cent of London people travelled on the roads by car, omnibuses, tramways and horse-drawn vehicles, with just thirty-six per cent choosing railways. In short, the traffic was chaotic and it was clear the problem was going to get far worse, with the Board noting: 'Horse-drawn vehicles continue to be supplanted with remarkable rapidity by those mechanically propelled.' London County Council hoped to keep slow-moving traffic close to the kerb to free up the centre of the road, but that plan was being thwarted by traders loading at the roadside. A proposal to take post out of the equation seemed irresistible, although it took a mammoth sixteen years for the line to open.

Construction didn't start until 1915, and was hobbled by the First World War and its competing demand for manpower. After the war came the General Strike. Nonetheless, it was fitted out in time to carry the Christmas parcel post in 1927, while the first letters were taken in February 1928. The single tunnels were 2.75 metres (9 feet) wide – big enough to accommodate twin lines – and lay some 21 metres (70 feet) beneath London in places. The line came closest to existing tube routes at Oxford Circus, where it veered near the Bakerloo line. The engineered workhorses that carried the mail took their power from a central rail, and travelled at up to forty miles per hour between stations and just seven miles per hour through them. Prior to stations, the line split into two single-track tunnels. The cars were sturdy, serviceable, electrically powered ones that survived teething issues to operate for at least thirty years, with each being thoroughly checked over after every 4,000 miles travelled. To mark its golden anniversary in 1977, two of the units dating from 1930 were painted gold. Its operational peak came after the Second World War when it was ferrying four million letters a day under London. In 1987, it became known as the 'Mail Rail' and was held in great affection among post office workers. However, its era was drawing to a close.

According to the Royal Mail, the costs of running the Mail Rail in the twenty-first century were some five times more expensive than road transport. Unions were sure this was because the system was being deliberately run down. Although there was support for the Mail Rail from London's government, which feared more than eighty lorries per week would use the roads if it wasn't running, Mail Rail nonetheless closed on 31 May 2003. A year later, the last Travelling Post Office ran in Britain, ending a long history that linked mail and train. Travelling Post Offices were carriages or trains devoted to the transport of mail, which was sorted by staff as the train raced through the countryside to different destinations. Some even had post boxes for use by travellers. A system to pick up or deposit mail bags from the side of the line without the train stopping first started appearing in Britain as long ago as 1866.

It seemed that a vital slice of railway history was coming to an end, as the joys of computers and the immediacy they offered were being embraced. Crucially, though, Mail Rail was mothballed rather than ripped up, which meant it could eventually be given new life, transporting passengers instead of parcels in a multimedia museum focusing on the story of post.

And another new age of travelling underground is going to begin with the opening of Crossrail, linking London's east and western suburbs. For three years, eight 1000-ton boring machines have been grinding through the land to create twenty-six miles of tunnel some 40 metres (130 feet) below the heart of the city. The three million tons of spoil taken away from the site have been deposited in Essex, where a new bird sanctuary has been created. The Elizabeth line will have forty-one stations and is expected to transport more people into London faster than ever before.

Invergordon to Wick

Series 4, Episode 15

Distance: 80 miles

Michael Portillo: 'Victorian tracks have brought me to the uppermost edge of mainland Britain. From my seat on the train, I have gawped in admiration at Scotland's grandeur. The railways in the Highlands brought not industrial revolution so much as continuity to enable communities to survive and traditional skills to flourish.'

When Victorian Britain comes under scrutiny, it's the mushrooming middle classes that are generally in the spotlight. Thrifty and self-reliant, their industrious behaviour started to change the shape of society, especially after some began to earn big money from their enterprises. Previously, Britain's social order had been a pyramid, with a wealthy, privileged few at the apex and the vast majority populating the bottom tiers. As late as 1882, a survey found that four-fifths of the land in the country was owned by just 7,000 individuals. Soon after that, the middle of the pyramid began bulging, yet the aristocracy had not gone away. Although the Industrial Revolution did much to dismantle the long-held hierarchy that kept the country's wealth circulating among a small number, the landed gentry and the philanthropy associated with it was still in evidence, and never more so than in the north of Scotland.

That's where the Duke of Sutherland decided to build his own railway in order to get better connections to one of the remotest corners of the country. Sparsely populated and with limited industrial means, the chances of the northern prong of Scotland having a railway line to call its own seemed limited until he intervened. The Duke stepped in when the Sutherland Railway, authorised in 1865 to run a twenty-six-mile stretch of line between Bonar Bridge and Brora, ran out of money and stopped five miles short of its target, at Golspie.

Unsurprisingly, he had few difficulties obtaining the necessary permission from Parliament and, as he was the sole landowner involved, he made a start on construction before authorisation was finalised. He didn't stop at the original plans and built a further eleven miles of track to Helmsdale, which opened in 1870. The following year, the Highland Railway took over the line's timetable and finally absorbed the Duke of Sutherland's Railway into its own operation four years after that.

There were two reasons behind the Duke's commitment to the venture. The first was the position of his home, Dunrobin, a glorious castle that resembles a French chateau and has been dubbed the jewel in the Scottish crown. There's probably been a castle on the site since the thirteenth century, but most of the outside that exists today was designed by Sir Charles Barry, the architect responsible for the Houses of Parliament, after Queen Victoria began a trend in home design north of the border through her attachment to Balmoral. The second reason was an abiding love of trains – and perhaps there was more than mere altruism at play here. The Duke of Sutherland, clearly a frustrated engineer, bought his own engine and rolling stock, and had a right to use it on the line, which was maintained until British Rail took over the country's railways decades later. Not just the owner, he was also a driver and on at least one occasion was behind the throttle as the train brought Queen Victoria for a stay at Dunrobin. In *Punch* magazine, he was known as 'the Iron Duke' for his railway obsession.

He had already invested separately in the Highland, Sutherland, and Sutherland & Caithness Railways before they finally all amalgamated. Overseas, he'd backed the small-scale Mont Cenis Pass Railway, built by engineer John Barraclough Fell across the Alps. Although it was a short-lived operation, running for just three years, it was something of an engineering triumph, given the gradients involved. It linked St Michel in France, and Susa, in Italy, and its trains carried passengers, freight and mail. From the British perspective, it sped up the journey of mail bound for India. The railway was quickly superseded by a tunnel beneath Mount Cenis completed in 1870. (Here, a bold plan was drawn up by a French engineer and dug by Italian labourers. When two working parties, heading in opposite directions, met in the bowels of the mountain on Christmas Day 1870, the event was considered so momentous it became front-page news across Europe.)

This wasn't the end of the railway extension in this part of Scotland either, with a line finally reaching Wick, via Thurso, built by the Highland Railway. The fourteen-mile-long Wick & Lybster Light Railway was up and running in 1903, thanks to a treasury grant of £25,000 and local subscriptions, also to be run by the Highland Line. It stayed in operation until 1944. Thurso's link to the network became crucial in the First World War, as men and coal were transported there for the British warships based between the tip of Scotland and the Orkneys at Scapa Flow. The trains became known as Jellicoe Specials, named for Admiral of the Grand Fleet John Rushworth Jellicoe. Scapa Flow remained the country's primary naval base in the Second World War. Meanwhile, herring landed at Wick became widely distributed when the catch was bountiful. More enduring traffic has taken to the line, it being the closest railway access to the northern tip of the country, John O'Groats. It's the destination of many end-to-enders, travelling the 874 miles there to or from Land's End.

While the Duke was famous for his love of locomotive power, another Scot who preceded him, but was equally well known in his day, was more disdainful. Born in Cromarty in 1802, Hugh Miller – firmly of the middle classes, was a writer, evangelical Christian and geologist, whose identification of fossils as ancient species brought him both fame and controversy in equal measure. After his premature death, the funeral route in Edinburgh was lined by thousands of people. One of his lesser-known works was a book about his travels through England, sometimes by train, in the style of *Great British Railway Journeys*. However, in his writings he doesn't exhibit a love of train travel, often opting to go by coach, nor any great affection for the people he encounters.

On one occasion, he stayed at the Manchester & Birmingham Railway terminus on a Sunday. As a fervent supporter of Scotland's Free Church, he was curious to know why people were not in church that day.

> I could hear the roaring of the trains along the line, from morning til near midday and during the whole afternoon; and just as the evening was setting in, I sauntered down to the gate by which a return train was discharging its hundreds of passengers, fresh from the Sabbath amusements of the country, that I might see how they looked. There did not seem much of enjoyment about the wearied and somewhat draggled groups; they wore, on the contrary, rather an unhappy physiognomy as if they had missed spending the day quite to their minds and were now returning, sad and disappointed, to the round of toil from which it ought to have proved a sweet interval of relief.

Nor did the scenery of England hold much pleasure for him.

I quitted Manchester by the morning train and travelled through a flat New Red Sandstone district, on the Birmingham Railway, for about eighty miles. One finds quite the sort of country here for travelling over by steam. If one misses seeing a bit of landscape, as the carriages hurry through, and the objects in the foreground look dim and indistinct and all in motion, as if seen through water, it is sure to be repeated in the course of a few miles, and again and again repeated.

One soon wearies of the monotony of railway travelling – of hurrying through a country, stage after age, without incident or advantage and so I felt quite glad enough when the train stopped at Wolverhampton to find myself once more at freedom and a-foot.

He did, however, take some enjoyment from the company of the third-class passengers he encountered. 'For the sake of variety, I had taken the penny-a-mile train; and derived some amusement from the droll humours of my travelling companions – a humbler, coarser, freer and withal merrier section of the people than the second-class travellers.'

Meanwhile, some present-day travellers might identify with the trip he had to London. 'There were long wearisome stoppages at almost every station – and it was within an hour of midnight and a full hour and a half beyond the specified time of arrival, ere we entered the great city.'

View from the train

The stand-out section of the journey is when the train tracks the coastline between Brora and Helmsdale, where unspoiled sandy beaches are occupied only by groups of resting common or grey seals, who gaze up unflustered by the sound of the train. At sea, you might glimpse dolphins and minke whales or diving seabirds.

Acknowledgements

Thanks to Karen Farrington for her impeccable research and writing for this book. Michael Portillo for writing the introduction and from Boundless, John Comerford (Executive Producer), Alison Kreps (Series Editor), Katie Wixon-Nelson (Line Producer) and Susanne Hamilton (Head of Production) for their assistance in selecting the journeys and supplying imagery from the series. To Sarah Williams at the Sophie Hicks Agency. From Headline Non Fiction, Iain MacGregor, Georgie Polhill, Cathie Arrington, Patrick Insole and Louise Rothwell.

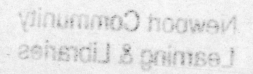

Picture credits

Plate Section

PILLGWENLLY

29-09-21